Essays and Addresses on Arab Laws

Essays and Addresses on Arab Laws

William M. Ballantyne

Routledge
Taylor & Francis Group
LONDON AND NEW YORK

First Published in 2000
by Routledge
2 Park Square, Milton Park, Abingdon, Oxon, OX14 4RN
711 Third Avenue, New York, NY 10017

First issued in paperback 2011

Typeset in Garamond by LaserScript Ltd, Mitcham, Surrey

British Library Cataloguing in Publication Data
A catalogue record of this book is available from the British Library

Library of Congress Cataloguing in Publication Data
A catalogue record for this book has been requested

ISBN10: 0–7007–1094–9 (hbk)
ISBN10: 0–415–66695–3 (pbk)

ISBN13: 978–0–7007–1094–2 (hbk)
ISBN13: 978–0–415–66695–4 (pbk)

Publisher's Note

The publisher has gone to great lengths to ensure the quality of this reprint but points out that some imperfections in the original may be apparent

Contents

Acknowledgements

In the course of over 50 years of professional practice, it has been my pleasure and privilege to work with many colleagues of the highest calibre. It would be invidious for me to mention individuals at the risk of inadvertently excluding others; thus in general I must content myself with expressing my thanks and appreciation to all.

Specifically in connection with the present volume, I would like to thank Kathryn Garratt, linguist extraordinary, who read and corrected the initial proofs; Khawar Quraishi, of 1 Hare Court who did the detailed research for Chapter XIV; and Alison Padfield, formerly of 1 Hare Court, who did much to construct Chapter IX.

1 Hare Court
Temple

Preface

It is for me sobering to realise that thirteeen years have flashed by since the publication of my 'Commercial Law in the Arab Middle East: The Gulf States', and its companion, the 'Register of Laws of the Arabian Gulf'. The latter is, of course, up-dated quarterly, but although there have been several reprints of 'The Gulf States', there has been no second edition: the material in the present volume may to a certain extent, serve as an alternative.

Although in its essence 'The Gulf States' continues to preserve its validity, there has been much legal development in the area during the last thirteen years. The 'Code of Civil Transactions' of the United Arab Emirates was promulgated in 1986, just too late to be incorporated in detail into 'The Gulf States' – a fairly exhaustive analysis of its provisions appears in this volume (Ch. IX). Bahrain has issued its commercial code, which is also the subject of a short article (Ch. VIII).

Other legal developments too numerous to mention in a preface figure in the individual chapters.

After due consideration, the various essays and addresses within this volume have been left as originally written or delivered. In a generous forward to my 'Legal Development in Arabia' (1980: Graham & Trottman) Sir Norman Anderson (recently and very sadly for us, departed to that other existence to which his deep faith has surely admitted him) wrote:

> "Inevitably as Mr Ballantyne himself remarks, an unedited collection of such articles and addresses cannot avoid a good deal of repetition; but the only feasible alternative would have been a

wholly new book which summarised, in successive parts, first the political and legal history covered in this series of contributions, then the current position (with all its uncertainties), and finally the course that future developments seem likely to take. But it may well be that the very repetition which a publication of this sort necessarily involves will serve, as nothing else might, to drive home the importance of the advice Mr Ballantyne continually – and rightly – gives: namely, that all who want to do business in this area:

1 *must*, from the very first, acquaint themselves with the *facts* of the legal position rather than rely on what others tell them to be the case on the basis of the way in which the law has, or has not, been enforced in the past;
2 must *ensure* that they conduct their business on the basis of a water-tight contract, drawn in Arabic, which includes (where this is appropriate) clauses concerning arbitration and choice of law which do not conflict with any enactment in the local law which may exclude the efficacy of these clauses, whether in whole or in part (as, for example, in regard to labour regulations), and which takes advantage of any concessions or exemptions which may be available.
3 must be *exceedingly careful in choosing local representatives, companies or directors, and the terms they lay down about the control that their shareholders exercise.*"

There is less 'overlap' involved in the present contributions; for such as there is, I cannot expect a better apologium. Some repetition between the parts is inevitable, where each part may often have had to serve as complete in itself. Not the least reason for this is the ever looming presence of that great common denominator in the Arab jurisdictions, Al Islam and hence the Shari'a. I hope that the contents of this volume serve to emphasise my own belief in the vast and increasing importance of this subject – vide, for example, the Coulson Memorial Lecture at Chapter X. There is also a very short Introduction to the Shari'a itself (Chapter VI).

When 'The Gulf States' was published, its main purpose was to serve as a text book for the LLM post-graduate course at SOAS. 'Arab Commercial Law' then occupied one term of a one year subject. That single term has long since been expanded into three, with a complete course entitled 'Arab Comparative Commercial Law' for which I continue to be responsible. The expansion has of itself necessitated the provision of the students with additional material, some of which is in the form of notes given to them *ad hoc*: some by way of essays or addresses published or delivered elsewhere. Most of the material in this volume has served that purpose, and a prime consideration for its publication now is to provide an additional text book for the course in the future.

I have referred to the terrifying speed with which the last thirteen years have sped by: another delay will see me, even if spared, at an age far exceeding the Biblical allowance. If I do not collate this material now, no-one else will.

An additional motive for publication now appears. During the course of nearly 50 years professional practice of Arab laws, I have amassed a vast body of material not only in the form of lectures and addresses, but also legal opinions given in a variety of matters. I have been persuaded that all this material should be collated and published.

Finally, this volume has no index, other than the initial table of contents. A detailed index, in a collection of this king, is not only unnecessary, but a nuisance. The date at which each chapter was delivered or published appears in the contents and thus represent the situation at that date. A reader who wishes to up-date the subject matter, can refer to my 'Register of Laws of the Arabian Gulf' which lists laws as they are gazetted, and is up-dated quarterly.

1

An Overall View: The Common Elements and a Comparative Study

From this comparative study I am excluding Iran. We all know something of the situation in Iran at the present time, and I am not in a position to contribute anything really constructive on the legal position in that troubled country. I doubt whether many people are, and I think we are very fortunate indeed to have Mr Alexander Aghayan to talk to us about Iran. Certainly Iran provides a shining, or glaring, example (depending which way you look at it), of the sheer motive force which one version (I stress this) one version of Islam can provide in the world today. I happen to be one of those who believe that there is a very real, effective, and heartfelt 're-assertion' (as I call it) of Islam at the present time and that this is something which must be understood if our relations with the Arab world are to survive: and this affects us very deeply as commercial lawyers, or at any rate should do so. In Islam the law is interwoven with the religion and vice versa, and we cannot differentiate between the two. Beyond pointing out, albeit superficially, the extent to which the Sharia currently applies in the countries we are discussing, I shall leave this theme to one, Professor Habachy, whom I am honoured to be permitted to call friend.

Now I wonder whether I may be permitted to digress shortly by way of reminiscence. In my opinion, this may be both relevant and useful in order to appreciate something of the really amazing changes which the advent of oil wealth has wrought in this area of the world.

To understand the present situation and balances, let us take a short look at recent history. In particular, this may enable us to get Egypt's contribution to the law of this area into perspective, and to understand some of the reasons for it. I will refer to this in a moment.

I first went to Cairo as a pilot in the Air Force in 1943 – it was a busy metropolis, more than half as old as time, stretching back many hundreds of years: and before that, of course, thousands more further along the river.

I first visited the Arabian Gulf in 1948. Then it took three days by flying boat; three delightful days during which you dined with the crew at night and during dinner agreed the take-off time in the morning. In 1948 Kuwait was a golden mud-walled town, a fishing port with some trade and a pearling industry: and behind it, desert: surrounded by a great wall built, so the story has it, in 90 days against threatened Saudi aggression.

Bahrain in 1948 with all its thousands of years of history and pre-history – neolithic, the Sumerians, the Phoenicians, the Greeks, the Portugese to name but a few: was it the Garden of Eden? – was in 1948 still a tiny community with a British adviser working with the Sheikh.

Dubai was a smuggling and trading port – I hope I have put those activities in the right order of priority – a little Venice stretching along its creek.

My first visit to Abu Dhabi was not until the 1960's and there was nothing there but a fort and a few barasti huts and again of course, desert.

Muscat under the old Sultan, could only be described as a medieval walled city: lanterns at night for walkers were obligatory, the town gates were locked at sunset and you could be put in prison for smoking in the streets.

Even in 1954 when I returned to Kuwait to advise the then Ruler, I found it virtually unchanged: it was really only as a result of the Abadan crisis, with the sudden demand for Kuwait crude, that the State suddenly took off economically: and

Saudi Arabia – in the 1960's Riyadh was little changed from the town which Abdul Aziz took by storm. In those days, in Kuwait, Bahrain, Qatar and what was then the Trucial coast, the British exercised extra-territorial jurisdiction over, broadly, all but Muslims and even some of those, and this extra-territorial regime did not end until 1961 (Kuwait) and 1971 (the rest of the area).

The point I am making is of course that this cataclysmic impact of oil wealth and social change, has come about really in a maximum of 25 years, and in some cases considerably less.

To me it is altogether remarkable that these Islamic societies in the Gulf have been able to adapt to the extent to which they have adapted to the dictates and needs of modern commerce. Perhaps the easiest transition has been in Bahrain, an island with a great tradition of settled civilisation over, as we have seen, many thousands of years, and where wealth has come gradually and in small quantities. But consider the others! In particular Saudi Arabia, where they owe a great debt to ARAMCO, as well as to their own undoubted acumen. Even so the conflicts are very apparent.

I well remember Sheikh Abdulla Saalem in Kuwait agonising over whether it was consistent with his religion to allow, on the cession of British extra-territorial jurisdiction in 1961, the introduction of a modern system of Codes. History shows that he did so; with the result that the Kuwait Codes have subsequently been the model for much other Gulf legislation (notably in Bahrain).

I hope that it may have been useful to make a short appreciation of this background, this recent history, in order to appreciate also the position at the present day.

What I would like to do now, if I may, is to take a look, on a comparative basis, at these various jurisdictions, and see what are the common factors which, for present purposes, we can attribute to them. I think the main touch points, as it were, are as follows, although we will no doubt be able to bring in others in discussion:

1 The Sharia Law of Islam which I can describe very loosely as the common law of the area, although that really is a misnomer and must be taken with several qualifications;
2 The Arabic language and this is a factor which is often put at the bottom of the list, quite wrongly, and under-emphasised;
3 That in general the civil law as distinct from the common law principles and codes tend to apply more and more: there are exceptions to this but they are increasingly few;
4 In the field of foreign investment and commerce, the need for national participation;
5 Taxation, where, with the exception of Egypt, there is a common philosophy overall;
6 The law surviving from the old extra-territorial jurisdiction;
7 The law, and I stress, the *law*, relating to the Israeli boycott.

Before taking a closer look at these factors however, I think we must have a clear picture of the constitutional status of the States with which we are dealing. This can be done very quickly for present purposes and may of course be developed by subsequent speakers. We are dealing with seven sovereign States, one of them, the United Arab

Emirates (U.A.E.) made up of a union or federation of seven Emirates, the degree of sovereignty of each of which would form an interesting study in international law far beyond the scope of this paper. In four of these sovereign States, Kuwait, Bahrain, Qatar and the U.A.E., the British Crown was formerly responsible for foreign relations, and as an adjunct to that, exercised the extra-territorial jurisdiction to which I have referred. I would stress that this was *not* a colonial regime; they were even at that time independent States in special treaty relations; they were Protected States not Protectorates. The fact that these relations were modernised with Kuwait 10 years before the others is significant. At that time Kuwait promulgated a comprehensive system of Codes drafted by Al-Sanhouri, the great Egyptian jurist, on civil principles and owing a great debt to Egyptian law.

In this context, I think it is impossible to over-estimate the debt which the Arab world owes to Egyptian law and lawyers. It is not surprising to find that the excellent Egyptian Codes, which were themselves based on the French Codes, have formed and will, in my opinion, continue to form the basis for lay legislation throughout the Arab world: not only are they excellent, but of course they are in Arabic and available and this in itself constitutes an insuperable advantage.

We are indeed fortunate in having my old friend Zaki Hashem with us who will tell us all about Egypt, and I would not have the temerity to try to go into any detail which is anyway not the purpose of this paper: but it is I think, interesting to draw one parallel – Egypt herself was subject to, or the victim of, Capitulations and until the end of the 19th Century had an almost impossibly complicated system of inter-conflicting consular jurisdictions. At that time an act of very great statesmanship swept away this complication, and substituted a national system of mixed courts which worked admirably and the judgments of which are still quoted with reverence today. (If anybody is interested in pursuing this subject, I would refer them to Judge Brinton's excellent book on the Mixed Courts of Egypt). It is, to say the least, a pity that similar tactics were not employed in replacing the extra-territorial jurisdiction or capitulations as we might call them also, in the Gulf. As it is, there is now considerable divergence between the legal situation in each of these States, and we have to seek for the common factors which we are now considering.

Turning now to those factors in more detail:-

The Shari'a

I need hardly remind this audience that these are all Islamic States. This is not at all the same as saying that Europe is Christian. Islam is part of the texture of Arab life and its cannon law the Shari'a is closely interwoven. This must be understood in order to have any comprehension, however superficial, of the basic philosophies of the subject with which we are dealing. In my opinion (and I would stress that it is *my* opinion) – even now, despite the considerable writing on various walls, I find myself in debate with learned colleagues on this subject – in my opinion, the Shari'a provides the key, and will continue to provide the key, to legal development in this area. At one end of the scale, are the cataclysmic events in Iran, which are obvious; Pakistan is another Islamic State, outside our area today, but to be referred to by analogy. I am not suggesting however that these are other than extreme, extraordinary manifestations of what I call the 'reassertion' of Islam; in the more moderate context this trend is, in my opinion, discernible also overall: the new Civil Code of Kuwait, as to which I have no doubt we shall be hearing from Dr Anis Kassim; the very guarded context in which 'lay' laws have been adopted throughout in Saudi Arabia – they are called 'Regulations' not 'laws' (pace the Ulama') – the recent constitutional developments in Egypt, where I believe the Shari'a has recently been proclaimed as *the* principal source of law as distinct from being *one* of the sources of law (about which Dr Zaki may be able to tell us more): and judgments and trends in banking in the U.A.E. (to which I shall refer later) – all are straws in the wind.

As the principles of the Shari'a may be strange to some of you may I explain very shortly that this system derives its authority basically from the Koran and developed through a system of traditions and sayings of the Prophet and interpretation, which process however, practically speaking, finished some hundreds of years ago.

The main object of this paper being to provoke discussion, I would like to make another controversial statement and quote from what I have written in another context:

> "It is often said that the Koran and hence the Shari'a provides all the principles necessary for the regulation of relationships even in the world of commerce. As with Christianity or other major religions, that would be true in the context of the ideal society, wherein every member accepted and obeyed its dictates under spiritual sanction."

I went on to say that in the context of society as it exists today, the lesser merits of man-made law must obtain because:

> "The inherent immutability of the Shari'a militates against its suitability in the system of international commerce which *man* has created and acceptance of this truth is reflected in the publication by most of the States of the Muslim world of commercial and other codes in replacement of the Shari'a which is now in many cases limited to matters of personal status" (Ballantyne: 'Legal Development in Arabia' at page 109).

As I have said, some of my old friends might disagree with this and I hope we might even have a lively discussion here about it. Be that as it may, I think the principle and the trends are increasingly recognised in particular in banking circles, where very active investigation is going on into the possibilities of 'Islamic banking' – seemingly, to me, a self-contradiction in terms! We shall be hearing from Professor Saba on the Shari'a: but shortly, in this context, I am sure we all know something of the difficulty or even impossibility of reconciling Shari'a principles with modern principles of banking and insurance. In a revival of the Shari'a, it seems to me that on the one hand such principles as the Sanctity of Contract (pacta sunt servanda), good faith etc. would not only survive but be enhanced – the sanction at the Shari'a being not restitutio or damages, but hell-fire! But on the other hand, the needs of modern commerce are not necessarily served in other respects.

To quote from myself once again:

> "the problem is that the Arabs have, to a greater or less degree, in wishing to adopt the existing international world of commerce, come face to face with the classic situation: an irresistible force against an irremovable object. As is not uncommon in these circumstances (not by any means only in the Arab world) the question has been begged on all sides. It will be, to say the least, interesting to see for how long and to what extent this apparent anomaly can continue." (Ibid, at page 121).

I think this is an obvious place in which to consider in rather more detail the constitutional and legislative background of the States we are considering, in order to appreciate the role which the Shari'a Law of Islam currently plays in their legal systems.

Of the States under consideration here, Egypt, Kuwait, Bahrain and the U.A.E. have written Constitutions largely on the same pattern (Egypt having provided the basic model for all), and containing provisions which are in some respects common form. Of immediate interest in the present context is the precept relating to El Islam: 'the religion of the State is El Islam, and the Islamic Shari'a is *a* principal source for legislation'. However, I have already pointed out that this provision has recently been changed in the Egyptian Constitution to give greater prominence to the Shari'a. Another interesting anomaly appears in the legislation setting up the Union Court of the U.A.E. which appears to ascribe to the Shari'a a more prominent role than is justified by the wording of the Constitution – it might be said I think that the Constitution of the Court is in this respect at variance with the Constitution of the State. Be that as it may, the wording in the Constitution of Kuwait, Bahrain and the U.A.E. is the same and it will be noted that the Shari'a is not stated to be *the* principle source of law but flexibility was deliberately maintained, in particular to enable modern commercial legislation to be promulgated.

Mr Qasim is going to talk to us about Kuwait, and in particular about the new Codes and I in no way wish to anticipate that: but the legal history of Kuwait is an interesting case in point and I would like to refer to it briefly.

Kuwait Judicature Law (Law 19 of 1959) established 'Lay' Courts having jurisdiction even in personal affairs. This was a rather dramatic step in a Muslim State at that time (I referred above to Sheikh Abdulla Salem's doubts in the matter). In personal affairs cases, in the case of a Muslim, the school of the Imam Malik was applied and the Majella (the old Ottoman Civil Code) continued to be prescribed in civil matters as previously; but the Commentary at that time to the Law (i.e. in 1959) went on to point out the need for basic legislation to stand beside the Islamic principles in the provisions of the Majella and promulgation of modern Codes of Procedure, Criminal Law, and Commerce quickly followed including an excellent Conflict of Laws (Private International Law) Code. Kuwait is still the only one of these Gulf States that has a Conflict Code. The Commercial Code (Law No. 2 of 1961) which was based upon Egyptian/French principles, contained the General Law of Obligations for Kuwait and other provisions which one would normally expect to find in a Civil Code. The reason for this was a deliberate move away from the principles of Islamic Law, contained in the Majella, in commercial matters: indeed the Commentary to the Commercial Code in explaining this situation is worthy of express note, because it puts State policy at that time beyond doubt:-

> "The reason is that the Majella, which is the Civil Code of Kuwait, has its provisions based upon those of the Islamic Shari'a, the Hanafi School, and the Kuwait Commercial Law *cannot*, being taken from Western Laws, have recourse to the Majella to complete its provisions; thus it is necessary to transfer to the Commercial Law a special book containing the provisions of Obligations in general and such provisions are taken from Western Law similar to the Commercial Law itself."

Thus, in the modern law of Kuwait, by a stroke of the pen, the role of the Shari'a was expressly limited to matters of personal affairs or status, and excluded from matters of commerce. Around this principle have grown the other Kuwaiti Commercial Laws touching upon Conflict, Banking, Commercial Companies, Industry etc.

Once again, I do not wish to intrude upon the field of my friend Mr Qasim who will be referring to the New Civil and Commercial Codes of Kuwait which came into effect on 25 February 1981. Suffice it to say here that it may be that the massive erosion of the Shari'a introduced by the Codes of the early 1960's seems to be in process of reversal. Of the other two States with full written Constitutions in the Gulf (and beyond having mentioned Egypt, I shall of course leave detail of the law of that country to Dr Zaki), Bahrain and the U.A.E., whose Constitutions appeared in 1973 and 1971 respectively, the position has never been so clear-cut with regard to the influence of the Shari'a as has been the case in Kuwait. Time only permits me to say here that in Bahrain to a much lesser extent, and in the U.A.E. and the individual Emirates to a sometimes greater extent, there is always the possibility that lacunae in specific Codes may be filled by the Judge by the application of Shari'a principles, and this must always be borne in mind by reference to the jurisdiction in each case. As a current practical example I would again refer to the recent Banking cases in Abu Dhabi.

Saudi Arabia has no written Constitution and the Shari'a is the Law paramount: such Regulations as have been passed are officially taken to 'regulate' the Shari'a principles – if it came to a conflict, it is difficult to see how some of these could be applied in derogation of the Shari'a.

In Qatar there is a rudimentary 'Constitution', which provides that the Shari'a is *the* principal source of law in the State, and I shall be referring to this in more detail when I come to deal with Bahrain and Qatar specifically.

Oman, like Saudi Arabia, has no written Constitution, and again the basic law must be taken to be the Shari'a but qualified once again, by modern laws which, however, tend to vacillate rather more between Civil and Common Law principles – and I leave the detail on this to my colleague Anna Monico.

The Arabic language

Arabic is the lingua franca of the area and the language of law and courts. Once again this is not at all the same as saying that French is the language of France, German the language of Germany etc. Anything else apart, the revelation of the Koran and the virtual explosion in society which followed spread a definitive version of the language over an immense area of the world. Here, language and thought are complementary to a limitless extent. In construing a law the definitive version of which is Arabic, it must be construed from the Arabic. In my opinion, an English lawyer can make a fair shot at construing an English translation of a French law: the same does not apply with the Arabic. You invariably get a diversity of translation, largely because of the richness of Arabic, and even more the different thought processes which made up the language. In what I may loosely call the West, we have our rules of interpretation and construction of the written word – rather more rigid at common law, rather more flexible at civil law: but in the construction of an Arabic law or particularly document, we find a fresh set of principles asserting themselves which are inherent in the thought processes which begot the language, and the language which progressively furthered the thought. Practically speaking, for the commercial lawyer, this is not an unmitigated disaster: *provided* there is full realisation of the situation. Increasingly, documentation must be in Arabic, and where this is not obligatory, it is almost always desirable. There should be an agreed Arabic version of a contract from the outset. Otherwise, to the substantive dispute which may develop under the contract, you are merely adding a linguistic dispute which will be almost inevitable; because no two people agree upon the right version of an Arabic translation! Arabic is a very beautiful language: lughat al Malāika the language of angels: but it is also lughat al 'Ḍad' the language of Dad (traditionally one of the more difficult letters in the Arabic language to pronounce): that is to say, it is very difficult.

Before turning to my next heading, I would refer to a practical consideration which comes to mind in dealing with the Arabic language – how is one to ascertain the current trends in legislation in this area, to keep abreast of laws as they are published? The answer lies happily in the principle of gazetting which is now common to most of these States. Egypt, Kuwait, Bahrain, Qatar, the U.A.E. (and the Emirates of Abu Dhabi, Dubai, Sharjah, Ras al Khaimah) and Oman all publish official gazettes regularly, and in all of these jurisdictions laws must be gazetted. Saudi Arabia unfortunately presents a difficulty; a kind of 'newspaper' called Umm al Qura is published but cannot be said to be exhaustive of all Decrees, Laws, Ministerial Decisions etc.

The Civil Law as distinct from Common Law

I have already expressed one of the main reasons for this, namely the excellence and availability of the Egyptian Codes in the Arabic language. That apart, in my opinion which I express with obvious regret as a basically common lawyer, the civil law, with its codified system, is more appropriate for this area than would be the common law. The common law embodies essentially a minuteness of definition much beloved by us within the cold shores of England, and tolerated even within the much larger shores of the United States; but in general that approach is not found attractive in Europe; and most certainly not in Arabia where the language itself absolutely redounds against it.

Like most generalities, the overall proposition that the civil law forms the basis for the lay legislation of these States must immediately be qualified. It is not, yet at any rate, of universal application. What does seem to be true however, is that such common law vestiges as exist are really remnants, and that new legislation is indeed exclusively based upon the civil law. May we examine this for a moment; in those Gulf States which have written Constitutions, (may I remind you – Kuwait, Bahrain, Qatar (but only to a certain extent), U.A.E.) these are, as I have said, based firmly on the Egyptian precedent. It is thus not surprising to find new legislation issuing under such Constitutions based on the same precedent. Of the others, Saudi Arabia has always based its Regulations (for example those relating to corporations; the fragmentary Commercial Code; Commercial Agencies Regulations; etc.) upon the Egyptian model: in Oman, the same trend is discernible in new legislation (examples: the Companies Law, Banking Law etc.) although it is true that there appears to be more of an admixture of principle in that particular jurisdiction. In fact, only in some of the Emirates of the U.A.E. (for example Dubai and Sharjah) might we expect legislation to appear more or less on a common law model. As not very much legislation does appear there anyway, this may be of somewhat academic interest at the present time.

It is not of course my role here to go in detail into the diversity of municipal law in these States: this is the role of my colleagues, although it will be my role to do that with regard to Bahrain and Qatar tomorrow. Thus, to illustrate my point under this heading, I merely refer briefly to:

Kuwait: as I have already said, a very comprehensive system of Codes ranging from the Constitution through the Judicature Laws, the new Civil and Commercial Codes (replacing very recently the old Commercial Code) and the Majella (or old Ottoman Civil Code based on the Shari'a) to Procedure Codes, Criminal Codes etc. all broadly based on civil principles and procedures.

Saudi Arabia: to which I have referred, Regulations on a similar pattern albeit fragmentary.

Bahrain: proving immediately an exception to the generality in that, as we shall see tomorrow, its laws of obligations are still drafted on common law principles: although there exists in Bahrain an anomaly whereby they would probably be interpreted in the courts increasingly from a civil point of view, and it is anticipated in any event that they will be replaced shortly by Codes based on the other system:

Qatar: with, once again as we shall see tomorrow, a comparative paucity of legislation but what there is (Civil and Commercial Code; Companies Law etc.) based on the civil model;

The U.A.E.: in which there is again a sad lack of 'Federal' or 'Union' legislation, due to what I can only describe as conflicts within the political structure (Abu Dhabi wants laws, Dubai does not!) but what there is shows the Civil influence.

The Individual Emirates: well, I have already referred to exceptions in these subsidiary jurisdictions: I call them subsidiary, but it should be noted (and this I think is important) that according to the U.A.E. Constitution, Emirate legislation is valid insofar as it does not conflict with Union legislation – our American friends will certainly find no anomaly here.

Oman: I have already referred to, and my colleague Anna Monico will be dealing with that jurisdiction in detail.

Foreign Investments: National Participation

This will not come as a surprise to anybody. It occurs to me that I am taking somewhat of a liberty in including this generality, really one of policy, in a short paper on comparative law! However, this is not an academic exercise, we are all commercial lawyers and looking for practical considerations. I am sure you all know that local participation by nationals is becoming increasingly necessary in all ventures carried on by foreigners. This is required or can be achieved in a variety of ways – the necessity for preponderance of local equity capital in corporations (Kuwait, Bahrain, Saudi Arabia, Qatar – I will refer to very notable exceptions in Bahrain when I talk on this subject tomorrow): the fixed percentage of equity depending upon the project (Oman): Foreign Capital Investment Laws (Saudi Arabi and Oman) etc. etc.

The necessity for a local sponsor or agent also applies virtually throughout the whole area, although with varying degrees of severity. Once again I am sure that all my colleagues will be dealing with this aspect in detail. The most liberal jurisdictions in this respect continue to be the Emirates, in particular perhaps Dubai and Sharjah. Commercial Agencies, which may often be defined as distributorships, but the definition of which must be very closely watched in every jurisdiction, increasingly have to be held exclusively by nationals, and indeed Commercial Agency Laws contain traps and difficulties by way of termination, compensation etc. which I have little doubt we shall develop in discussion at some length.

Inevitably, to the foreign investor against this background, the protection of his investment looms large. This is a huge and separate subject, involving inter alia complicated aspects of State contract – because, in the nature of things, in these countries many, if not most, of the large contracts are State contracts. I do not need to stress to you Ladies and Gentlemen, that the conclusion of a proper contract and the protection conferred by it are absolutely of the essence. That apart, where there are written Constitutions, they provide for the inviolability of private property, and that ex-propriation may only be effected for the public benefit and against due compensation. It is, I think, relevant to refer here to the Summit Conference of Islamic States which took place not long ago at Taif in Saudi Arabia, and at which a draft Islamic Charter of Human Rights was put forward and adjourned for further study and eventual promulgation by a further conference: and it is important to note that this principle of the inviolability of private property was unequivocally stated in the Charter, which was intended to apply to Muslims and non-Muslims alike.

Taxation

This may be thought an unusual heading in a short comparative study: systems of taxation do of course tend to vary normally from State to State, and the only common element is that it is a common curse! In the present instance, however, there is in fact a common origin for taxation throughout the area in that, with the exception of Egypt, all taxation legislation was introduced as the basis of the fundamental change in the structure of royalty payments that occurred under oil concessions some thirty years ago. Prior to this change, royalties were paid under existing concession agreements at the now almost incredible rate, on average, of Rupees 3, Annas 8 per ton! It was then devised (I believe first with respect to Venezuela) that if the oil producing countries could be induced to pass fiscal legislation imposing taxation whereby the concessionaire oil companies might be charged, in lieu of the royalty payment system, then by arrangement with the home countries of such companies by way of tax credits a very much increased 'royalty' might be paid to the producing country and, of course, insofar as that payment constituted an income tax the concessionaire company would obtain a corresponding credit at home. This was the whole reason for the introduction of taxation in the area. (I stress again Egypt is an exception to this: taxation was introduced into Egypt for the more usual economic reasons not associated with oil). The tax laws are virtually identical, with the exception of Saudi Arabia, where United States draftsmen were involved (in the rest of the Gulf they were British); and one essential corollary to all is that we are dealing throughout the area with taxation on corporations only. There is no taxation on individuals: there was until recently in Saudi Arabia but it has been abolished. There is one interesting and relevant feature of this tax situation. Having regard to the motive behind its introduction in the first place, it was originally intended to limit taxation to oil companies producing petroleum from the ground. The original tax laws in most of these jurisdictions were therefore so limited (for example Kuwait, Qatar). However, the revenue authorities of the United Kingdom declined to accept such discriminatory legislation as coming within the definition of 'income tax' and for that reason the laws were extended to include all bodies corporate whatever their commercial activities. Bahrain was, and continues to be, an exception; the Bahrain legislation did not have to satisfy the U.K. authorities, and thus the Bahrain legislation was, and is, limited to oil producing companies. I shall say more of this when I come to deal with Bahrain as a tax-free area.

The Law surviving from the Extra-Territorial Jurisdiction

I think I have dealt largely with this already to the extent to which time permits: it is still a factor. These survivals are to be found in, for example, the Contract Laws of Bahrain and the Southern Gulf which are still on the common law pattern: Laws of Civil Wrongs (Torts): and in the Penal Laws: and, in the Emirates, where the only method of incorporation is still by a Charter from the Ruler concerned – although we have been promised a Union Company Law for some considerable time.

The Israeli Boycott

We are not concerned here in any shape or form with politics, and the only point I want to make about this is that it is a sanction imposed by law. The Arab League agrees upon the principles, and each member State enacts the law to give effect to them. This is what has been done: so in each case you are dealing with a law in the country in question: and it is, of course, in each case a law going very much to public policy and you certainly cannot in any way contract out of it. There is no time to go into this in any detail, but for those who do not know of it I would refer them for such detail to the House of Lords Report of the Select Committee on the Foreign Boycotts Bill which is an extremely useful reference document in this respect.

That deals very shortly with the common comparative factors to which I have referred. I am rapidly running out of time and will have to end, but perhaps I have just time to engage in the most dangerous practice of prophecy. I would have liked to have dealt in far more detail on the comparative basis with the various heads in the summary, which I think you have had in advance, and which I have in fact not followed with any accuracy. In particular, I would have liked to have dealt on a comparative basis with the Conflict of Laws and jurisdiction and with Arbitration in rather more detail. However, I am sure all these comparisons will come out during the course of this conference. The latter subject, in particular, is going to be dealt with next by my colleague Dr Dilger – and I hope that we can develop some of the subjects in panel at the end.

As to prophecy – I stated at the outset that I thought the key to progression in this area lay in the extent to which there was likely to be a re-assertion of Islam in the law; and I stressed to a certain extent also how I thought this was already coming about. In my view, this is indeed the key to the future and in considering it one essential feature has to be borne in mind: legislation in these States can be achieved very quickly with the possible exceptions of Egypt and Kuwait – in the latter State, elections have recently been re-introduced, the Constitution in that respect having been in abeyance for some years (as is still the case in Bahrain). I have no doubt in my own mind that this is the trend, and the Western world will simply have to live with it and adapt to it. I shall be, personally, very interested to see what our other Speakers think about this.

I would like to advert to Corporation Law. I have already referred briefly to this aspect of course. Egypt, Kuwait, Saudi Arabia, Bahrain and Qatar have Company Laws on the continental model, that is to say generally speaking with companies ranging from the Societe en nom collectif through the Societe anonyme, save that in Qatar only the latter may be formed. The Emirates of the U.A.E. still have a charter system, while Oman has a hybrid Company Law to which Anna Monico will refer. In the corporate field however, a large number of international corporations have been formed between States as partners or shareholders. There is a diversity of these: and again their analysis and definition would form an interesting study – whether they be creatures of international law, possessed of objective personality; an amalgam of the municipal laws of the States concerned; what would be the liability in each case of the shareholders or partners (i.e. the States): these are matters deserving of further study, on which comparatively little has been done in the international legal field. Not the least problem is the extent to which these entities would be recognised as such in courts other than those of the member States. Certainly the first step always is a careful analysis in the Arabic language of the Treaty and Statutes setting up the corporation.

II

Arab Comparative Commercial Law

In 1983 Noel Coulson came to me and asked me if I would contribute one term's lecture on the subject of modern commercial laws of the Arab, in particular the Gulf, States. The title which we devised for that course was 'Comparative Commercial Law of the Middle East', and the plan of the year's course was:

Term 1 – The Shari'a
Term 2 – A Historical 'Bridge' and introduction to the Codes of Egypt and North Africa
Term 3 – The Modern Commercial Law

The course proceeded upon that basis for four years, and led to the devising of a new one. In this there were really two initiatives in one: firstly, it was now possible to obtain an LLM in exclusively Arab law subjects:

Shari'a I being a general introduction to the Shari'a
Shari'a II the law, succession and personal law in the Shari'a
III Arab Comparative Commercial Law:
IV A dissertation.

Now, it is, of course, with the third of these, Arab Commercial Law, that we are concerned this evening, and of which this is the inaugural lecture, and this brings me to the second initiative. It is intended that as well as forming part of the LLM package to which I have referred, this particular course, which will consist of 25–30 lectures as time permits, stretching over the academic year, should remain available to practising lawyers as a separate package. To that end, my lectures have been timed to take place in the evening at

18.00, and the scheme is to have about an hour's lecture – it may be less, I sometimes think that an hour is too long for a concentrated subject of this nature – followed by a 'workshop' during which not only the subject matter of the lecture will be discussed, but also practical problems arising from the practice of law in and with the Arab jurisdictions. Such workshops have operated very successfully in this School in other legal subjects, I believe Chinese law is one outstanding example. The LLM students will be free to stay on for the workshop and particularly perhaps, in view of the diversity of nationality usually represented, will be able not only to absorb knowledge from the practising lawyers, but also contribute specialist knowledge from their own jurisdictions.

Now, the title to course III has been chosen with considerable care and I want to come on to that and analyze it in a moment. First, however, just one more word about the general parameters of the course. It will be essentially practical: but that is not to say that we shall leap immediately into a consideration of current commercial problems without adverting to the general principles of law, the study of which must precede any understanding of our subject. In the jurisdictions which we are considering, it is absolutely essential that these basic underlying principles be grasped – indeed this is the same in any system, but a fortiori in considering the Arab world. How often am I asked: 'Why do we not have more cases?' Well, there is more than one answer to that, but the immediate one is that it is quite useless to read cases without having a full knowledge of the legal system of the jurisdiction in which they are delivered. As an aside, I may record my own gratitude to the classical system which forced me to learn Latin and Greek and contrast the great damage done in my own legal education by the war. That meant that my time at Cambridge was very much curtailed. After the war I was obliged to embark upon a legal career without the sound basis of jurisprudence upon which it would otherwise have been based, and for many years I suffered from that deficiency, from the lack of that basis. Thus, I do stress this: a fortiori in the Arab jurisdictions – we shall not make that mistake in this course. We must get the principles well established.

This brings me on to my last general point: the object of this course is not to enable anyone to practice 'Arab law' – there is no such thing, as we shall see in a moment. The object is to give an introduction and, as I have said, a solid base from which one can proceed. I recall that in 1939, I think it was, in the course of my awesome first approach to the study of Arabic I sat at the feet of the great Professor Tritton. He emphasized the need for a classical approach to the study of Arabic – he drew upon a blackboard a wheel with a hub and spokes. He said the classical language is the hub of the wheel; if you master that, then you can wander at will down any one of the spokes to a particular colloquial form or dialect; but it is a very different matter starting at the perimeter and trying to work your way back to the hub. Well, I hope it will be apparent as we progress that what we are trying to do here is to establish the hub of our jurisprudential wheel, if I can put it that way, upon which we can then wander at will into any jurisdiction in the Arab world and have some idea of the background and perhaps in particular, in the case of practising lawyers, the questions to ask lawyers in the country concerned. Also, of course, I would hope in many cases our hub will, if I can mix metaphors, serve as the spring-board for future studies, and that many will go on to learn Arabic (for this course is essentially in English – I shall say more about that) and to master the laws of one or more of the Arab jurisdictions.

Now the content of this course is dealt with as succinctly as possible in the paper advertising it as follows:

> It will deal on a comparative basis not only with the modern Arab Commercial Codes, both inter se and with Western jurisprudence, but also with the Shari'a, the extent to which it does or might apply in the various Arab jurisdictions, and, again, an analysis of the Shari'a provisions in commercial matters in comparison with the modern laws.

We can leave that there for a moment. Suffice it to say that the object is to study modern Arab commercial laws in comparison with Western laws; at the same time bear in mind that in a particular instance and varying from jurisdiction to jurisdiction, the Shari'a law may be relevant: may indeed be paramount; and thus to assess what the Shari'a says about each particular incident of commercial law which we are considering. This is an ambitious programme.

Now I want to come on to the title – Arab Comparative Commercial Law. As I have said already, this has been carefully chosen and requires analysis. Not 'Arab Commercial Law' – as we shall see in a moment, there is not yet a lex arabica, or more particularly a lex mercatoria arabica - not even Arab commercial laws. Let us consider these words in detail:-

Arab

We do not happily have to try to define here what is meant by an Arab, as that is more difficult than it sounds. Suffice it to note that we are here dealing with 18 separate jurisdictions from Morocco in the West through to Oman in the East; that is the significance of the word Arab in our present context. Eighteen separate jurisdictions, taking the United Arab Emirates as one jurisdiction although it itself comprises seven Emirates each with its own peculiarities and laws. Now we shall see that all these jurisdictions do have laws in common but they do not have a common law. I think we must right at the outset get this into perspective. If we asked ourselves the question, is there a lex arabica, is there a lex mercatoria arabica, we must return a negative answer at the present time. In many cases in practice in the Arab world there is a transnational approach between the various jurisdictions: in all of them, the comparative approach has, as we shall see, a peculiar relevance because of the common features which exist between them: these common features exist (notably of course the Shari'a itself) to an extent which is not discernable in other jurisdictions: but that is very far from saying that there already exists a lex arabica. To assume that there is a body of law which can be so entitled would be a dangerous error at the present time. The comparative processes which are so relevant may in the future lead to a truly common body of law, but such a designation would only truly be safe to assume in my view if there occurs common legislation by the Arab States to justify it. Unfortunately at the moment there are few signs of this and thus each jurisdiction must be taken as individual. Now, as in other non-Arab jurisdictions where authority is not available within the particular forum, it may be relevant to adduce authority, doctrine and jurisprudence from other Arab jurisdictions in priority over other sources, but that is at the moment as far as it goes. However, among the common processes which we can deduce from an overall study there is of course the one element which is unique to the Islamic States and that is the Shari'a law. The role of the Shari'a and its extent in the jurisprudence of the Arab States will of course be one of our main topics in this course, and let there be no mistake: in today's climate political, economic and social, this is a subject of overwhelming and increasing importance. I don't think any student of contemporary history could doubt that for a moment: the increasing reassertion of the Shari'a is apparent.

Comparative

With the foregoing firmly in mind, we can deal at this stage briefly with 'comparative law'. We might say even more briefly that there is no such thing. Professor Gutteridge (a Trinity Hall man) put it very neatly: 'It is a method of study not distinct branch or department of law'. However, it is a method of study which is peculiarly apposite to an introductory study of Arab laws. Indeed, in my view, the comparative approach is achieving ever increasing significance in the study of law generally and I shall want to go into that in more detail later in this course, but this is particularly so in the Arab jurisdictions and we shall see the reasons for that in a moment; but we shall be continually seeking for points of concordance between the systems. This brings us on to:

Commercial Law

In the comparative inter-Arab studies which follow we shall quintessentially be considering contract. May I be forgiven for quoting again at some length from Professor Gutteridge because he puts it better than I ever could:

> "Commercial law is, strictly speaking, merely one aspect of the law of contract, but its volume and the importance of its subject-matter have elevated it to the rank of an independent branch of the law in general. The value of comparison seems to be beyond doubt in this instance. Diversity of law affects commerce more sensibly than any other form of human activity and constitutes an impediment to the free interchange of goods which is the life breath of trade. International commerce is ambulatory in nature, and transactions may often range over a very wide area, thus rendering them subject to several different systems of law. Private international law has failed to provide a remedy for this state of uncertainty, and men of business have been driven to seek their own remedies. These generally take the shape of either the use of standardised forms of contract designed to supersede or modify the legal situation or the communication to the business world of details of the foreign rules of law which give rise to difficulties. In either case, the value of comparative investigation of commercial law is so obvious as to make it unnecessary to labour the point. Commercial law also offers the

> most favourable opportunities for the process of unification which necessarily involves comparison of the relevant laws."

This is even more relevant in the Arab jurisdictions. As to '*law*' – we shall be dealing with the Shari'a up to the extent to which it applies: and the *civil law* system. There is alas little relevance left to the common law in the Arab jurisdictions. It may ultimately contribute in the comparative process as one of the general principles of law, but such occasions are increasingly rare.

Now, what are the features which we find to be common to the Arab jurisdictions overall? I think these must be distinguished as follows:

1 Al Islam
2 The Shari'a – the law of Islam
3 The Arabic language
4 The Constitutions
5 Civil and Commercial Codes on a common model
6 An interchange of judges
7 The influence of Egyptian writings and judgments

We must consider each of these factors in turn. Taken in the aggregate they represent a powerful cohesive force which dictates a degree of propinquity between the various Arab jurisdictions which it may be said does not exist elsewhere. It is of course true that some of these features are equally common as between Western jurisdictions – in the West we find common constitutional models; we find of course common origins for the great European Codes; we find where there are lacunae in the law of a particular forum that it may be relevant to invoke authority from another jurisdiction. However, for reasons which will become apparent to us, where such common features exist in the West they in no way provide the cohesive force which they constitute in the *Arab* world; and of course, in addition we have the unique features of Al Islam, the Shari'a and the Arabic language.

We must now consider briefly each of these sources.

Al Islam – The Shari'a

We can bracket these two together: the Shari'a is of course the canon law of Al Islam.

It is surely unnecessary to inform this audience that in dealing with the Arab world we are dealing with all Islamic States. It is perhaps not so obvious that this is not at all the same as in dealing with the Western world we are dealing with Christian States! For the Arab, his religion is inextricably interwoven with his life. The percepts of Al-Islam are ever present in his thoughts and speech: the Quran says 'Ye who believe, mention (or remember) God often, praise him both early and late', and the cry of the mu'aththin rings out five times daily from the mosque, calling the faithful to prayer. The Shari'a is the law of that religion. In looking at the strong reassertion of Islam which we are witnessing in the Arab world, we are looking also at the reassertion of the Shari'a law.

Just as the Constitutions of the Arab States prescribe Al-Islam as the religion of the State, so do they, in greater or lesser degree, prescribe the Shari'a as a source of legislation. There are degrees of prescription, which we shall study as we go along. In Saudi Arabia and Oman, for example, there are no written Constitutions (this is not strictly so: Saudi Arabia has the old written declaration of the Hijaz, but this is not a Constitution in the modern sense: nonetheless it prescribes Al-Islam as the only source). The extent to which the Shari'a does in fact apply as a source of legislation must be one of our main objects of study in this course, and, as I have said, there is diversity: for example, in Qatar and, since 1980, in Egypt, the Shari'a is *the* main source of legislation. In Kuwait, Bahrain and the U.A.E., the Constitution prescribes the Shari'a as *a* main source of legislation. In the Constitution of Jordan, although, as would be expected, Al-Islam is clearly stated to be the religion of the State, there is no mention of the Shari'a as a source of legislation.

Thus, in dealing in any particular jurisdiction in the Arab world, the practising lawyer must ask himself at the outset the degree to which, if at all, the Shari'a is applicable to the problem which he is considering. In some jurisdictions (e.g. Kuwait, and now, since its new Commercial Code, Bahrain in commercial cases) it may have no relevance; in others, such as Saudi Arabia, it may be omnipotent. The lawyer who does not undertake this preliminary investigation is acting very much at his peril; for, as we shall see, at the Shari'a many modern commercial contracts would simply be illegal and void. We shall of course consider these matters seriatim as this course continues. This essential element is often neglected even by Arab lawyers.

The Arabic language

One cannot possibly over-emphasize the importance of the language in the study of Arab laws. There can be no doubt that the availability of the original Egyptian Codes as drafted by that great jurist Al-Sanhouri in the Arabic language played a large part in their being adopted, as adapted by Sanhouri, by many other Arab jurisdictions – Iraq, Syria, Libya, Kuwait, Qatar – and as models for many others. Allied to the exigencies of the language, the genius of Sanhouri spread the format of these Codes throughout the Arab world. However, the matter goes much further than that: the official language of all these countries is Arabic, the courts accept pleading and documentation only in Arabic, as would be expected, and the thought processes involved in and reflected in the Arabic language introduce an additional element into interpretation and construction.

In my experience of practice in both common and civil law systems, I have found that the fundamental difference between the civil and the common lawyer lies in a basic difference of approach which probably defies analysis. In the Arab countries, this difference is compounded again by the veneer of Arab thought reflected in the language. The whole essence of this course is that it is in the English language. That I hope will be its value, and I shall do my best to bridge the gap and to give an entreée, as it were, to those thought processes which are so essential to practice in the Arab jurisdictions, and which are reflected in the Arabic language. However, I must stress at the outset that those who wish to pursue their studies (and I do hope there will be many of you), really, if they are to progress further, must learn Arabic and learn it to some effect.

I believe the most difficult task which I shall have in this series of lectures will be to instil in non-Arabists some understanding of the atmosphere inherent in Arab thought as reflected in the language: concomitant with this will be to instil some idea of the thought processes involved in the Shari'a. In the classical writings on the Shari'a we find what the Western lawyer would regard as an obsession with grammatical analysis of language. This approach must be appreciated, and I will endeavour to give examples of it as we go along. That brings us immediately to that mystical book, the Quran (and I hope I am not offending anybody by describing it as such).

The revelations recorded in the Quran in that wonderful language really beautify and set the standard for the Arabic language overall. Let us try to get a little of the atmosphere by recalling that marvellous book, 'Al-Ayam', written by the blind author Taha Hussain, I suppose at the turn of the century. In that, he describes his initial education in Cairo – what a fascinating and vivid account it all is. I seem to recall that one volume of the book was translated into English, and it would be well worth getting hold of a copy. Now, I am not suggesting that the education of the modern Egyptian lawyer bears much relation to the early education of Taha Hussain, who studied to be a Shaikh at Al-Azhar. However, the account in 'Al-Ayam' helps one to understand the mental approach, the thought processes, which are reflected in the Arabic language and thus form an essential element in the construction of Arabic. By the time he was twelve, the young Taha Hussain had mastered the whole Quran by heart. He had to be able to declaim from any given sura or revelation at the dictate of an examiner. He then progressed to master the 'Alfiyya', the basic thousand verses of Arabic grammar, all in rhyme. The point I am trying to make is, I think, that the language per se, the very language in itself, takes over right from the beginning. This is very difficult, but I think it could be put this way: that the thought processes which create the Arabic language in order to convey them then become subject to the control. of the actual language and the sound of the language itself. I cannot dwell on this, but as a matter of construction, let me take a short example: the hallowed precept in the continental codes, the civil codes: les conventions légalement formeées tiennent lieu de droit à ceux qui les ont faites. Now this, or something like it can be found in the French Code, the Italian Code, the German Code – really wherever we look. It of course reflects the basic maxim *pacta sunt servanda*, and we can usually translate it that contracts legally concluded constitute the law of the parties. It is not surprising to find that because of the civil basis of the Arab Codes, it is common to them also – al-aqd shari'at al-muta'aaqidin. Now literally translated that means that the contract is the law of the parties, but, of course, left at that it is absolutely meaningless. In searching further for a meaning, in interpreting that provision, Arabic comes into play, another element in construction. I shall try very hard to put this across as we progress on the course.

On this question of sanctity of contract, let us make a short excursus: it illustrates, as we go along, one of the distinctions which we shall have to make between the Shari'a and the secular laws.

The Shari'a recognizes in full the sanctity of contract. I quote from a modern decision, the remarkable award of Professor Reneé Dupuy in the Texaco Arbitration:

> "The observance of contract, generally speaking, is proclaimed by the Quran (see in particular Sura V.1), and the practice of the Prophet, which is the second source of law in Islam (Bukhari III

> 187). The writings of Muslim jurists uphold the same principle, in particular Ibn Qudama, a jurist of considerable authority in the Hanbali School, which is predominant in Saudi Arabia . . . This principle applies not only to agreements completed by private persons, but also agreements entered into by the sovereign. Thus, under the Shari'a nobody, neither the sovereign nor any official is exempt as a matter of privilege."

Well, as a general principle that is fine: but when we look into it more deeply, we find the basic differences which distinguish the Shari'a philosophies from those of modern Western systems. May I here translate a passage from 'Masaadir Al-Haqq' of Sanhouri: he puts it, in Arabic of course, better than I can and he is an outstanding authority. He does not follow the usual course and put the main difficulty on the basis that the Shari'a knows no general theory of contract per se, but only types of nominate contract: although that is of course the case. However, he is of the opinion that we can, in our time, go far to extracting, by analogy from the specific examples of nominate contract given by the Shari'a, a general theory. No, he does not put the difficulty there, i.e. in the matter of nominate contract; he highlights the matter somewhat differently:

> "Thus, those nominate contracts mentioned by the doctors of law are only those contracts which most frequently occur in the transactions of the time. If civilization has evolved other contracts *which satisfy the conditions laid down in the jurisprudence, such contracts are lawful.* It is on this legal (shar'i) policy that the new Iraqi civil legislation is based" (let us recall in passing here that it was Sanhouri who drafted the Civil Code in Iraq, among others).
>
> Article 74 of the Iraqi Code enumerates the types of contract in accordance with their objects. Then this is followed by a general provision, Article 75, as follows (Sanhouri quotes):
>
> > "The contract may embrace anything else in respect of which the obligation is not forbidden by law or contrary to public policy or morals."
>
> However, the scope of public order in the Islamic jurisprudence is wider than that in Western jurisprudence. The prohibition of contracts contrary to riba or gharar greatly extends such scope in the Islamic jurisprudence: so also does the theory of condition as

applied to the contract increase the extent of such scope to a large degree.

Thus, the principle in the Islamic jurisprudence is freedom of contract within the bounds of public order; *but the multiplicity of the principles which are considered to go to public order narrow such freedom.*

Let us return and complete our list:

The Constitutions

It suffices to note at this stage that where there are written Constitutions, these are more or less based on a common form. As the reason for this is basically the same as the reason why there are common Codes, I shall now pass immediately to:

Civil and Commercial Codes on a common model

I have already briefly alluded to this in reference to the genius of Al-Sanhouri and the subsequent availability of the basic Codes in Arabic.

In 1949 Egypt promulgated its new Civil Code. This was drafted by Sanhouri, and has survived virtually unamended for nearly 40 years. In 1942, when he was working on the Code, Sanhouri announced that he had used comparisons of more than 20 modern Codes, the jurisprudence of the Egyptian Courts, and the Islamic Shari'a.

Now, as we progress in this course we shall of course study the sources of the Arab laws in detail. However, it was quite apparent that Sanhouri's preoccupation and main difficulty in drafting the Egyptian Code was to try to build a bridge between the Shari'a and the dictates of modern commerce. In this course I shall try to point up the conflict between the *immutable tenets* (i.e. the Quran and Sunna) of the Shari'a, and in particular the modern economic scene. In 1980, I wrote:

> "The problem is that the Arabs have to a greater or lesser degree, in wishing to adopt the existing international world of commerce, come face to face with the classic situation: an irresistible force against an irremovable object. As is not uncommon in these circumstances (not by any means only in the Arab world) the question has been begged on all sides. It will be, to say the least, interesting to see for how long and to what extent this apparent anomaly can continue."

Well, the anomaly does continue, and increasingly the position is accentuated by current political circumstance; it will be our task in this course to assess these anomalies along with the importance of this conflict between the Shari'a and Western (and, indeed, modern Arab) legal concepts, and this we shall do on a comparative basis as we go along. The dream of Sanhouri was that the Shari'a could be increasingly adapted to such needs, and that modern Codes could be increasingly made to conform more with the Shari'a, so that by some kind of compromise the two could meet. There is no sign of that happening, and, indeed, I regard it as in the ultimate analysis, probably impossible.

The Interchange of Judges

One aspect of the overwhelming influence which Egypt, its laws and lawyers had upon the other jurisdictions of the Arab world lies in the supply by Egypt of judges for their courts. This is particularly true of the courts in the Arabian Gulf which on the cessation of the British Extra-Territorial Jurisdiction (Kuwait 1961, Persian Gulf 1971) had no trained lawyers with which to staff their courts. They were thus obliged to import judges and, for reasons which will already have been apparent to us, they looked in particular to Egypt. This was a natural process – the first Gulf Code to be promulgated was the Kuwaiti Commercial Code of 1961 written as we have seen by Al Sanhouri and it was fairly obvious that in these circumstances Egyptian judges would follow. It must be evident that this situation again makes for uniformity, a transnational approach to the interpretation of the Codes.

The Influence of Egyptian Writings and Judgments

This is almost a sequitur from what we have been saying. Jurisprudential writings in many of the Arab jurisdictions are simply not to be found: in particular again, the Gulf area. It is not surprising that the one work which is certain to be found at the right hand of every judge sitting in an Arab court is the monumental Al Waseet of Al Sanhouri, his 10-volume Commentary on the Egyptian Civil Code. The other book which is almost always present somewhere is the Majellat al Ahkam Al'Adliya, commonly known as the Majella, the Ottoman Codification of the Shari'a which was put together in the 19th Century. Most judges have this available just in case a Shari'a point comes up!

So we have all these unifying factors; let us remind ourselves of what they are:

1 Al Islam
2 The Shari'a
3 Arabic
4 The Constitutions
5 Civil and Commercial Codes
6 An Interchange of judges
7 Influence of Egyptian writings and judgments.

This situation encourages us, particularly where there are lacunae, where there are gaps in any particular system, to adopt the comparative approach and look for points of uniformity, for points of concordance in order to fill them. Of course, we find increasingly that this approach is to a limited (if increasing) extent valid also in Europe – let us remind ourselves that a French judge, for example, cannot decline to give judgment on the basis that there is no law; he must adduce a principle from somewhere. But, due to the factors which I have briefly outlined this is a much more potent consideration in the Arab jurisdictions than it is in Europe.

With this general background in mind we shall embark upon our comparative study – comparative to a certain extent between the jurisdictions: comparative to a certain extent with European law: comparative above all as between the Shari'a and secular law, which, I stress again, obtains in greater or lesser degree according to the jurisdiction concerned.

An ambitious programme. We clearly cannot look in detail at 18 jurisdictions, and our picture will have to be painted essentially with a broad brush in many respects. I propose to try to deal with it on the following pattern:

Sources of law

We shall analyse the sources of law prescribed by the various Constitutions and Codes, from the Shari'a itself through to custom etc. As I have said, we cannot possibly cover all the jurisdictions and in the main we shall take the most modern Civil and Commercial Codes, those of Kuwait, as illustrating one end of the scale, and we shall take Saudi Arabia as representing the Shari'a par excellence at the other. In between we shall find varying shades.

The Shari'a

I cannot of course assume that my audience will have any knowledge of the Shari'a and it will be necessary therefore to give a short introduction to the subject. I stress that this will be short and will aim in the first instance to paint once more with a broadbrush: thereafter, as we consider each incident in the Codes in the modern context, we shall try to see what the Shari'a says about the same incident. I think that it would be useful if I were to anticipate the main difficulty in all this right at this initial stage, and I would like to quote from Noel Coulson's book in which he puts the difficulty with his usual incisiveness:

> "Muslim jurisprudence . . . is the revealed will of God, a divinely ordained system preceding and not preceded by the Muslim State, controlling and not controlled by Muslim society."

Now, this is really concentrated. Let me elaborate a little. In considering the adaptation or the modernization of the Shari'a to fill the needs of contemporary circumstances, we are immediately dealing with an essential contradiction: the whole essence of the Shari'a as a religious law is that it is not intended to develop according to the dictates or needs of society; quite to the contrary, society and its circumstances are to be controlled, circumscribed, by the Shari'a. Society is supposed to evolve according to the dictates of the Shari'a. Now, clearly, if that had happened, then there would be no conflict and no irresistible force against an irremovable object. But it did not happen, and there is now much talk of new ijtihad, new emerging doctrines based on the Shari'a which will, so to speak, up-date it and bring it into line with modern conditions. This, of course, involves a basic conflict, an essential floundering around trying to surmount *immutable* provisions of the Shari'a. It is in this that lies, to me, the whole insurmountable problem in seeking to adapt the Shari'a to some concepts of Western commercial law which offend basic and immutable provisions of the Shari'a.

A topical example may serve to highlight this difficulty, and perhaps fix it in our minds. Let us examine the matter by reference to the Charter of the Islamic International Court of Justice promulgated by the Islamic Conference in January 1987. The principle provisions of the Charter from our point of view are as follows:

(From the Preamble)

> "The fifth Islamic Summit Conference . . . desiring to set up a principal judicial organ to decide disputes in accordance with the provisions of the Islamic Shari'a and the principles of public international law . . .

(Article 1)

> The Islamic International Court of Justice is the principal judicial organ of the Islamic Conference Organization, is founded on the principles of Islam and the sources and basic rules of the Islamic Shari'a . . .

(Article 27)

> (a) The Islamic Shari'a is the basic source relied upon by the Court in its judgments.
> (b) The Court shall refer to international law and biparty and multiparty international agreements, or international custom in force, or the general principles of law, or judgments issuing from international tribunals.

(Article 28)

> (a) Arabic, the language of the Quran, is the first language of the Court, and Arabic together with English and French are the accredited official languages."

Here we find our irresistible force and irremovable object again. We must moreover recall the Hague conferences, which confirmed the Shari'a itself as a general principle of law as referred to in Article 38 of the Statute of the International Court of Justice. What if the other sources referred to here are contrary to the Shari'a? Presumably they must be ignored. What then happens to a modern investment treaty?!

I have no doubt that we shall debate these matters during this course, but let us always throughout bear this essential position in mind. This is the difficulty.

Comparative study of the Codes

Having laid a firm basis in our Constitutions, in our sources of law and with at least some idea of what the Shari'a is all about, we shall then proceed to study the principles of law as laid down in the various

Codes: and we shall do this on a comparative basis adverting also to the position at the Shari'a as we go along.

We shall appreciate the differences between personal and real rights.

We shall identify the sources of rights in the civil and Islamic jurisprudence: contract, individual volition, the illegal act (tort: delict and qausi delict), enrichment without cause and the law. In particular, we shall spend time on contracts – the elements of contract – the congruence of wills – validity of consent – deceit – duress – object and cause – nullity and its consequences – the effect of contract and its termination – breach, damages, etc.

Now, it will be apparent that these headings present a picture more familiar to the civil than the common lawyer. I have already given the reason for this: the Codes are Egyptian thus French/European based.

Egyptian law

Mr Ian Edge is at present in Cairo on a research project, but he will be returning to contribute to the course from his knowledge of the historical contribution of Egyptian law to the Arab systems, and indeed to provide material on the Egyptian Codes and background. This will probably be during the second term of the course.

We shall throughout introduce concepts of private international law, of conflict, and we shall see, and indeed stress, that of course the comparative approach provides no substitute for the observance of principles of private international law.

Specific Commercial matters

Having thus laid a solid foundation in our comparative study of the Civil and Commercial Codes and the Shari'a, we shall proceed to consider specific commercial incidents. A lot of these will of course already have been adverted to in our study of the Commercial Codes where they are dealt with specifically; but we shall hope to cover such matters as: Foreign Capital Investment, Banking, Negotiable Instruments, Commercial Agency, Arbitration, the Laws of Corporations, etc. etc. The extent of these specific studies will of course be dictated by the time available. I would stress again: we shall not luxuriously advert to specific matters and specific cases at the expense of building a solid foundation for our edifice.

This is an ambitious programme. There is a wealth of material needless to say, and my task is to encapsulate it. One is inspired by the challenge: I do not believe there to be any comparable course anywhere in the world – even my friends in Cairo tell me that one does not exist in Arabic in this format.

So, we might end with Pascale: 'If I had had more time, I would have been briefer.'

III

A Short Introduction to the Shari'a

'Shari'a', from the root Shar' (also used as an alternative expression to Shari'a), is the road to the watering place, the clear path to be followed: in our context the common law of Al Islam.

Shari' 'the legislator is used for the Prophet, but more frequently to denote the divine legislator, Allah.

> "Now we have set thee on a clear path (Shari'a) of commandment; follow it, and do not follow the whims of those who do not know (Quran XIv 18).
>
> He hath enjoined on you (shar'a) the religion which he commended unto Noah . . . (XLII 13).
>
> To every one of you we have given a divine law (Shir'a) and a clear way. (V 48)."

If one may venture to summarise the main difficulty facing the lawyer when obliged to advise on the possible effects of the Shari'a in a modern commercial transaction, it may be classed as: uncertainty. The Shari'a is a religious law, consisting of bare principles revealed in the Quran, to which society is obliged to subscribe. Those essential principles are not to be diluted by the changing needs of society as viewed by society, which on the contrary must develop within the parameters prescribed by the principles. I have written in another context:

> "It is often said that the Qur'an (and hence the Shari'a) provides all the principles necessary for the regulation of relationships even in the world of commerce. As with Christianity or other

> major religions, that would be true in the context of the ideal society wherein every member accepted and obeyed its dictates under spiritual sanction; and, in the modern commercial world, this would envisage also such obedience, in general, internationally by members of other cultures, including States. This is unfortunately at the moment unthinkable; and in the context of society as it exists, the lesser merits of man-made law must obtain. It is in the latter context that the Shari'a must be viewed and, in its very nature, necessarily found wanting. It may be said that it is the material world that is at fault in this, and that either of the religions to which I have referred, restored to their essential validity amongst us, would do a better and more adequate job; but that is another subject and a deep one."

The Shari'a does not seek to propound general principles of law; it rather deals with, specific instances, or transactions, and propounds rules relating thereto. There is no law of 'contract'; no law of 'torts': there are examples of nominate contracts with rules applicable thereto, from which general principles must be deduced by analogy.

The object of this paper is to give a very short introduction to a complex subject.

In pre-Islamic Arabia society was based on the tribal unit, which governed itself through a body of unwritten rules evolving largely with the backing of the consensus of the community – in other words customary law. Law enforcement was the responsibility of the wronged individual: within the tribe, through ad hoc arbitration before a suitable hakam, who was popularly a priest of a pagan cult claiming supernatural powers: between tribes, through force of arms.

In contrast, at Mecca flourishing trade had led to the beginnings of development of commercial law, with public arbitrators and officials charged with the collection of diya (blood money): and Medina, an agricultural area where forms of land tenure were recognised. However, even in these two centres legal rules were based on customary practice and consensus.

In 610 AD there commenced that extraordinary series of revelations to the prophet Mohammad which now make up the Quran.

By 622 AD the Muslim community had become firmly established at Medina and religious faith became the unifying force rather than the tribal ties – the Prophet acquired political and legal sovereignty while the will of God as expressed in Quranic revelations came to supersede tribal custom in many respects.

The Quran, described by the late Professor Coulson as 'the bare formulation of the Islamic religious ethic' set a new accepted standard which would later be reduced to a set of legally formulated rights and obligations, and remedies where these were disregarded.

Examples of basic notions in the Quran are compassion for the weaker members of society; fairness and good faith in commercial dealings; and incorruptibility in the administration of justice. More particular provisions were also included – for example relating to alcohol and usury: however, these also were really proscribed in terms of their effect on the soul of the indulger, not their effect on society and the legal incidents of preventing or punishing them.

There are over 6000 verses in the Quran. Only 500–600 can be regarded as legal provisions and these are mostly concerned with religious duties and worship. About 80 verses are concerned with strictly legal concepts and many of these relate to particular problems rather than giving comprehensive treatment to general topics. Most of them were revealed during the Prophet's ten years at Medina and a large proportion contained provisions concerning married women, demonstrating a genuine effort at social reform, but on the whole they were designed to mitigate customary practice, not to replace or revolutionise it. Many of the Quran provisions are manifestly incomplete and lack guidance as to sanctions to be implied against their infringement. In order for the law of God to be applied in practice, operative parts had to be supplied from elsewhere. It was the Caliph 'Umar for example, who expressed the fervent wish that before he died the Prophet had left with them a definition of Riba.

It is a matter of history that between 622 AD and 750 AD Al Islam created a vast military empire stretching from the Pyrenees to the Khyber Pass.

Once the Prophet was no longer available to settle disputes, a vast corpus of legal decision began to be ascribed to him the validity of which probably constitutes the source of the greatest single controversy in early Islamic legal history. However, during his lifetime he was undoubtably faced with many legal problems not least arising out of interpretation of the provisions of the Quran. It is not surprising therefore that as remarked above, we find ad hoc solutions to particular problems with no attempt to formulate a 'code'.

It may be said that the main preoccupation at this time and during the early Caliphate was with inheritance and financial matters due to the problem of what to do with the unprecedented influx of wealth. Great flexibility and inventiveness were shown by the Caliphs.

In 661 AD we find the shift of the centre of power from Medina to Damascus. One cogitates continually upon Spangler's proposition that the idea creates system and the system promptly destroys the idea. True to form, religion now became the servant of the administration and many foreign concepts and institutions were absorbed. Full-time Qadhis were first appointed but a large part of their work was still administrative and only gradually did they carve a niche for themselves as legal experts and authorities on religion. There was however as to be expected much regional variation, as their basic function was to apply the local law in the region to which they ministered: there was, for example, a marked contrast between Medina and Kufa.

The Qadhis thus came to control and adapt customary law against a background of ethical considerations enjoined by the Quran. Legal solutions were once again based on expediency, perhaps because events at the time were too rapid for systemisation. The Umayyads were responsible for establishing a practical system of legal administration not a science of jurisprudence.

750 AD saw the Abbasid period. There was much political discontent involving Arab racial discrimination against non-Arab converts allied to a religious revival (a desire to return to purely basic precepts of religion) leading to rapid evolution of early schools of law. Representatives of such schools were appointed as government legal advisers (for example Abu Yusuf, chief Qadhi to Harun, composed a treatise on fiscal and penal law - the Kitab Al Kharaj). The rift between doctrine and practice had not yet arisen. At this period Medina and Kufa were the most influential schools and there was much review of local practice in the light of the Quran itself. For example, Riba at this point was interpreted to mean any gain resulting from chance and not previously precisely calculable in advance.

Within the schools the opinion (ra'y) of individual scholars gradually merged into a consensus of opinion within the school, and the concept of sunna (beaten path) appeared – the ideal doctrine established in the school, previously used to mean customary practice in both Jahiliyya (pre-Islamic period) and among Muslims.

Ra'y gradually gave way to analogical reasoning (qiyas) from a basis of consensus: ra'y still emerged occasionally as an exception in the form of istihsan (equitable concessions, public interest etc. requiring a divergence from strict qiyas). Then the sunna or established doctrine of a school came to be traced back to a pious originator ('Umar at Medina, Ibn Mas'ud at Kufa etc.). The process eventually ended with ascription to the Prophet, leading to a chain of tradition.

By 770 AD opposition to the early and constantly evolving schools was encountered: we find a rigidly doctrinaire approach to the substance of the law and its jurisprudential basis emerging – the accommodation of current legal practice became abhorrent and the law lost touch with practical needs and circumstances. As an example, an extreme doctrine of Riba in the bartering of commodities appeared at this point which appeared to lack point or purpose in relation to actual transactions. The ascription of a Sunna to the Prophet became all important and was backed up by Hadith (traditions) of varying authenticity, all of which however were supplied with a chain of authorities (isnad) beginning with the Prophet.

From 770 to 800 AD we find an uneasy co-existence of the consensus and doctrinaire approaches, with the doctrinaire gradually gaining the upper hand. During this period appeared the first written compendium of law, the Al-Muwatta' of Malik ibn Anas, a scholar at Medina, who gave his name to the Maliki school of law. One of its features was the attempt to make previously allowable rules based on local practice as special dispensations (rukhsa) from rigid doctrine. However, Malik felt free to reject the tradition (Hadith) of the option of the Majlis (khiyar al-majlis) ascribed to the prophet, because it was contrary to current practice at Medina. He regarded the supreme criterion in this respect as consensus of opinion and thought that there was nothing so sacrosanct about traditions from the prophet or other precedents that enabled them to override such authority in cases of conflict.

This early compendium set the pattern for later legal literature: but once again as pointed out above, points were dealt with piecemeal, and although topics came to be grouped more logically, no attempt was made to deduce general theories, for example, of contract.

At Kufa at this time there was a considerable divergence reflecting a more cosmopolitan and class-based society with higher status accorded to women. The Quran was interpreted in the light thereof and in general society was more receptive of the influence of foreign legal systems. The leading authority of this school at this period was Abu Hanifa (died 767) who gave his name to the Hanafi school of law but there were considerable divergences of opinion even among his pupils Abu Yusuf and Ash-Shaybani.

Local allegiance to the schools came to be replaced by allegiance to the authors of the first legal treatises: thus at Medina we find the Maliki school (although Ibn al-Qasimi developed its systematic foundations): whereas the Kufans had the Hanafi school (although it might be said that Ash-Shaybani was its true founder).

As a general picture we find many other minor schools active, conflict rife, which conflict became crystallised into the ahl al-ra'y (the early schools based on consensus) and the ahl al-hadith (the doctrinaire traditionists). This was an ideal atmosphere for the appearance of a great jurist – Muhammad ibn Idris ash-Shafi'i – to fill the need for a unifying process (born 767 AD). It is perhaps not too succinct to say that whereas previous scholars had been concerned mainly with the ethics of a situation, ash-Shafi'i concentrated on its legal implications. His greatest impact was in the realm of jurisprudential method with the aim of unifying the law. This culminated in his work 'Risala'. Perhaps nothing may serve so well to illustrate the difference between traditional writings on the Shari'a and what would be regarded as normal for a legal text book today, than to quote the first paragraph of Shafi'i's introduction:

> "In the Name of God, the Merciful, the Compassionate.
> Abu 'Ali al-Hasan b. Habib b. 'Abd al-malik, on the authority of al-Rabi' b. Sulayman al-Muradi, from al-Imam Muhammad b. Idris . . . al-Safi'i, said:
>
> 1. Praise be to God (Allah) who created the heavens and the earth, and made the darkness and the light; yet the unbelievers attribute equals to their Lord. Praise be to God to whom gratitude for one of His favours cannot be paid save through another favour from Him, which necessitates for the giver of thanks for His past favours to repay it by a new favour which (in turn) makes obligatory upon him gratitude for it. Those who describe Him cannot attain to the utmost of His greatness, which is as he has described Himself (in the Qur'an) and above what His creatures can attribute to Him. I praise Him with such praise as is obligatory on account of His kindness and the might of His majesty. I ask help of Him: The help of one save in whom there is no power or might at all. I ask Him for His guidance: The guidance whereby no one who takes refuge in it will ever be led astray. I ask Him for His forgiveness for whatever (offence) I have already committed and for what I have deferred – with the pleading of one who confesses himself in a state of servitude and

> who knows that none but He can forgive his offence and save him from it. I bear witness that there is no god but God alone, who has no associate whatever, and that Muhgammad is His servant and Apostle."

The introduction continues with admonitory religious exultations.

In essence Shafi'i prescribed four major sources of law (usuul): Firstly, the Quran with indicated means of interpretation and supplementation of its limited substantive provisions, especially precedents of the Prophet Muhammad, seen as second only to the word of God. Secondly, Hadith (traditions) as evidence of the sunna or behaviour of Muhammad: but Ash-Shafi'i raised Mohammad from primus inter pares, to a source of divinely inspired legal decisions, the wisdom of God. Thus the Hadith were to be a source of divine will complementary to the Quran. Sunna was only nominally second to the Quran and the Quran came to be interpreted in the light of the practice of Muhammad. Essentially Shafi' was primarily concerned to resolve contradictions in divine revelation and establish uniformity of doctrine: failing all other devices later rules abrogated earlier rules. However, the Quran and Sunna could not abrogate one another but only former provisions within the one or the other.

Thirdly, Ijma' to which however Shafi'i gave a new connotation. Consensus must be that of the entire Muslim community. This in fact ruled out consensus as an effective force of law once the Muslim community had spread outside Medina and fulfilled his aim of eliminating local diversities.

Fourthly, Qiyas or analogical reasoning – a particular form of ijtihad (the exercise of one's own judgment) which must however conform to the dictates of divine revelation and consensus.

Shafi'i repudiated individual opinion (ra'y) and istihasan.

Shafi'i went a long way to reconciling the traditionists (ahl al-hadith) and the ahl al-ra'y: the subsidiary function of human reason in law 'was never after him seriously challenged'. (Coulson).

In the century following the death of Shafi'i the Sunna became the focal point and the hunt for traditions was pursued by law reporters rather than jurists, the latter confining themselves rather to evaluating the material unearthed. The substance of an authentic Hadith was unchallengeable: if at all, it must be attacked through its authenticity, its chain (isnad).

By the end of the ninth century the great collections of Hadith of Al-Bukhari and Muslim had been compiled. It must be admitted that many Hadith are probably apocryphal but on the other hand there was no particular reason why any Hadith should be definitely rejected unless good reason could be adduced. However, they were accepted as authentic by Muslim jurisprudence as a whole and therefore had a marked effect on legal development.

Contrary to Shafi'i's aim and wish, even more schools of law appeared. Amongst those which must be especially noted was that of Ahmed ibn Hanbal, the musnad or chain of traditions of which contained 80,000 traditions. The school rejected human reason in any form as a source of law. This had its effect even on the Maliki and Hanafi schools although they were reluctant to revise their whole systems and continued to recognise subsidiary but additional usuul or sources of law (istihsan, the ijma' of Medina etc). Even the Hanbalis eventually came to recognise that qiyas (comparison) was unavoidable in practice.

Now the expansion of the area of law covered by divine revelation led to rigidity of doctrine and the lively enquiry of the early stages of development slowly and eventually stagnated. Law in Islam was the command of God, there was no room for speculation as to its nature, and the function of jurisprudence was solely to discover the terms of that command.

By the tenth century we have the classical theory of law, that is to say the generally accepted formula for the process of discovery of the divine will, resting on the same four usuul of Ash-Shafi'i, but fundamentally different from his scheme. We find the introduction of the concept of ijtihad (deduction) as the process of recognising the manifest meaning of the Quranic rules or deriving a novel rule by analogy therewith. The Sunna was regarded as dominant even almost to the extent of repealing a Quranic provision. However, the difference between analogical reasoning (ijtihad) and qiyas (comparison) was somewhat unclear.

In the classical theory, Ijma' (consensus) constituted a guarantee of the whole system of usuul. Following Shafi'i's dictate this was the agreement of qualified legal scholars in a given generation and deemed infallible. It was based upon the tradition 'My people will never agree upon an error'. Ijtihad on the part of an individual, could come only to a tentative conclusion about the will of God whereas a consensus of all the jurists (ijma') was incontrovertible and infallible. In insisting upon universal consensus as a prequalification for the operation of ijma', Shafi'i had appeared to grant it minor importance but it became crucial in the classical theory. However, once formed, even under the classical theory, it became immutable. Thus, the doctrine of ijma' in fact set the seal upon flexibility in the law, ijtihad withered away and what is referred to as 'the closing of the door of ijtihad' occurred in the early 10th century. The result was rigidity, with jurisprudential activities being circumscribed by taqlid (tradition), confined to the analysis of established rules. Jurisprudence became an introspective science practised for its own sake confined to endless elaboration of rights and duties.

The science of jurisprudence (fiqh) regulated the practices of faith, medical hygiene, social etiquette, law and morality with its exponents (fuqaha) as the guardians of the Islamic conscience. Hence, as a matter of principle, acts and relationships were measured on a moral scale: mubaah, makruh and haram (permitted, abhorred and forbidden). From the 10th century onwards, legal literature consisted increasingly of exhausting commentaries upon the works of Malik and the other founders of the schools and their immediate successors. Once 'discovered' the law must be obeyed with no question of variation according to time and place – ideally the religious State and society must conform.

What is important to note for present purposes, is that since the 15th century four main schools have survived covered by Islamic legal philosophy with the blanket authority of ijma'. The Shafi'i and Hanbali schools coincide more often than any other two because both are based upon legal theory with elaboration following. The Hanafi and Maliki schools existed before the theory of usuul was formulated but later strove to transcend their 'local' origins and in doing so approached somewhat nearer to the other two. Their common and distinctive feature however, is the admission of supplementary sources of law, which are in fact the classical expression of just those elements of the early schools which Shafi'i strove to eliminate (istihsan, istislah, the ijma' of Medina).

While it is difficult to generalise in a complex subject, it may be said that the Hanafis and Malikis diverge in the matter of the scope of the law and the role of the courts, in that Maliki emphasis is on the intention of a person in assessing the validity of his conduct, a moralistic or subjective approach; whereas the Hanafi concentration is on external conduct, a formalistic or objective approach. The Hanbalis go further than any other school in integration of law and morality.

However distinct the four schools, Islamic legal philosophy sees them as inseparable manifestations of a single essence. Ash-Shar'ani (circa 1530) asserted the differences arising from the result of ijtihad in the absence of explicit guidance from divine revelation and spoke of the latitude of interpretation rather than divergence, quoting the Hadith:

> Difference of opinion among my people is a sign of the bounty of God.

The Shi'ites

Thus far we have spoken only of the four Sunni schools all of which are at least united on the incidents and nature of political sovereignty.

However, sectarian divisions began during the civil war (AD 656–661) between Ali and Mu'awiya which produced the Shi'ites and the Kharijites. The Shi'ites recognised Ali as the true successor with their leader divinely appointed. The Kharijites reject all notions of heirship and descent and require piety and personal capability only for leadership – the leaders to be elected and even deposed by vote of the community.

For the Shi'ites, only the Imam, being divinely inspired, is qualified to deduce new rules. They have also their own collections of Hadith. They are split into numerous smaller divisions e.g. Zaydites, Twelvers, Isma'ilites. No credence is given to ijma' or evidence of practices of the early Muslim community.

However, these ideals have been belied in practice and various Shi'ite branches have allowed ijtihad, the use of reason, concept of zann etc and awaiting fulfilment of the ideal conditions inherent in their basic beliefs.

It is hoped that this very short survey will help to provide a background against which may be viewed the difficulties inherent in an application of the Shari'a to a modern commercial legal problem. Many of the papers in this volume refer to this difficulty and to the way in which various States in the Arab world have perforce dealt with it – from a complete and rigid adherence in Saudi Arabia to the Shari'a as the only law, to the adoption by such States as Bahrain and Kuwait of modern commercial codes.

The Majella

No introduction to the Shari'a, however short, would be complete without a reference to the Majella. This remarkable compilation was spawned by the Tanzimat, the legal reforms which took place in Turkey at the end of the 19th century. In so far as it was possible to 'codify' Shari'a principles in comprehensible form the Majella did so. It did so based on the Hanafi school of jurisprudence. It has frequently been said that the two books to be found at the right hand of probably every judge in the courts of the Arab world are Sanhouri's commentary on the civil code of Egypt, Al Wasit, and the Majella. The Majella is an invaluable work of first reference, from which to glean the basic principles which enable one to progress further in enquiry into any particular case by further reference of course to the precepts which obtain in the particular school governing the matter in point. (The Majella is available in English in the translation made by Judge Hooper – The Civil Laws of Palestine and Trans-Jordan: Vol. 1, The Mejella (London: Sweet & Maxwell, 1938), the whole of which has been printed in successive issues of the Arab Law Quarterly).

Further, reference must now be made to the 'Saudi Majella' – The Majellat Al Ahkam Ash Shari'a of Ahmad bin 'Abdullah Al Qari, (Abdul Wahab Ibrahim Abu Sulaiman and Muhammad Ibrahim Ahmad 'Ali (Tihama publications, Jedda, 1981)). This compilation was started on the initiative of the late King Abdul 'Aziz Al Saud, whose original intention was to create a compendium of Shari'a rules based upon all four schools. In the event, it is based upon the Hanbali school, the official school followed in Saudi Arabia. It thus constitutes an admirable source of Hanbali law, with copious footnote references to Al Mughni and the Sharah Al Kabir, the leading reference works on Hanbali law. There is also a very useful system of cross-referencing to the Ottoman Hanafi Majella. Unfortunately, the Saudi Majella is not available in English.

IV

Arbitration in the Gulf States: 'Delocalisation': A Short Comparative Study

The purpose of this paper is to consider the concept of 'delocalisation' in the context of arbitration legislation and practice in the States of the Gulf Co-operation Council (GCC). Those States are, in north-west to south-east progression around the Gulf, Kuwait, Saudi Arabia, Bahrain, Qatar, the United Arab Emirates and Oman: if we consider the Emirates, the constituent parts of the UAE, as seven at least semi-sovereign States, we are considering thirteen jurisdictions. It is patently impossible, within the scope of this short report, to go into minute detail on each jurisdiction, and therefore a comparative overview of the divergencies and similarities between the jurisdictions with reference to our topic would seem most useful.

The main consideration here is to examine the extent to which, if at all, an arbitration may be delocalised, or lifted out of the jurisdiction of the courts of the forum, and the extent of court intervention. It must be said at once that the GCC States do not at the present time constitute ideal or even advisable fora in this context. The keynote is uncertainty, as will appear from this report. There is no concept of 'international' as distinct from 'national' arbitration: there is no philosophy even approximating to that inherent in the recent legislation in France.[1] I refer hereafter to those incidents in which court intervention is expressly envisaged in existing legislation; but it must, of course, always be borne in mind that, unless expressly excluded by legislation, the court may always be supposed to have inherent supervisory or intervening jurisdiction. This is particularly so against the constitutional *Shari'a* background which exists in all the GCC States. In so far as we have little more than this background to rely on in those three or four jurisdictions where modern commercial arbitration occurs purely as a matter of practice, without any enacted legal basis, it must be reviewed briefly at the outset.

The main factor characterising these jurisdictions is that they are all Islamic states, and, as a concomitant to that, they have to a greater or less degree a backcloth of the *Shari'a* law of Islam, the Muslim law.[2] This system stems in essence from the Quran and the Sunna, the Hadith, etc. in the seventh century onwards, and it ceased developing, in the sense in which Westerners would understand development, centuries ago. The extent to which this system incises upon commercial arbitration in the GCC States varies enormously. For instance, if we take such emancipated jurisdictions as Kuwait and Bahrain, we find that the *Shari'a* has minimal relevance, while it is maximised in Saudi Arabia or Oman, with Qatar and the various UAE jurisdictions (with the exception, to a certain extent, of Abu Dhabi) occupying a somewhat hazy middle ground. It has to be said immediately, however, that there are distinct signs of a reassertion of the *Shari'a* law; the trend is now to react against the sudden importation of Western codes into these countries through, of course, Egypt, whose system was based upon the French. It is now felt in many quarters that this was done too hastily, and that the proper way now is to have a close look at the *Shari'a*, and to extract and incorporate into legislation such principles as may be adapted to modern commercial conditions. I am one of those who is extremely sceptical of that approach, although I say this with great deference to my many Arab friends. The *Shari'a* is one of the great systems of law, but it is not, in my view appropriate in many respects to what the world has made of commerce. In this, it may well be that commerce, not the *Shari'a*, is at fault – but the fact remains.

A further point of uncertainty to be kept in mind is that, with the exception of Kuwait and Bahrain, there are important lacunae in the secular legislation relating to arbitration, and that therefore the relevance of the *Shari'a* and the extent to which it may be relied upon to fill any such gaps, must be ascertained in any given case. Definition of the qualifications of arbitrators, and of arbitrable matters, are two points which spring to mind. On the latter point, while it is a common provision, or practice, that only matters admitting of '*sulh*' (or 'settlement') may be submitted to arbitration, in almost all these jurisdictions all provisions relation to *sulh* are drawn from the *Shari'a*. It should be mentioned here that *sulh* is in fact a more restrictive concept than *aimable composition*. The Kuwait Civil Code defines it as a contract whereby two parties resolve a current or future dispute between them 'by (virtue of) each of them relinquishing a comparable portion of his claims' (Art. 552), and the latter phrase applies to this aspect of arbitration as it is conceived throughout the area. Kuwait further provides that *sulh* is not permitted in other than property claims in matters going to public policy. This would appear to be the limit of available definition of arbitrable matters in secular legislation in the GCC States.

There are written Constitutions in Kuwait and Bahrain, where the *Shari'a* is prescribed as *a* principal source of law; in Qatar, where it is *the* principal source; and in the UAE, where again it is *a* principal source, but its relevance is enforced by the judicature laws issuing in the UAE under the Constitution.[3]. In Saudi Arabia and Oman, we are dealing virtually with *Shari'a* jurisdictions. When we consider a modern commercial arbitration in the light of the *Shari'a*, we find immediately further considerable difficulties. For example, if the *Shari'a* were to apply *per se* to an arbitration, we would find that there were stringent powers in the *qadi*, the religious judge, to intervene; we would find that an arbitration clause, other things being equal, is revocable by the parties right up to the time of the award; there is no provision in the *Shari'a*, as I understand it, for the hearing of future disputes – arbitration is limited to present disputes; there would be no question of the consideration of foreign law; there is restriction on the number of cases which are arbitrable; and there is question in any event to what extent the *Shari'a* is applicable or appropriate to be applied to non-Muslims, while where a Muslim is concerned the *Shari'a* always applies, the location being irrelevant. These provisions are, of course, qualified by secular legislation, in greater or lesser extent, over the area, in particular in judicature laws which further define the role of the *Shari'a*.

Returning to our topic, we now consider four areas where interaction between the judicial system and the arbitration process may be anticipated, and compare the degree to which such interaction takes place in the various jurisdictions.

Instituting the arbitration (including defences staying/excluding court jurisdiction, and the court's role in setting up the tribunal)

Agreements to go to arbitration in both present and future disputes are recognised by enacted legislation in Kuwait, Saudi Arabia, Bahrain, Dubai, Sharjah, Ra's al-Khaima and Oman; by implication in Abu Dhabi (the Civil Procedure Code makes no restrictions in this respect); and as a matter of practice in Qatar. They are also recognised in the Qatar Draft Civil and Commercial Procedure Code, a document of somewhat uncertain status, which is referred to and applied by the courts as they think appropriate or useful, in order to accustom the country by degrees to a modern court procedure system, as one recent judgment has it. We shall refer to this Code hereafter, because it is in use, although it should be borne in mind that it has not been gazetted and is therefore not law.

In Kuwait and Bahrain, arbitration, which is regulated by a special Chapter in their respective Civil and Commercial Procedure Codes, may be instituted by parties with a valid arbitration agreement without reference to the courts. However, the courts may be asked for assistance in all cases of difficulty in forming the arbitration tribunal; the duly appointed arbitrators are subsequently responsible for notification of parties, fixing time of sessions, etc. This procedure is generally adhered to in practice in Dubai and Sharjah, which still apply the same Anglo-Indian-based Contracts Law as does Bahrain; however, these Emirates as yet have no Procedure Codes regulating the practice of arbitration sanctioned in the Contracts Law, and there is no provision for court assistance in appointing arbitrators. In all the aforementioned jurisdictions, should a recalcitrant party to an arbitration agreement attempt, in the event, to bring an action before the courts, the other party may rely on the arbitration clause and the courts could be expected to refuse to accept the case: Kuwait has attempted to put the matter beyond doubt, in that the court is stated to have no jurisdiction to hear a case where a valid arbitration agreement/ clause (*compromis* or *clause compromissoire*) is relied upon by one or both parties. Indeed, even prior to the new Codes, in a case in which I was personally concerned (*Kuwait Oil Company* v. *Idemitsu Tankers*) in 1980, the Court in fact declined the case because of the existence of an arbitration clause relied upon by the defendants. The matter does not, of course, go to public policy in any of our jurisdictions,[4] and parties may always waive the arbitration clause, either expressly or by implication, and submit to the court's jurisdiction.

The use of the term 'jurisdiction', or the defence of 'lack of jurisdiction', in this context is somewhat special (as the Explanatory Memorandum to the Kuwaiti Code acknowledges), and has been the subject of some controversy, especially in Egypt. It is perhaps best regarded as a procedural device (a) to emphasise that a judge cannot overrule a party relying on the arbitration clause, and (b) to ensure that this defence is raised at the outset, before consideration of the substance. An interesting view of the problem is taken by Abul Wafa, an eminent and lucid (although currently somewhat 'heretical') writer in the field of procedural law in Egypt. He views any reference to a 'defence of lack of jurisdiction' in relation to arbitration as an unfortunate mis-use of the term: he maintains that a finding of 'lack of jurisdiction' implies referral to another court having jurisdiction, and only a violation of the legislative rules apportioning jurisdiction among the various courts can lead to this defence. He further holds that there is no justifiable and arbitrable case where no court has jurisdiction, and that, for instance, the reason that the Egyptian Code precludes arbitration abroad in matters in which the Egyptian courts have sole jurisdiction is that this places the matter *within the jurisdiction* of a foreign court.

It could of course be said that the Kuwaiti Code bears him out, in continuing to refer to 'the court having original jurisdiction to hear the case', and 'the competent court', and in providing for such court to resume jurisdiction at the stage of enforcement, appeal or application for setting aside – as do other jurisdictions where there is no mention of lack of jurisdiction in the arbitration context. Furthermore, a defendant in Bahrain, for instance, relying upon the defence of 'non-hearing of the case and adherence to the arbitration clause pursuant to the agreement' (Art. 236, Bahrain Civil and Commercial Procedure Code) could expect to produce the same effect as if he were in Kuwait relying upon the court's 'lack of jurisdiction'.

Abul Wafa would clarify the situation by requiring a defence of non-acceptance (or equivalent terms, which he discusses) of the case where the parties' right of resort to all courts is denied by agreement. He points out that this defence still precludes the court from hearing the case if either party relies upon it, because the existence of the arbitration clause and concomitant waiver of parties' right of resort to the competent court deprives the case, albeit temporarily, of one of its formal legal requirements, and the court *must* refuse to hear it.

The immediate objection to this is that defences of non-acceptance are generally adduceable at any stage of proceedings, and this was no doubt a consideration in Kuwait's choice of solution (an exceptional defence of lack of jurisdiction not going to public policy and capable of waiver by the parties apparently being thought preferable to an exceptional defence of non-acceptance which must be raised at the outset). Abul Wafa's solution is more radical in that he would have *all* defences of non-acceptance raised at the outset, but this, of course, lies outside the scope of this paper. It suffices to say here that Article 173 of the Kuwaiti Code, taken in conjunction with the section of the Explanatory Memorandum relating thereto, leaves no doubt that a valid arbitration agreement would always be respected.

Current practice in Qatar also allows parties to a valid arbitration agreement to institute proceedings without reference to the courts. However, the Draft Civil and Commercial Procedure Code has imported the Abu Dhabi Civil Procedure Code's provisions concerning types and methods of arbitration, and we shall therefore consider Abu Dhabi first, and then return to the Qatar Code.

Abu Dhabi recognises three categories of arbitration: contractual arbitration, which is agreed upon and may be carried through to the award stage by the parties, without reference to the courts; judicial arbitration, whereby parties to a dispute already before the courts may persuade the judge to allow them to submit certain or all points of the dispute to arbitration, the arbitration award then being incorporated in the court judgment; and court-registered arbitration, in which one party to an arbitration agreement may register it, in the manner of an action, with the competent court, which then notifies the unwilling party and invites him to state any objections he may have: if the court overrules such objections, the dispute must then go to arbitration. In judicial arbitration the court has wide powers of intervention, including cancellation of the whole proceeding if it sees fit in case of protracted complications in selecting the tribunal. Unless the agreement which becomes the subject of a court-registered arbitration has been carefully drafted to preclude such intervention, all provisions applying to judicial arbitration apply to it.

The Qatar Draft Code broadly speaking reproduces the above provisions, and adds Jordanian-based provisions concerning a party's right to apply for halt of any court proceedings by relying upon an arbitration agreement: the court rules to refer the case to arbitration if the party can convince the court that it is and always was his intention to adhere to such agreement. The Qatar Draft Code subjects all forms of arbitration to an equal and stringent degree of court control, and omits Abu Dhabi provisions which alleviate such control to a certain extent under court-registered and contractual arbitration.

In Saudi Arabia and Oman, arbitration is set in motion through the relevant competent authority. In Saudi Arabia, this is provided for in the new Arbitration Regulation issued by Royal Decree 40 of 1403, and for our purposes this authority would normally be the Committee for Settlement of Commercial Disputes or the Grievance Board (since government bodies, which are within the latter's jurisdiction, may submit to arbitration with the authorisation of the Prime Minister); however, the term as used in the Arbitration Regulation could also refer, for example, to the *Shari'a* Courts or the Committee for Settlement of Labour Disputes, depending upon the nature of the dispute. In Oman, the enacted arbitration provisions, contained in the 1984 Procedure for Hearing Cases and Applications for Arbitration before the Authority for Settlement of Commercial Disputes, cover only commercial arbitration in matters subject to the jurisdiction of the Authority, and all arbitration tribunals are headed by one of the three judicial members of the Authority, with the parties each nominating one arbitrator of its own.

There are no provisions in Oman concerning any reluctance by a party to honour an arbitration agreement, and one can only assume that the matter would be settled at the discretion of the Authority. The Saudi Arbitration Regulation, however, places arbitration on a sounder basis. Parties with prior agreement to arbitrate and/or a duly drawn arbitration document, deposit the latter with the competent authority in order to obtain 'accreditation' thereof by the authority. Article 7 of the Regulation has a double effect: it provides that where there is a prior agreement to arbitrate in future disputes, or where the competent authority has accredited the arbitration document relating to a particular dispute, the substance of the dispute 'may not be heard other than in accordance with this Regulation'. This at once establishes (a) that parties may not resort to the *Shari'a* practice of abandoning or withdrawing from Arbitration once it is duly provided for or set on foot; and (b) that Saudi Arabia does not recognise agreements to arbitrate under any rules other than those it has laid down.[5]

In Saudi Arabia the competent authority will respond to requests for assistance, as in Kuwait and Bahrain, in case of difficulty in forming the tribunal. In Qatar, the court steps in, under the Draft Code, without the need for a request for assistance. In Oman, and in Abu Dhabi (except in contractual arbitration), the court either appoints arbitrators nominated by the parties, or may appoint those of its own choosing should the parties decline or fail to make a nomination.

Kuwait is the only one of these jurisdictions to provide specifically that the courts may rule on urgent matters pending the outcome of arbitration, although parties may expressly reserve such matters to the arbitrators. There is room, however, for argument that as a matter of general principal, or common sense, courts of urgent causes, interim matters, etc. will continue to have the powers they have when a matter is before the competent court, as regards things which will not wait until the arbitration tribunal is formed.

Again, Kuwait is the only jurisdiction to specify that only arbitrators who were named in the arbitration agreement may be empowered to arrive at an '*aimable composition*' or '*sulh*', but there is no other restriction in Kuwait, and none in our other jurisdictions, concerning the stage at which arbitrators may become conciliators. To return briefly to Abul Wafa, he opines that the important factor is that the person of the conciliator should be known to the parties before they can validly commit themselves to accepting a conciliatory solution – their confidence in such person being crucial to the effectiveness of the solution – and that any other restrictions are superfluous. Abu Dhabi and the three Emirates still applying the Law of Contracts[6] make no mention of *sulh* proceedings in secular legislation, and although it is understood that arbitration leading to *sulh* takes place in practice in Dubai and Sharjah, it would seem that only arbitration at law is recognised in Abu Dhabi.

Stipulations concerning rules of law and procedure

Arbitrators are specifically released from the constraints of fixed procedure in Kuwait, Bahrain and Oman, with the exception of that laid down in the arbitration provisions (or anything which may be laid down in its own regulations by the Authority in Oman). In Kuwait, however, the parties themselves may prescribe procedure to be followed by the arbitrators. Arbitrators are however bound by rules of (domestic) law, except in proceedings leading to *sulh*, when as a general rule public policy would seem to be the only criterion for restrictions, although, as we have seen, only Kuwait makes this point expressly. It should be noted that Kuwaiti domestic law, in its Conflict of Laws Code (Law 5/1961) envisages the application of principles of foreign law to the merits of the case; while in arbitration in Bahrain, under the Procedure Code, Article 237, the parties are free to apply the rules of foreign law (or even institutional rules) to their arbitration, provided that the proceedings take place and the award issues in Bahrain. (In both Kuwait and Bahrain, awards issuing outside the jurisdiction would be treated as foreign awards for purposes of enforcement, and this may be taken to be the case in all the other jurisdictions.)

There are no provisions in the remaining jurisdictions concerning rules of procedure or law to be followed by the arbitrators. In view of the tight control exercised over proceedings and enforcement by the Saudi competent authorities, and by the court in Abu Dhabi in judicial and court-registered arbitration (and *cf.* the Qatar Draft Code), it can be anticipated that arbitration would need to adhere closely to rules followed by the competent authority/court itself. In addition, awards in contractual arbitration in Abu Dhabi and Qatar (Draft Code) are submitted to stringent examination at the enforcement stage, and this is also the practice in arbitration in Dubai and Sharjah, and there is nothing to prevent these last two Emirates and Qatar (currently) from re-examining the facts and effectively re-hearing the case, so that any attempt to follow rules at variance with those of domestic law would be futile. Remembering that in Qatar there is no enacted legal basis for arbitration, and contractual freedom being limited only by public policy and morals (under Civil and Commercial Law 16/1971) a wide variety of arrangements and rulings relating to arbitration agreements may be envisaged. Judges to whom application would be made for enforcement, and who come from a variety of legal backgrounds, tend to apply their own native law to fill gaps in Qatar legislation, rather than turning to the *Shari'a*, although the latter, and particularly the Ottoman *Majella*, is referred to; while government contracts, and especially the Public Works General Conditions of Contract, which make wide use of arbitration clauses, tend to specify ICC Arbitration Rules. It will readily be seen that a full discussion of possible rules of law and procedure applying to arbitration in Qatar is beyond the scope of this paper.

Subsequent occasions for court intervention

Once arbitration is established and arbitrators appointed, courts can be requested to intervene on a number of occasions.

Cases may be brought in court in Kuwait and Saudi Arabia for disqualification and removal of arbitrators, upon the same grounds upon which a judge may be removed. The Bahrain Code omits to make provision concerning arbitrators, but does include provisions for the disqualification and removal of judges, which could be expected to apply in the case of arbitrators. In the other jurisdictions lacking codified provisions, *Shari'a* rules concerning both appointment and disqualification of judges, and also arbitrators, might be invoked.

In all GCC jurisdictions with statutory arbitration provisions (including the Qatar Draft Code) there is provision for a statutory time limit within which the arbitrators must issue their award, but (except under the Qatar Draft Code, or in judicial arbitration in Abu Dhabi) the parties may agree on a different time limit, and may extend or apply for extension of time limits. However, where a time limit as fixed is exceeded, any interested party may apply to the court/ authority to take over the hearing of the dispute. (In the case of the two above-mentioned exceptions where the court-stipulated time limit is exceeded the Qatar/Abu Dhabi court automatically (re)commences hearing the case.)

The foregoing constitutes the limit of expressed intervention during the course of the arbitration proceedings under the Saudi Regulation, the remainder of the competent authorities' control being exercised at the deposit of Award and enforcement stage. Kuwait, Bahrain and Qatar additionally allow application to the court to compel attendance of witnesses and production of evidence, while Abu Dhabi seems to imply in its Article 87 that it is incumbent upon the court to intervene in this matter in the two types of arbitration in which the courts take an active part, since the said Article goes on to state that, however, it may only intervene on grounds of contempt of court should the arbitrators raise the matter with it. Oman is vague on this point: the President of the Authority may impose a negligible fine upon uncooperative witnesses, but it is not clear who brings the matter to his attention, or whether he can compel the attendance of the witnesses. Bahrain and the Qatar Draft Code further provide for administration of the oath to witnesses by the arbitrators, with the result that bearing false witness lays the perpetrator open to a charge of perjury, and he may be subjected to criminal proceedings on that count; again, it is not clear whether this is at the discretion of the arbitrators, or whether the court's intervention is mandatory.

Only Oman and Kuwait go on to make express provision for further court intervention in the proceedings, Oman dealing with the matter shortly by importing a section of Kuwait's Article 180, which provides for halt of the proceedings if the arbitrators come upon something outside their jurisdiction (e.g., a point of law needing to be clarified), or if they uncover forgery, falsification or other criminal acts connected with the proceedings which require to be settled by court judgment. Despite the absence of statutory provision in the other jurisdictions, it is, of course, unlikely that courts would refuse to look into such matters should the arbitrators or the parties raise them.

Thus we are left with Kuwait, which, having started out as the jurisdiction most firmly in support of the sanctity of the arbitration agreement, goes on to provide the most obstacles to its smooth implementation. In addition to the above-mentioned provisions, Article 180 of the Kuwait Procedure Code also allows the arbitrator to halt the proceedings pending the resolution of any other question which he sees as vitally affecting his award, and the parties may agree to suspend the proceedings for a period of up to six months; the arbitrator may also make application to the court having original jurisdiction for an Order for judicial assistance. Kuwait also allows appeals by the parties in actions for removal of an arbitrator.

Provisions allowing appeals and applications for setting aside to be brought before the courts; enforcement of final awards accepted by the courts

As regards appeals from the arbitration award itself, and applications for setting aside the award, both the Kuwaiti and Bahraini Codes envisage such remedies. The Kuwaiti Code which issued in 1980 has taken the step of abolishing appeals to the competent Appeal Court unless the parties expressly provide therefor. Even then, there can be no appeal if the award is the result of *aimable composition* (*sulh*), if the arbitration concerned a matter on appeal, or if the case was below a certain minimum value. Bahrain still allows appeal to an Appeal Court unless the parties have expressly waived their right in this regard, but also precludes appeal in *sulh* and arbitration at the appeal stage of a case. Both allow applications for setting aside on grounds of various irregularities with respect to the arbitration agreement itself, or for invalidity of the award or of the proceedings, or where there are grounds which would permit of petition for retrial in a case before the courts: these grounds include such things as fraud, or concealment or forgery of documents material to the award by any of the parties, inconsistencies in the award or inadequate representation of a party. An appeal must be registered within a fixed time limit, and before the court has made the award enforceable, and, as has been said, the parties have a choice as to the admissibility of appeals; applications for setting aside are always admissible, despite any agreement to the contrary, and may be brought at any time that relevant facts come to light. Applications are heard by the court having original jurisdiction, and in Kuwait, if the court sets aside the award, it may then consider the substance of the dispute.

It may be noted here that it is not made clear in the Kuwaiti and Bahraini Codes, or in the case of contractual arbitration in Abu Dhabi, what ensues should the court itself find some impediment to enforcement of the award, and the same uncertainty holds for Bahrain and Abu Dhabi in the case of a successful application for setting aside. Such matters are naturally also problematical in those jurisdictions where there is no expressed legal basis for arbitration, or no statutory proceedings laid down therefor.

In Saudi Arabia, the award is open to objections raised before the competent authority by either party within fifteen days of its deposit with the Authority – no grounds for objection are specified – and the Authority rules upon such objections before any party may apply for enforcement of the award. There is nothing in the Arbitration Regulation preventing the objections raised from entailing a review of the facts and effective re-trial of the dispute.

In Qatar, under the Draft Code the award is deposited with the court, and it is not until the interested party applies for its enforcement that the court must notify the party against whom the award was made that he has seven days to register any objections. The court has wide powers, either at the instance of the objecting party, or of its own accord, to correct 'slips of the pen' in the award; to return it to the arbitrators for amendment if it is obscure or contrary to law (the award becomes void if the arbitrators fail to comply); and to cancel the award if the arbitrators or the parties are found to have been guilty of improper behaviour, if the award is out of time, or if it is void for any other reason. If the award is set aside, the court hears the case. If all objections are overruled, or if there are none, or once they have been satisfied, the court may ratify the award and it becomes enforceable. It must, however, be remembered that while courts in Qatar may allow themselves to be guided by the Draft Code, the current practice in the absence of enacted legislation is to obtain enforcement of the award by its embodiment in a court judgment, and, as we have seen, there is nothing to prevent a review of the merits of the case by the judge.

In all the above jurisdictions (Kuwait, Bahrain, Saudi Arabia and Qatar (Draft Code), an award is enforced upon application by a party, under a court order (or ratification), which is issued after the expiry of any period allowed for appeal or objection, and after the court or competent authority has assured itself that there are no impediments to the award's enforcement. Enforcement procedures are as for court judgments. The apparent homogeneity is, of course, marred by variables in what each jurisdiction would regard as an impediment.

The Abu Dhabi Code provided the model for the Qatar Draft Code as regards motives for amendment by the court, return of the award to the arbitrators and setting aside the award, so that there is no need to repeat those provisions, except to remark that Abu Dhabi has an additional provision making contravention of general principles of justice a ground for cancellation of the award. It is unclear, in the Abu Dhabi Code, whether such matters are raised by the court of its own accord, or by the parties. The implication seems to be that the court is responsible for amendment and ordering the arbitrators to carry out amendments, while Article 92(2) suggests that it is the parties who must move to have the award set aside. The award is invalidated if not amended by the arbitrators as instructed by the judge. Under the terms of Article 96, as we have seen, the parties may draft their agreement to arbitrate in disputes which are not already before the court, so as to exclude some or all of the court's powers under the above provisions. In contractual arbitration, deposit of the award by one party is treated as a case filed against the other, and the latter is notified and given a time limit by the court within which to raise objections, which the court will review: if it overrules such objections, and if it can find no grounds in the Procedure Code for rejecting the award, it must accept the deposit thereof.

In all three types of arbitration in Abu Dhabi, if the court accepts the award, it must embody it in, or make it the subject of one of its own judgments. The award is then no longer assailable, and the judgment itself may only be challenged if it differs wildly from the award itself.

In Dubai and Sharjah, the award has no legal basis until it is embodied in a court judgment, and there is nothing in law to prevent the court reviewing the facts before issuing such judgment. Again, once the judgment issues, only this, and not the award, is open to appeal, and in practice the appeal is only admissible where the judgment is materially different from the award.

Oman alone makes the award of the arbitration tribunal absolutely unchallengeable: once it is deposited with the Authority for the Settlement of Commercial Disputes, it is final and enforceable by the operation of law, presumably in the same way that the Authority's own judgments are enforced. This is a logical provision, since appeal could only lie to the Authority, which is closely involved in the arbitration, while one of its own judicial members always has the deciding voice, as president, in any arbitration tribunal. Thus, Oman's is seen to be a form of institutional arbitration. Article 68 in fact makes provision for the Authority to deal with disputes concerning, and appeals (*ishkalat*) against, the execution of the award (such as can be raised against execution of judgments in other jurisdictions): this is a curious provision, since there is no parallel means of protesting against execution of the Authority's own judgments, and Oman has no Procedure Code other than the one regulating the Authority, nor a Courts Law which might indicate the procedure for such protests.

Before concluding, it should be noted that Kuwait has set up its own form of institutional arbitration under Article 177 of the 1980 Civil and Commercial Procedure Code. Arbitration tribunals may be set up under the auspices of the Ministry of Justice, headed by a member of the judiciary and completed by experts in the desired field chosen from a schedule of such experts maintained by the Ministry. Parties who choose this method have their dispute heard without fees, and will avoid some of the delays caused by any eventual application to the courts for assistance, since the Ministry's tribunals may themselves issue orders compelling witnesses to testify, compelling the production of evidence, and obtaining judicial assistance from other courts. Awards in such arbitration are not open to appeal, but application may, of course, be made to have them set aside on the grounds previously recited for setting aside in Kuwait.

Notes

1 New Civil Code Art. 494 *et seq.*

2 For a general analysis of this subject, see the author in (1985) 1 ALQ 3 *et seq.*

3 See the author in (1985) 1 ALQ *loc cit.*

4 *Quaere*, however, Art. 7 of the Saudi Arbitration Regulation (Decree 40/1403) which seems to envisage that once parties have duly agreed to arbitrate, the process is irreversible!

5 It should, however, be noted that Saudi Arabia has subscribed the ICSID convention of 1960.

6 A code based on English law, a survival from the British extra-territorial jurisdiction.

References and Further Reading

Ahmad Abul Wafa: *Arbitration (Altahkim bilqada' Wa F'alsulh)* Alexandria (1964) (Arabic). *Optional and Mandatory Arbitration*, Alexandria (1978) (Arabic) (in particular at pp. 114–123).

Samir Saleh: *Commercial Arbitration in the Arab Middle East*, London, Graham & Trotman (1984) (English) – an excellent analysis of arbitration law in the Arab states.

V

The States of the GCC: Sources of Law, the Shari'a and the Extent to which it Applies[1]

This article seeks to give a brief outline of the bases of jurisprudence in the States of the Gulf Co-operation Council: Bahrain: Kuwait: Oman: Qatar: Saudi Arabia: The United Arab Emirates.

The *Shari'a* runs like a golden thread through the jurisprudence of the Gulf States. In this article we shall consider the sources of that jurisprudence and one of our main tasks will be to assess the extent of the role played by the *Shari'a* in each Gulf jurisdiction. In confronting any legal problem, perhaps the first question to be asked is: to what extent, if at all, does the *Shari'a* affect the matter? The answer may vary from 'not at all' in a problem falling within the Commercial Code of Kuwait to 'basically' in a problem in Saudia Arabia, while in the other jurisdictions, the answer may be somewhere between these extremes. Overall, we must record and always bear in mind the *uncertainty* engendered by the looming presence of the *Shari'a* which should be one of the factors to be borne in mind in weighing the benefits and risks of any commercial contract in the Islamic countries.

A comparative approach is essential in this area. Not the least reason for this is the lacunae which exist in the codified law. It may be said that in this respect the need to resort to general principles increases in inverse proportion to the quantum of specific substantive law or specific conflict rules, as the case may be, which is available. We therefore have to consider the sources of law prescribed in the various codes, where we shall find, as might be anticipated, that the legislator has given to the judge in many cases the right, in fact the obligation, to supplement codified provisions or to introduce principles where such provisions do not exist.[2]

The Constitutions form the backdrop to all legal considerations, and the role of the *Shari'a* as prescribed by these Constitutions as a source of law is important.[3] I would like to stress the essentiality of ascertaining at the outset the basic constitutional position: this is true both where a detailed constitution is laid down in writing, as in Kuwait, Bahrain, Qatar and the UAE; where it is prescribed also in writing but in broad principle as in Saudi Arabia; and where it is unwritten, as in Oman.

Saudi Arabia

We may deal briefly with Saudi Arabia where we find the *Shari'a* as *the* source of law on an almost unalloyed basis. There is a parallel body of secular 'Regulations' to which, due to the sensitivity of the '*ulama*', the word 'law' cannot be applied: these would in my view be void if contrary to express provisions of the *Shari'a*. In this connection, we recall the writings of Ibn Taymiya of the Hanbali School, (the School applying in Saudi Arabia) and his teachings that laws are valid unless expressly forbidden in the *fiqh*.

Oman

Touching also briefly on Oman here, because it, too, falls outside the pattern of our other jurisdictions and indeed outside the pattern in the Middle East generally, we find the Sultan at the head of the hierarchy, relying upon the *Shari'a* of the Ibadi School.[4] However, reference to Oman must be qualified in this respect, because it certainly legislates *sub nomine* 'laws' and in such codes as the Banking Law and the Commercial Companies Law for example we find that the *Shari'a* has for several years been by-passed to an extent which we do not find in Saudi Arabia.[5] (But see now the Omani Constitution of 1997.)

The picture needs to be updated to take account of the promulgation of the new 'Procedure for Hearing Cases and Applications for Arbitration before the Authority for Settlement of Commercial Disputes'. The creation of the new Authority will be discussed more fully in future issues of the *ALQ*, but it will be noted here that it has wider powers than its predecessor, the Committee for the Settlement of Commercial Disputes. The sources of law to which it is referred in issuing its judgments are, however, little changed.

Article 44 of Sultani Decree 32 of 1984 prescribes:

> . . . decrees and laws in effect in the Sultanate; contracts between the litigants provided that such do not conflict with the laws, public

> order or morals; established and observed customs in the field of commercial activity; and that which will achieve justice between the adversaries and lead to stabiltiy in commercial transactions.[6]

Here we note the authority which the written law of Oman, in common with the other codes which we shall consider, ascribes to the contract between the parties: the principle of *pacta sunt servanda*, a principle which the *Shari'a* subscribes.[7] It may be thought that the latter two dictates of Article 44 confer considerable latitude upon the Authority, although, again, the ever present backdrop of the *Shari'a* must be constantly adverted to.

Kuwait

Kuwait took a bold step by establishing in 1961 a secular system of commercial law.[8] That continued to be the situation until 1977 when, in response to the general reassertion of the *Shari'a* in the area, Kuwait set up a committee to review the laws in the light of the Islamic law. Two results of this were the new Civil and Commercial Codes, which took effect in 1981. Kuwait is currently reviewing its Constitution in the light of the *Shari'a* and of course the burning question is whether it will make the *Shari'a the* source of law.

It is relevant in this connection to consider the confusion occasioned when Egypt took this step in the latter days of the Sadat régime. Egyptian judges at that time did not know whether to give effect to the change directly, or whether to await legislation – the predominant problem, as always when one is concerned with the *Shari'a*, being banking interest. The immediate effect in the Courts was that each judge acted according to his own judgment, resulting in conflicting judgments, until the Court of Cassation took the unprecedented step of sending a circular which stated that a constitutional change did not necessitate any change in the practice of the Courts in this respect unless and until subsidiary legislation was passed dealing with the subject. This perhaps dubious directive points at the quandary which such States face when they have to measure their current stage of legal and economic development against the *Shari'a*. It may perhaps be argued that it is not conclusively significant whether the Constitution states *the* or *a* principal source of law; but it surely must be significant when a change is made from the latter to the former. If a law, particularly a basic law, is changed, then it is assumed that the amendment was intended to produce some effect.[9]

Article 1 of Law 67/1980 issuing the Kuwaiti Civil Code finally expressly abolishes the *Majella*, the Ottoman attempt to codify the Hanafi School of Islamic Law. Law 67/1980 also repeals other laws, but these are not germane to our present topic.

Article 3 of the new Civil Code is however extremely relevant. By this Article, the Civil Code as a general law is expressed to be without prejudice to specific legislation; in other words, the Civil Code lays down the general pattern of the law but specific laws take precedence. This Article's full significance becomes immediately apparent in that one specific law, indeed the very next one to be promulgated in Kuwait, is the Commercial Code. The cogent point here is that, although the Civil Code includes, as we shall see, many *Shari'a* provisions, the Commercial Code is nevertheless able to preserve commercial transactions to a large extent from incursions of the *Shari'a*.

One outstanding example lies in the matter of *riba* or more specifically here, interest on loans. This is, of itself, a large and difficult subject with which I hope to deal in a later article; it suffices to note here that while Article 547[10] of the Civil Code expressly provides that loans shall be free of interest, the Commercial Code as a 'special' law allows interest on 'commercial' loans and indeed contains detailed provisions as to its regulation.[11]

Article 1 of the Civil Code itself warrants translation in full:

> "1(1) – Legislative provisions apply to the matters to which such provisions relate both expressly and by implication."

Here we have a typical civil law approach to construction of a statute: quite simply, if by implication the provisions apply to a situation, then they should be applied.

> "1(2) – If there is no legislative provision, the judge gives judgment in accordance with Custom. If there is no Custom, the judge deduces his opinion taking guidance from the dictates of the Islamic jurisprudence (*fiqh*) most in accord with the reality and interests of the country."

'Custom' here is '*ᶜurf*' not '*ᶜaada*' (that is to say it is custom with a capital 'C' and 'deduce' is '*ijtahada*' which is used to express the classical concept of deduction of a (legal) conclusion in the *Shari'a*).

On the face of it, if this is a hierarchical structure, a pyramid of authority, then Custom may apply even if contrary to the dictates of the *Shari'a*, inasmuch as the latter is *a* not *the* main source of law. We recall again the reasoning of Ibn Taymiya that where legislation or custom is not *contrary* to the *Shari'a* it may be applied – bearing in mind however that Ibn Taymiya was a Hanbali not a Maliki. However, if or when the Constitution of Kuwait is changed to make the *Shari'a the* main source then, in order to give significance to the change, in my view it must be interpreted to mean the exclusion of Custom which conflicts with the *Shari'a*. It may be added that the learned commentator on the Civil Code regards the latter as already being the correct view of Kuwaiti law, even on the present wording of the Constitution. His Commentary is a learned piece of analysis which we must study in some detail because of its relevance not only as far as Kuwait is concerned (it is published with the Code and thus has legal force), but because it expounds on general principles which are important for other Arab countries as well. There is a general Introduction which confirms that the Civil Code sets out the general principles which were totally lacking in the *Majella*. It may be recalled that the general definitions in the Introduction to the *Majella* are very abstruse – in English, they often mean very little even in Judge Hooper's first-class translation[12] – and the commentator to the Kuwaiti Code suggests that they belong not to enacted legislation, but to learned works on Islamic jurisprudence. He then points out that although such general principles are not missed when there are already established general principles, or specific laws which fill the gap (he cites the priority of legislation over other sources of law, and the principle of non-retroactivity of laws, which is enshrined in the Constitution), yet there are many situations where all is uncertainty, and which demand a codified background of general principles.

Proceeding to the prescribed sources themselves, the commentator opines that it goes without saying that Custom must not offend what is best translated as 'public policy or morals' ('*al-nitham al-ᶜ aam wa husn al-aadab*'). He then states:

> "Customs ('*ᶜaadat*' – i.e., with a small 'c') which contradict the social, political, economic or moral principles upon which the community rests, can never be elevated to the rank of Custom (*ᶜurf*) even if of long duration; in a country such as Kuwait, whose religion is by the Constitution Al-Islam, it is not possible that anything which contravenes one of the bases or established precepts of Islam should constitute Custom."

Thus, it will be seen that we have a controversial point here, when the wording of the Constitution is compared with the Commentary to the

Civil Code – a point which may become even more controversial in the future. Be that as it may, the commentator observes that Iraq and Egypt also followed this pattern (although as we have seen the latter has recently made a change in the favour of *Shari'a*), then cites other Arab jurisdictions which give the *Shari'a* precedence over Custom, or omit Custom entirely.[13] The commentator goes on to observe that Custom is the people's original source, the innate method of regulating the details of life's transactions, and moreover that both the Qur'an and the Sunna accept it as such. He quotes from the Qur'an:

> "Oh, believers do not consume your assets as between you in vain, unless it be by way of commerce by mutual consent."

and from the saying of the Prophet as reported by Muslim:

> "You are most knowing in your worldly affairs."

and from another saying reported by Ahmed:

> "As for your religious affairs that is for me; as for your worldly affairs, in that you are the most knowledgeable."[14]

Therefore, continues the commentator, Custom has been said to constitute a law (*shar'i*) precedent, and therefore placing custom after *Shari'a* principles would be misleading when the noble *Shari'a* has it as one of the major sources.

The Commentary to the Kuwait Civil Code proceeds to record that there is nothing to be feared in directing a judge to deduction (*ijtihad*), in that the uniform qualifications required of judges, and the supervision of the Court of Cassation, would ensure that the deduction is sound, that right guidance is taken from the Islamic *fiqh* (jurisprudence), and that there is uniformity of opinion. Right guidance is moreover ensured, says the Commentary, by not restricting judges to any one School of Law, or to the preponderant dictates thereof, and by adopting such principles as most accord with the reality of the country, etcetera, and with the general principles relied upon by Kuwaiti legislation overall; a judge must redound against principles of *fiqh* which conflict with provisions of Kuwaiti legislation, otherwise legal chaos would result.

The Commentary's last really important point in our present context is that:

> "It goes without saying that no provision of the Code precludes the judge from taking guidance – by the side of the provisions of

> the Islamic *fiqh* – from the general principles of law, or the principles laid down in international treaties or other pieces of legislation, or deducing his opinion from provisions established by the judiciary and jurisprudence, whether Kuwaiti or otherwise, as long as they agree with the situation of the country, and the benefit of the community, and are for the realization of justice.
>
> Nonetheless, the Code has not sought to parallel the Egyptian and some other Arab legislation in applying the principles of the law of nature and the principles of justice, having regard to the obscurity and ambiguity inherent in these two expressions . . ."

Here we find an express recognition of the judge's need to apply general principles in the modern context, and the comparative approach expressly recommended.

In summary, although we find that the new Kuwaiti Codes have perhaps made little difference in principle to the basic commercial legal position in Kuwait thus far, the future is another matter. One has only to consider, for example, that a specific law under a general law may well be repealed or amended, leaving an unmodified general law. All depends on future policy and we must recall the trend towards reassertion of the *Shari'a*.

Finally, it must be said that only in the rarest of cases would it be relevant now to invoke common law argument in Kuwait. The Codes are complete, they are first-class, and they are civil law based, and behind them we have all the jurisprudential dictates set out above.

In the other States however, the position is different. It is not so incisive, there are varying degrees; in some of them the tradition of English law is more recent and there are survivals, in the form of surviving elements of British extraterritorial jurisdiction.[15]

Qatar

It is convenient to consider Qatar in proximity to Kuwait because the Qatari Law of Civil and Commercial Matters is a truncated version of the old 1961 Kuwait Commercial Code. It is clear that the legislator at the time thought to adapt the latter to Qatar's needs in the main simply by leaving out passages of varying length while occasionally importing passages of Egyptian legislation which Kuwait had, in principle, discarded. The result is an incomplete Code giving rise to many uncertainties, which a judge has to resolve according to his experience and inclination. Although we have constantly to remind ourselves that there may be a qualification where there are, for example, Palestinian, Jordanian or Sudanese common law trained judges sitting, as a basic precept we would expect to find a civil[16] court in Qatar advert to the principles of civil law, particularly as applied in Egypt, or in other States of the Gulf with a similar system, in order to fill the lacunae. This is not, of course, to say that where the legislator, although basing himself upon the Egyptian Code, has expressly omitted in context sections from that Code in drafting the Qatar Code, a judge may ignore such omission, and apply the Article of the Egyptian Code. It may be submitted that where, in context, an article is expressly omitted then there must be deduced from that the clearest intention on the part of the Qatari legislator not to include it and a judge must conclude accordingly that its provisions do *not* form part of Qatari jurisprudence. Be that as it may, in practice judges overall tend to refer in the first instance, to Sanhouri's Commentary 'Al-Waseet', and it is also still common for a judge in Qatar to refer to the *Majella*, despite the fact that Qatar adheres not to the Hanafi School but to the School of Ahmed, as the Hanbali School is referred to throughout the writings.

It is provided by the Qatari Law 13/1971 'Regulation of the Courts of Justice'[17]:

> Article 5: The Civil Court shall have jurisdiction to determine all civil and commercial matters and cases of personal status for non-Muslims.

This gives the Civil Court a wide brief. The one exception, cases of personal status involving Muslims would be referred in Qatar to a *Qadi* or *Shari'a* judge. It is interesting that, this apart, the Courts law in Qatar makes no express provision for a *Shari'a* jurisdiction, but provides for all matters to be heard by the Courts set up under this Law.[18]

We turn now to the Civil and Commercial Code of Qatar.[19] I translate the relevant provisions of the Code for present purposes as follows:

> "Article 1: The tenets of this Law shall apply to all matters embraced expressly or by implication by the provisions hereof as well as to all commercial acts engaged in by any person even if not a merchant.
> Article 2: In prescribing principles which apply to merchants and commercial acts regard shall be had to contracts recognized by law, which constitute the law of the contracting parties.

Article 3: If there is no contract or if there is but it is silent as to (a particular) provision or the provisions set out in the contract are void, the legislative provisions contained in this Law shall apply. Article 4: In the absence of the legislative provision which can be applied, the judge shall adjudicate in accordance with custom, special or local custom taking precedence over general custom, and in the absence of custom the principles of the Islamic *Shari'a* shall be applied."

We recall that in the Qatari Constitution the *Shari'a* is prescribed as *the* main source of law and that this latter provision is more stringent in the application of the *Shari'a* than are the written Constitutions of other States in the area. The vital point at issue here is, of course, the extent to which in the Qatari system, the *Shari'a* must, in view of the wording in the Constitution, be regarded as paramount: that is to say, must the sources of law referred to in the Civil and Commercial Code, be read subject to the proviso that they be not contrary to the *Shari'a*? Is the apparent hierarchy of authority referred to in the Code pyramidal, or must all the sources therein indicated be regarded as essentially subject to the dictates of the *Shari'a*? It is, of course, in this situation that a judge in an Islamic jurisdiction often finds himself in an unenviable position to which I have referred in another context as that of an irresistible force against an irremovable object.[20]

The matter is, of course, controversial. However, the *Shari'a* is not prescribed in the Qatari Code to be the *sole* source of law and in my opinion to give absolute paramountcy to the *Shari'a* in the context of the Qatari Civil and Commercial Code would be a false interpretation of the provisions of Qatari law. Most, if not all, modern commercial contracts contain provisions which would be illegal at the *Shari'a*; many of the provisions of the Qatari Codes would be similarly illegal; and it cannot in my view have been the intention of the Qatari legislator to subject his legislation to such an impossible test. If this view is right, then similarly, Custom could be applied, even if not always in accordance with the *Shari'a*. Once again, I hasten to qualify this view. It would not be valid, in my view, where the Code or the other prescribed sources in Qatar were silent; in such a case, then the *Shari'a,* as *the* principal source of law, must be called upon in the first instance to fill the lacunae.

We advert now to the express provisions of the Code quoted above.

First, we note a similar provision to that in the Kuwaiti Code that all tenets of the law apply to matters expressly or by implication covered by it. We thus find the prescribed sources in the Code to be:

a) The contract between the parties (if any) and provided it accords with the law; here again we find adherence to the hallowed principle of *pacta sunt servanda.*
b) Express legislative provision.
c) Custom.
d) The *Shari'a.*

In Article 4 of the Code we find, of course, the usual directive to the judge where he finds no guidance in the prescribed sources and, as in Kuwait, he is ultimately directed to the *Shari'a.* The parallel with Kuwait is not surprising having regard to the origin of the Qatari Code. If the view that I have tentatively advanced as to the role of the *Shari'a* in the context of the express provisions of the Qatari Code is correct, then similarly in my view Custom could be applied by the judge even if not always in accordance with the *Shari'a.*

Bahrain

We recall the provisions of the Bahrain Constitution prescribing the *Shari'a* as *a* principal source of law.

Against that ever-present backdrop, we record that Bahrain has as yet little legislation on the civil model and no Civil Code as such and we therefore find that the sources of law are still prescribed in the Judicature Law of 1971.[21] That Law provides:

> "in the event the judge finds no provision of law capable of application, he shall deduce the basis of his judgment from the principles of the *Shari'a* and the provisions thereof, and in the absence of any such provision, Custom shall be applied. A particular Custom shall be preferred to a general Custom, and in the absence of Custom the tenets of natural law or the principles of equity and good conscience shall be applied."

Thus, in the event of a lacuna in enacted legislation, the judge is expressly directed firstly to the principles of the *Sharia.* However, it is instructive to compare this formula with those of Kuwait and Qatar to which we have referred; it has some interesting features. Firstly, the formula seems to envisage that secular legislation may be preferred to the *Shari'a*, the inference being that it may not be in accord with the *Shari'a.* Secondly, and very significantly, it is envisaged that the *Shari'a* may be deficient in supplying a solution to a particular problem – in that case Custom applies. We then revert to the ever-present question, as to whether such Custom would be applicable if contrary to the tenets of the *Sharia*? Finally, the judge is directed to 'the tenets of natural justice or the principles of equity and good conscience'. Once again, are these tenets or principles to be applied in defiance of the *Sharia* or only if in accord therewith?

These are difficult questions indeed. Bahrain is a modern State with a fully developed commercial community and an emancipated banking system on the modern occidental model both domestic and offshore. There is still a dearth of commercial legislation in Bahrain in view of which reference to commercial and in particular banking custom becomes increasingly relevant. If the principles of the *Shari'a* were to be applied strictly to these matters, then many aspects of such commerce and banking would be found to be illegal. Practically speaking, it is unlikely that this conflict would at the present time be allowed to develop but these anomalies must always be borne in mind.

With regard to the secular law and the principles which might be applied by a judge sitting in Bahrain we note that the law of contract and tort in Bahrain is still common law based and that consequently it would be relevant to adduce common law precedent although in many respects reliance may also be made and is made in practice upon Egyptian and other authorities on the civil side. It may be submitted that a comparative law argument should thus carry considerable weight. The position with regard to the common law will change when the new Civil and Commercial Code which has been so long awaited in Bahrain, and which is based upon Egyptian civil principle, is issued.

The United Arab Emirates (UAE)

We now consider the UAE and its Emirates, dealing first with the position in the Union jurisdiction, and then with some of those Emirates which have preserved their own separate systems. Although the UAE Provisional Constitution has the *Shari'a* as *a* principal source of legislation, when we turn to the Law setting up the Union Supreme Court – which started its existence as the Constitutional Court in the Union, but has subsequently gathered authority and now has a separate Cassation Division – we find this Law[22] providing, in Article 75:

> "The Supreme Court shall apply the provisions of the Islamic *Shari'a*, Union Laws, and other Laws in force in the member Emirates of the Union *conforming to the Islamic Shari'a*. Likewise it shall apply those rules of Custom and those

principles of natural and comparative law *which do not conflict with the principles of that Shari'a.* (Italics added)."

Thus, although we here have a Constitution which recognised the *Shari'a* as *a* principal source of law, we have a Law setting up the Supreme Court of the land which appears to be providing that the *Shari'a* shall be *the* principal source, because by its terms any measures which are contrary to the *Shari'a* would seem by express provision to be invalid. This highlights the complexity of a study in these jurisdictions, and the vital importance of first assessing the constitutional position, and then the possible role of the *Shari'a* in order safely to give an opinion or to adjudicate upon a commercial problem. By comparison with Kuwait, where the ambiguities are minimal in the face of comprehensive Codes with a solid backing of Egyptian and continental law, the rest of our area is strewn with difficulties in this respect.

Again, Union Law 6 of 1978, which set up the Union Courts of First Instance and Appeal, and transferred to these courts the jurisdiction of the local judicial bodies of certain of the Emirates (Abu Dhabi, Sharjah, Ajman and Fujairah), prescribes the following sources of law in Article 8:

"The union Courts shall apply the provisions of the Islam *Shari'a*, Union Laws, and other laws in force, just as they shall apply those rules of custom and general legal principles *which do not conflict with the provisions of the Shari'a.* (Italics added)."

The net effect of these provisions is to make the Islamic *Shari'a the* principal source of law in those Emirates to which the Law applies (it does not have the same relevance in the local courts of Dubai, Umm al-Qawain and Ra's al-Khaima, which remain under the control of their respective Rulers, although the degree of relevance is open to argument). Any difference in wording between Article 75 of Law 10/1973 and Article 8 of Law 6/1978 cannot be regarded as significant in view of the fact that appeal lies from the Union Courts in the Emirates to the Union Supreme Court.[23] One may also note that any challenge to the constitutionality of Union Laws 6/1978 and 10/1973 on the grounds that their prescribed sources of law go beyond the Constitution itself in giving legal priority to the Islamic *Shari'a*, would be heard before the Union Supreme Court itself as the Constitutional Court of the State. It may be accepted that the Supreme Court would remain bound by its terms of reference, since to uphold such a challenge would be in effect to rule that its own constitution is contrary to the UAE Constitution. In any event, as a matter of interpretation, once the Constitution has prescribed the *Shari'a* as a principal source of law, there is seemingly no reason why subsidiary legislation should not exercise discretion in degrees of severity provided that it obeys the basic constitutional dictate. Thus, in those Emirates where all courts are federal courts, the Laws setting up such courts may be considered declaratory of the legal status of the *Shari'a* as a source of law.

As regards the Emirates which have not opted to apply for incorporation into the Union Courts system, we shall assess them later in this article against the background of the Laws in force in each individual Emirate. The Constitution of the UAE provides for existing Emirate legislation to continue unless and until replaced by a subsequent Union measure; there is no express dictate that such existing legislation must be constitutional in accordance with the provisions of the new Constitution although, in my opinion, that is a matter of law, whether expressed or not.[24]

Even so far as concerns the Emirates which have abandoned their individual courts systems, there is a need for analysis of Emirate law, in the main because of Article 12 of Law 6/1978, which reads:

> "Subject to what is provided for in this Law, there shall be adherence before the Union Courts to the procedures, principles and regulations currently in force before the local judicial tribunals and in particular, those relating to litigation procedures, ways of impugning judgments, and means of their execution, until such time as the Law regulating the procedures before the Union Courts is issued."

To date no such Law has been issued, and we shall investigate the interaction here of Abu Dhabi law with Union Law, since this is the jurisdiction which provides the largest abundance of material for study.

Reference must be made to the Abu Dhabi Court Law 1968 and the Abu Dhabi Law of Procedure in the Civil Courts 1970. The former Law limits the jurisdiction of *Shari'a qadis* to 'personal affairs'. Accordingly, unless the parties should otherwise agree, cases involving commercial matters are dealt with by Civil Judges. The Law of Procedure in the Civil Courts states that:

> "In any matter not covered by a provision in the laws of the territory the Courts of the territory shall as appropriate apply

> the dictates of justice or conscience or the general principles of justice *provided that guidance shall be sought therein from the jurisprudence of the Islamic Shari'a*."

Article 8 of the Union Courts Law 6/1978 is a much stronger injunction to respect the *Shari'a* than is Article 5 of Abu Dhabi Law 3/1970 cited above, and it is significant that the majority of the Civil Chamber of the Abu Dhabi Court of Appeal has taken the view that Articles 61 and 62 of the Abu Dhabi Civil Procedure Code, which allow the Civil Court to require the levying of interest upon a judgment sum until the full amount due had been paid, had been invalidated by Union Law 6/1978. In that case[25] the bank concerned failed to recover interest on a loan because the majority of the Court held interest to be illegal at *Shari'a* Law, although there was a strong dissenting opinion from one member of the Court, who declared the matter to be controversial at Islamic Law, and argued that it would be wrong, indeed dangerous, 'to issue a decision based on absolute religious belief'.

As we shall see in a moment, when we consider some constitutional judgments issued by the Supreme Court which illustrate the uncertainty surrounding the matter of prevalence among the sources of law, a higher Court took the opposite view. In any event, the lower Appeal Court decision is not binding as regards later cases, there being no strict rule of *stare decisis*, but it does demonstrate the overall trend in Abu Dhabi towards questioning the legality of interest, and of secular practices generally, and it may be assumed that like Union Courts in Sharjah, Ajman and Fujairah would follow any lead given by Abu Dhabi. There has never in fact been any incisive ruling in the matter of the legality of banking interest in the UAE: it remains a recognised risk, while the true sanction is perhaps not so much a matter of law as of creditability.

We now have to consider briefly the situation in the non-subscribing Emirates of Dubai, and Ra's al-Khaima (and Umm al-Qawain) – very briefly in the latter case, since there is scant published material concerning the workings of justice in that Emirate.

In Dubai the *Shari'a* Courts have residuary jurisdiction in all but the few specific matters in which jurisdiction has been granted by Decree to the Civil Courts; in particular, the latter have jurisdiction in banking matters and any financial transactions in which a bank is involved, so that any consideration of the legality of interest would come within their province. Article 14 of the Dubai Courts Law 1970 provides that the Civil Court shall exercise its power in accordance with (1) the laws in force in the Emirate; (2) the provisions of the *Shari'a*; (3) the rules of custom and usage, provided the same be not in conflict with the laws, or public order or morals; and (4) the rules of natural justice, law and equity. Thus we again find the admission of general principles of law.

In the absence of any Dubai legislation on banking, the Civil Judge finds himself directed towards the *Shari'a* by this Article, yet in practice, the Dubai Courts have in the past taken the view that interest is not illegal. The extent to which Dubai may be affected by trends emanating from Abu Dhabi is difficult to assess, but it is worth restating that Dubai as recently as 1979[26] reinforced its own autonomous system of courts by establishing a Dubai Supreme Court of Appeal to replace the old Appeal Court.

In Ra's al-Khaima, the situation is broadly the same, the *Shari'a* Courts having residuary jurisdiction (Courts Law 1971, Art. 9) and the Civil Courts having jurisdiction in banking matters (Decree 9/1971, Art. 1(2)). The sources of law are identical to those prescribed in Dubai, as they are for the Civil Court of Appeal formed by Decree 14/.1971. (In the context of the significance of the order in which sources of law are laid down, it is interesting to note that in both Dubai and Ra's al-Khaima, the *Shari'a* Courts have prescribed for them 'the Laws in force in the Emirate . . . and the provisions of the noble Islamic *Shari'a*'.)

Reverting now for a moment to judgments of the Constitutional Division of the Supreme Court which illustrate the trend in attitudes as regards the relevant importance of the prescribed sources of law: we return first to the Hilal Case, in which the Supreme Court was asked to rule on the constitutionality of Articles 61 and 62 of the Abu Dhabi Procedure Law (3/1970). the Supreme Court held that the Articles were constitutional and continued to be so by virtue of Article 148 of the Union Constitution which provides that laws in force before the promulgation of the Constitution were to remain valid unless or until repealed or amended. This, of course, begs the question of whether:

a) interest is or is not legal at the *Shari'a*;
b) the provisions of the *Shari'a* must be regarded as paramount which, in view of the strong wording of the Courts Law, could well be argued to be the case.

This judgment is, in my respectful submission, wrong.

In this context we refer to another judgment of the Constitutional Division of the Union Supreme Court: 1982 Case 1/Year 8.[27] Here a number of cases were referred by the Abu Dhabi Appeal Court for guidance as to the constitutionality of criminal penalties imposed by the Abu Dhabi Alcoholic Drinks Law of 1976. The point at issue was the difference between the *Shari'a* penalties (the *hadd* punishments) and those imposed by the Abu Dhabi secular law. The Court referred to the Constitution, and to the Union Courts Law which, we recall, contains the apparent hierarchy of authority to which we have referred. The Court further referred to the conflict between the said secular law and the *Shari'a* as prescribed by Union Law 10/1973 Article 75. Having regard to the provisions of the Constitution prescribing the *Shari'a* as a principal source of law, must the *hadd* punishments be applied in substitution for the punishments prescribed by the Abu Dhabi secular law? The Court said that as a general principle this falls to the legislator to decide, not to the Court; the duty of the Court is merely to decide where necessary whether the legislation passed is constitutional. The Court then mentioned the directive in the Union Courts Law that laws were to be applied if in accord with the Islamic *Shari'a* thus, said the Court, does the local Abu Dhabi Alcoholic Drinks Law accord with the *Shari'a*? The Court referred to the penalties of imprisonment and fine for drunkenness prescribed by the Abu Dhabi law 'without prejudice to any other punishment prescribed by the penal code or any other law'. The Court pointed out that the crimes in issue here constituted drunkenness in a public place, *not* the *consumption* of liquor (italics added) – the latter is of itself punishable at the *Shari'a* by flogging according to the true Sunna. The Court said that the crime of drunkenness here in issue, for which the penalties are prescribed by the Abu Dhabi Law (Art. 17), does not contravene the provisions of the *Shari'a*, because the *Shari'a* does not prescribe a punishment for this particular crime – and it is with the crime of drunkenness in a public place that the accused are indicted in these cases. The Court was of the opinion that at the *Shari'a* this would be a matter of *ta'zir* (discretionary) not *hadd* (prescribed and mandatory) according to all the authorities. Thus, in the judgment of the Court, the penalties prescribed by Article 17 are not inconsistent with the *Shari'a*. The penalties prescribed at the *Shari'a* for Muslims drinking alcohol are different; thus the said Abu Dhabi Law is not unconstitutional.

To the uncomplicated mind, it may seem difficult to envisage drunkenness in a public place, without the prior consumption of alcohol!

Be the foregoing as it may, a later judgment seems to record a shift in emphasis. This recent case[28] once again dealt with the Abu Dhabi

Alcoholic Drinks Law, and seems finally to have put the paramountcy of the *Shari'a* in the UAE system beyond doubt. It thus merits consideration in detail. The constitutional division of the Union Supreme Court, sitting at Abu Dhabi on 25 December 1983 was again concerned with the interpretation of the Constitution in a number of cases raised by the Abu Dhabi Union Appeal Court. Again, the constitutionality of Article 17 of the Abu Dhabi Alcoholic Drinks Law 8/1976 was under consideration. The Attorney General's Office had demanded the imposition of the *Shari'a* penalties.

The Abu Dhabi Criminal Court had sentenced the accused to six months' imprisonment and a fine of DH1000 in accordance with paragraph 2 of Article 17. Both the accused and the Attorney General appealed. The Appellate Court said that the Abu Dhabi Law was a local law as referred to in Article 8 of Union Law 6/1978. The Court referred to Article 13 of that Law as follows:

> "Until the issue of the special law relating to the procedures of applying the *Shari'a hadd* punishments, the punishments provided in this Law shall be considered as 'estimated'."

The Appellate Court recorded that the Union Supreme Court applies the *Shari'a* and quoted Article 75 of Union Law 10/1973. Both lower and Appellate Courts must apply these principles. The Court pointed out that there was an apparent conflict between Law 6/1978 which enjoins the imposition of the penalty provided by Article 17 of the Alcoholic Drinks Law by application of the principle of *ta'zir*, and Union Law 10/1973 relied upon the Attorney General in demanding a sentence of flogging; the latter in accordance with Article 75 of Union Law 10/1973. Both laws are Union Laws, said the Court, equal in legislative weight, but differ in the punishment for drunkenness, thus creating a conflict, and calling into question the constitutionality of Law 8/1976. The Court referred to Article 7 of the Constitution stating that 'the Islamic *Shari'a* is a principal source of legislation' and asked, should the legislator have paid heed to this principle in framing Law 8?

Such were the issues in the Court of Appeal. In view of the apparent conflict, the Court referred the matter to the Constitutional Division of the Supreme Court.

In this case, the Constitutional Court referred expressly to Article 7 of the Constitution and faced squarely the question: 'Is the *Shari'a* the *sole* official source of law, superior to secular legislation; or are there other sources beside it?' The legislator dealt with this by making the

Shari'a the fundamental and principal source for everything issuing from the Authorities by way of legislation by his provision in Article 75 of Union Law 10/1973. The result, said the Court, is that the desire of the State was quite clearly expressed in the Constitution that its legislation be Islamic, and furthermore the legislator has chosen that the law (*shari'a*) of God is the principal source for all legislation and 'who can be better than God in law?' The Court went on to say that the Islamic *Shari'a* absolutely forbids liquor and the Judgment contains many quotations from the Qur'an and the Sunna and a long homily to these effects.[29]

The Court concluded that the *ta'zir* punishment provided for in the Abu Dhabi Drinks Law in no way prejudices the *hadd* punishment, but is a guide to the *Qadis* in sentencing *also* for the specific incidents of drunkenness in a public place, for the protection of the public weal. For this, imprisonment and fine are both recognised forms of punishment and if the public weal so requires there is no objection to *adding these punishments to the hadd.*[30] The Court said that the intention of the said Article 13 was not to suspend the *hadd* punishments for the following reasons:

1 The overall intention of the legislator is clear.
2 The *hadd* is from God and the legislator has no right to vary or suspend the same: the other punishments may be added.
3 The Qur'an and Sunna etcetera are from God and it is inconceivable that they can be waived.
4 A contrary view would mean that if a Muslim drinks alcohol in private or public without getting drunk, he would be subject to no punishment – this is completely at variance with the provisions of the *Shari'a*.
5 If the legislator has, as explained, taken the *Shari'a* as the fundamental source for all legislation, it is thus above all other laws. Article 17 of Law 8/1976 provides that the penalties therein prescribed shall be without prejudice to any other penalty prescribed by the Penal Code or any other law – *a fortiori* the *Shari'a*.

On the basis of the foregoing, said the Court, there is no conflict: *ta'zir* can be joined to *hadd*.

This judgment makes it quite clear that the *Shari'a* is paramount. This was of course a criminal not civil matter, but it may be submitted there can be no distinction in this respect in the philosophies applied by the Supreme Court and this decision constitutes a weighty precedent in criminal, civil and commercial matters.[31]

Conclusion

What are the main points to be drawn from this very complicated overall picture? First one should realise the growing emphasis to be given to the *Shari'a*. Secondly, this should always be analysed against the backdrop of the constitutional law of each State. Thirdly, the keynote is *uncertainty*: with the possible exception of Kuwait in commercial matters, the *Shari'a* could intervene to a greater or less degree in most jurisdictions.

In Kuwait the situation is incisive, with the sound basis of comprehensive codes on a civil law basis. In Saudi Arabia, at the other extreme, we find the *Shari'a* paramount, as developed in so-called Regulations out of deference to the '*ulama*', the learned doctors of law. In Bahrain, we find common law/civil law in that order: the Laws of Contracts and Torts based on common law, with a civil law patterned Commercial Agencies Law and Companies Law, and a Civil and Commercial Code along Egyptian/French lines currently in draft form, the promulgation of which will progressively abolish the common law element.

In Qatar we have a civil-based Code, and, for example, agency and company law also on that basis; but where there are lacunae there is still some room for common law supporting argument. Again in the UAE there is a civil emphasis, notably in the Companies Law, and in other specific laws, although there are as yet few codes: as far as the Union is concerned civil principles are set to oust the vestiges of common law. In the individual Emirates, however, this may take longer, although Abu Dhabi already gives the emphasis to the civil approach. Dubai, Sharjah and Ra's al-Khaima still apply the same Contracts Law as Bahrain, so that one starts with the existing common law, and introduces civil law as appropriate. It is not inaccurate to say that one may validly apply this approach in the remaining Emirates – Ajman, Umm al-Qawain and Fujairah.

Lastly, Oman is in a category of its own: the Banking Law and the Companies Law are good cases in point. It would be necessary to seek out all relevant precedents and arguments introducing civil and common law on a comparative basis.

Thus, the practical approach to any problem in the area is first, where necessary and appropriate, to go to the Constitution. Then the Codes must be considered. We turn to our prescribed principles to fill any gaps: we must accord due weight to each one as prescribed. Eventually, we go to commentaries, Sanhouri being paramount, and to common law books and precedents where we have a common law element. This brings us to court decisions: it has been stressed that one cannot always determine whether the courts would remain bound by prior decisions, but we recall that we are dealing with relatively small communities, and a limited number of judges, and even absent a mandatory rule of *stare decisis*, in practice it is unlikely that a judge will contradict himself on the same facts.

Notes

1 The material in this article formed the basis of a lecture in the series 'Comparative Commercial Law in the Middle East' delivered by the author to the LLM course at the School of Oriental and African Studies, University of London.

2 Quotations from the various codes in this article are my own translations from the original Arabic.

3 Kuwait, Bahrain, UAE: '*a* principal source of law'; Qatar: '*the* principal source of law'.

4 See Anna Monico, 'Oman' in *Proceedings of the Seminar on Middle East Law IBA*, 1981, pp. 135 *et seq.*

5 *Op. cit.* pp. 148 *et seq.* for a good overall statement of the situation.

6 Oman Official Gazette 286/1984.

7 Note the provisions of the Omani Banking Law which appear to confer upon contracting parties the right to choose both jurisdiction and law.

8 Kuwaiti Commercial Code, Law 2 of 1961.

9 See the recent Egyptian judgment in *Rector of Al Azhar* v. *President of the Republic and others*, 4 May 1985.

10 Article 547: 'Loans shall be without interest'. See also Article 305: 'Any agreement providing for interest in respect of the use of an amount of money or delay in performance of an obligation shall be void'.

11 Commercial Code. Articles 101 *et seq.*

12 *The Civil Law of Palestine and Trans Jordan*: Vol. 1, *The Mejelle* (London: Sweet & Maxwell, 1938).

13 Syria, Libya, Sudan, Jordan put the principles of the *Shari'a*, the *fiqh*, ahead of custom; Somalia *et al.* eliminate custom entirely. The Somali Civil Code prescribes first the *Shari'a* then the principles of sound justice.

14 'Render therefore unto Caesar the things which are Caesar's; and unto God the things that are God's' (New Testament, St Matthew xxii. 21): the comparison is irresistible!

15 Exercised by the British Crown by Order in Council (made under the Foreign Jurisdiction Acts) until 1961 in Kuwait; until 1971 in Bahrain, Qatar, and the UAE (then the Trucial States).

16 That is to say, other than a *Shari'a Qadi.*

17 Qatari Law 13/1971 Gazette 7/1971.

18 Recall, nevertheless, the prescription in the Constitution of Qatar as the *Shari'a* as *the* principal source of law.
19 Law 16/1971: Gazette 7/1971.
20 Ballantyne 'Legal Development in Arabia', London, Graham & Trotman, 1979, p. 121.
21 See also the author's chapter on Bahrain and Qatar in *Proceedings of the Seminar on Middle East Law IBA*, 1981, particularly pp. 95 *et seq.*
22 Law 10/1973.
23 See Law 6/1978, Article 7, and Article 4 of Law 17/1978 regulating the conditions and procedure for appeal before the Union Supreme Court.
24 *Contra*, however, the recent Egyptian case noted *supra* at note 9.
25 Civil Appeal No. 5/1979: *Abdullah Rashid Hilal* v. *The International Bank of Credit and Commerce.*
26 Dubai Law 2/1979.
27 UAE *Gazette* No. 100.
28 Published in UAE *Gazette* 135/1984.
29 Perhaps not surprisingly, the Court did not advert to the Qur'an at Surat II:219: 'They ask you about alcohol and games of chance. Say: in both there is great sin and benefits to the people: and the sin thereof is greater than the benefit . . .' (Al Boqara). We may also, however, recall: Surat IV:43: 'Oh ye who believe: Draw not near unto prayer when you are drunk, that you may know what you are saying . . .' Surat V:90: 'Oh ye who believe, alcohol and games of chance and idols and divining arrows are only an infamy of Satan's handiwork. Avoid it that mayhap you will succeed.'
30 All emphasis supplied
31 See also the Judgment of the Union Constitutional Court on 5 June 1983 in a reference by the Union Appeal Court of Sharjah (Case 209/1981). Here the Court in dealing with the constitutionality of the Law of Control of Alcoholic Drinks in Sharjah 1972 held that the said Law was constitutional and the punishments therein prescribed valid; but went on to say that the imposition of the *Hadd* punishment is obligatory on a Muslim who drinks alcohol, whether the same be accompanied by another prescribed *ta'zir* punishment or not. The Court referred to its judgments No. 1/Year 8 dated 8 November 1981; and No. 14/Year 10 dated 30 January 1983, both dealing with the Abu Dhabi Alcoholic Drinks Law. For two further cases on this subject see UAE *Gazette* 124 and 129.

VI
The Shari'a

It is a great honour for me to be here. Having said that, please appreciate the diffidence which I, one of the People of the Book, feel at appearing with these noble and learned colleagues on a platform devoted to the Islamic *Shari'a*. We are sitting here in Cairo, one of the very citadels of jurisprudence in the Arab world, not least in the field of the *Shari'a*; one mentions the name of Al-Azhar with the greatest of respect. It is impossible to overestimate the debt which the world of Arab jurisprudence owes to Egyptian jurists. We look at the Codes of virtually all Arab countries, and that debt is immediately apparent; while at the right hand of every judge and practitioner lies the monumental *Al-Wasit* of the late Abd al-Rizzaq al-Sanhouri. My mother tongue is English. My Arabic is heavy from a long sojourn in London. Also, I shall be speaking to a large proportion of Western lawyers, for whom I shall try to bridge the gap of comprehension in dealing with the *Shari'a*, and set the stage for discussion. I therefore ask leave from my Arab friends to speak in English. Where I refer to Arabic texts, I shall quote these in both languages. I acknowledge my own shortcomings in the Arabic language, the language of *dhad* and the angels.

The first and last time the IBA convened a conference on Arab laws was in Hamburg in 1980. I had the honour to sit on the panel on that occasion. The conference was a small one, but a great success. However, one lesson was learnt: the great value of that conference lay in the question and answer sessions and in the interventions from the floor which followed the speeches. Unfortunately, those were not recorded. This time, we shall not make that mistake. Everything will be on tape, and we shall concentrate on interventions.

I have spent nearly 40 years now concerned exclusively with Arab laws.

I may say with sincerity that I come here not so much to contribute but to learn. I certainly do not stand here as an expert in the substance of the *Shari'a*. In nearly 40 years practice in the Gulf States, the incursion of the *Shari'a* into commercial law has *in practice* been minimal. May we mentally underline the words 'in practice'. It has always been necessary to bear firmly in mind that in all the Arab countries, the *Shari'a* stands constitutionally as the, or one of the, main sources of legislation. In an Arab jurisdiction, therefore, the first essential and often difficult task of the practising lawyer is to ask himself: To what extent is the *Shari'a* relevant in this matter? The answer may vary from 'Not at all' in Egypt or Kuwait in a commercial matter: to 'Essentially' in Saudi Arabia. In various jurisdictions there are varying shades. It is my view that consideration of the *Shari'a* will very rapidly assume increasing importance, even dramatically in the immediate future. Anyone who ignores the possible role of the *Shari'a* in a transaction does so at his peril.

We are not by any means dealing with an academic subject. In my view the *Shari'a* is the most important topic at this Conference. Yet, when I suggested it as such at our initial meetings in London, there was opposition; Arab opposition at that. 'Everyone wants to hear about joint ventures and arbitration, not the *Shari'a*.' I simply do not agree.

In practice, I have found a lamentable, if understandable, ignorance, even non-adversion to the *Shari'a* among Western lawyers. This is understandable for several reasons:

a) The importance to which I have referred is in no way appreciated – even many Arab colleagues tend to play down the *Shari'a* as old-fashioned or *passeé*. This is a dangerous attitude. In the current reassertion of the *Shari'a* which we are witnessing, and shall witness in ever-increasing momentum, the *Shari'a* will be ignored at our peril.
b) The economic circumstances: in the euphoric conditions which have existed in the oil States over the last years, where the profit motive has outweighed all others, lawyers trying to get the thing right have really been rather a nuisance. Well, times have changed and are changing.
c) Reluctance to advert to the unknown: A centuries-old religious law? The ostrich puts his head in the sand. In any event, insert a

> proper law clause into your contract, and if possible a foreign jurisdiction or arbitration clause, and all will be well. I am sure that I do not have to spell out to *this* audience the folly of such an attitude in general. Let us take a practical example. A syndicated loan agreement will invariably contain such a jurisdiction and proper law clause; but a 'Closing Opinion' must be sought as to the validity of the agreement according to the law of the borrowing country. One has dealt with dozens of such Opinions. Every one contains a proviso that if the *Shari'a* were to be applied, the loan agreement would be assailable at the *Shari'a* for many illegalities. The most obvious one is, as we all know, the prohibition of interest on monies lent. We shall refer to that in a moment. But it really goes further than that.

It is trite to say here that in dealing with the Arab world, we are dealing with all Islamic states. It is not so trite to point out that this is not at all the same as saying that in dealing with the Western world, we are dealing with all Christian States! For the Arab, his religion is inextricably interwoven with his life. The precepts of *al-Islam* are ever-present in his thoughts and speech. The *Qur'an* says, 'Oh ye who believe, mention (remember) God often, praise him both early and late', and the cry of the *muaththin* rings out five times daily calling the faithful to prayer. The *Shari'a* is the law of that religion. In looking at the strong reassertion of *al-Islam* which we are witnessing in the Arab world, we are looking also at a reassertion of the *Shari'a* law. That word 'reassertion' is important. We are not facing a revival or revivification of Islam, because Islam has never been dead or even quiescent.

I have referred to the fact that the Constitutions of the Arab States prescribe the *Shari'a* as a source of legislation. Sometimes this is expressed to be *a* main source of legislation (Kuwait, Bahrain, the UAE); in some (Qatar, and since 1980, Egypt) it is *the* main source of legislation. The first question that should always arise in the mind of the practising lawyer, therefore, is the extent to which the *Shari'a* applies or could apply in a particular matter, and we find that the position is often blurred. The keynote is uncertainty. It is even more blurred in countries such as Saudi Arabia and Oman, where there is no written Constitution (this is not strictly so, in that Saudi Arabia has the old written declaration of the *Hijaz*, but this is not a Constitution in the modern sense). We do not have time here to look into all these niceties, although we may do so in discussion afterwards.

I have already referred to the obvious example of illegality at the *Shari'a* of interest on monies lent, and shall do so again in a moment. We take this only as a burning practical example – there are many other incidents of the modern commercial contract which could be indicted for illegality were the *Shari'a* to apply. But – how have the Arab countries dealt with the question of interest?

Let me say at once that the only way in which these doubts arising from a possible application of the *Shari'a* may be dispersed is by express secular legislation. It is politically very difficult, if not impossible, for an Arab State to promulgate such legislation, and here again we find, in many cases, uncertainty – the whole subject matter is evaded and the position is again blurred. Even where incisive legislation exists (and it is rare), who can say that it may not be challenged before a Constitutional Court as being contrary to the *Shari'a* as prescribed in the Constitution? Of the Gulf States, only Kuwait has legislated incisively in this respect. Whereas the 1981 Civil Code of Kuwait, as might be expected, forbids the charging of interest on loans, the Commercial Code of the same year, as 'special' legislation, expressly permits it. In other countries, the issue is swept under the rug but it nonetheless exists. In general, it has not been allowed to arise in practice. I can evidence many recent cases in the UAE where the position is changing, and where it *has* been allowed to arise; it has also arisen in Saudi Arabia; it could arise in the other jurisdictions. May I suggest again that we take this as an example: there are many other incidents of the modern commercial contract which could be assailed at the *Shari'a*.

The fact is that, in the modern international commercial context, the *Shari'a* is an embarrassment. It is always somewhat invidious to quote from oneself, but I will nonetheless do so from a book which I wrote in 1980:[1]

> "It is often said that the *Qur'an* (and hence the *Shari'a*) provides all the principles necessary for the regulation of relationships even in the world of commerce. As with Christianity or other major religions, that would be true in the context of the ideal society, wherein every member accepted and obeyed its dictates under spiritual sanction; in the modern commercial world, this would envisage also such obedience in general, internationally, by members of other cultures including States. This is unfortunately at the moment unthinkable, and in the context of society as it exists, the lesser merits of man-made law must

> obtain. It is in the latter context that the *Shari'a* must be viewed, and, in its very nature, necessarily found wanting. It may be said that it is the material world that is at fault in this, and that either Islam or Christianity, restored to their essential validity amongst us, would do a better and more adequate job. Be that as it may, the inherent immutability of the *Shari'a* militates against its suitability in the system of internal commerce which man has created. Acceptance of this truth is reflected in the publication by most of the States of the Muslim world of Commercial and other Codes in replacement of the *Shari'a*, which is now in many cases limited to matters of personal status."

I have referred already to the profit motive, which has in the past tended to obscure all else. Now, however, we all know there has been a change of scene. As part of that change, the Arabs are above all looking to *al-Islam* in the field of jurisprudence, and have for some time been questioning the rectitude of having, in many cases, adopted legislation stemming from occidental non-Muslim sources, instead of basing it upon the *Shari'a*. I would refer in this context to studies which are in progress, under the auspices of the Islamic Conference, by the Learned Academy of Jurisprudence – I have not yet seen any material emanating from the most recent conference at Kuwait, but no doubt one of my colleagues will be able to enlighten us in this respect.

We thus have overall a scenario where in many Arab States the *Shari'a could* be applied in a commercial transaction, even if in general it is not so applied. This obviously makes for a basic uncertainty which could only be removed by express legislation. Well – does this matter? The answer is, yes, it does, and in order to understand that, we have to turn to a short description of the *Shari'a* itself, and an even shorter consideration of the incidents which distinguish it from occidental jurisprudence. The *Shari'a* is, of course, the sacred law of Islam, an all-embracing body of religious law regulating, in theory, the life of every Muslim in every aspect. Essentially, the *Shari'a* is derived from and has its roots in the *Qur'an* and the customs of the Prophet as incorporated in recognised Muslim traditions. I think that the accepted and not-too-orthodox view must be that these two sources are immutable. Where there is an express provision (*nuss*) at this level, then it is mandatory and absolute. I believe there are those contemporary authors who pretend that even such express provision may be diluted or shaped to contemporary needs, but I do not believe that this is a view which would find other than very limited acceptance. It is based upon the requirements of *maslaha* or benefit to the community. May I quote a recent writing by my colleague here, Professor Abu Majd:

> "The sanctity of the word of God and the guidance of his Prophet does not *derive* from a tie with the past, recent or distant . . . Come, let us call things by their names and say that we are bound by the Book, following the true *Sunna* . . . But this does not involve sanctifying the opinions of men and devotion to following the ancients . . . indeed, that is a heresy which is abhorrent, as related for us by the *Qur'an*, and most forcefully to be eschewed by its adherents."[2]

Here, the learned, author is, I understand it, opening the door to a new *itjihad* but not, of course, laying express provisions of *Qur'an* and *Sunna* open to change. But – can the overall position be ambiented within this framework?

Coming downstream, as it were, from these basic precepts, we find the *Shari'a* developed over centuries by the consensus of Muslim scholars, and reasoning by analogy. Let us make a further generalisation by adopting the Arabic word *itjihad*, which I will translate for present purposes as logical and reasoned deductions and developments emanating from the basic principles to which we have referred. Given the immutability of the basic precepts, it is in the field of a new *itjihad* that the necessary flexibility to interpret the *Shari'a* according to the needs of modern international commerce rests. We shall consider in a moment whether that is legally possible to the extent necessary to satisfy those needs.

As a body of religious law, the *Shari'a* has been and is applied in different parts of the Muslim world in different ways, and particularly in different degrees of strictness. The deductive processes were established by the doctors of law by the Middle Ages. There are four main schools, or trends of doctrine: the *Hanafi*, the *Maliki*, the *Shafi'i* and the *Hanbali*, the latter being the school applied in Saudi Arabia. I find the *Shari'a* and its application extremely complex, not least because its main lines of thought were established so long ago. It is for this reason that many Islamic States, as I have already indicated, have been obliged to provide, by modern legislation, for the needs of contemporary commerce. It is also the reason why, in major international arbitrations, it was decided that the pure principles of the *Shari'a* must be replaced or supplemented by modern concepts. I may quote three which I have no doubt are well known to all of you:

In *Petroleum Development (Trucial Coasts) Ltd.* v. *the Shaikh of Abu Dhabi*,[3] the Arbitrator, Lord Asquith, rejected the Islamic law as applied in Abu Dhabi as not being competent to regulate a modern commercial instrument. He accordingly applied, and I quote, 'principles rooted in good sense and common practice of the generality of civilised nations – a sort of modern law of nature', as the yardstick in the award. (Incidentally, the learned Lord entirely overlooked the fact that at the time in Abu Dhabi there was British extraterritorial jurisdiction, but we need not dwell on that here.)

Again, in *Ruler of Qatar* v. *International Marine Oil Company Limited*,[4] the Arbitrator, while considering the law of Qatar to be the proper law of the Concession Agreement, declined to apply it. The *Shari'a* law in the Shaikhdom of Qatar was (and indeed is) Islamic law of the *Hanbali* school, which the Arbitrator held to be inappropriate to govern a modern oil concession. To quote from the Award: '. . . There are at least two weighty considerations against that view (i.e., the adoption of Islamic law). One is that, in my opinion, after hearing the evidence of the two experts in Islamic law, Professor Anderson and Professor Milliot, there is no settled body of legal principles in Qatar applicable to the construction of modern commercial instruments'. The learned Arbitrator then referred to the Award of Lord Asquith of which I have made mention, and went on to say: 'I have no reason to suppose that Islamic law is not administered there (i.e. in Qatar) strictly, but I am satisfied that the law does not contain any principles which would be sufficient to interpret this particular contract'; and he continued: '. . . Both experts agreed that certain parts of the contract, if Islamic law were applicable, would be open to the grave criticism of being invalid. According to Professor Milliot, the principle Agreement was full of irregularities from end to end according to Islamic law applied in Qatar. This is a cogent reason for saying that such law does not contain a body of legal principles applicable to a modern commercial contract of this kind'. (I should say that that is not now the position in Qatar, which has for some 20 years had a Civil and Commercial Code based upon the Kuwaiti 1961 Commercial Law.)

Lastly, in this context, in the famous *Aramco Arbitration, Saudi Arabia* v. *Arabian American Oil Company*,[5] the Arbitrators, Professor G Sauser Hall (Referee), Sir Saba Habachy KBE (Arbitrator appointed by Aramco), and Muhammed Hassan (Arbitrator appointed by Saudi Arabia), while holding that the proper law of the Concession Contract was the law of Saudi Arabia, which they found to be Muslim law as taught by the *Hanbali* school, and while adverting fully to the rule of *pacta sunt servanda*, which they correctly found to be fully recognised in Muslim law, yet held that the reégime of oil concessions had remained embryonic in Muslim law, and found it necessary to fill 'the gaps in the law of Saudi Arabia' by resorting to world-wide custom and practice in the oil business and industry, world case law and doctrine and pure jurisprudence. Sir Norman Anderson and Professor Noel Coulson put the matter with their usual lucidity: '. . . a system of law which attained its formal perfection centuries before the demands of modern technology, finance and marketing were dreamed of' . . . 'But, as we see it, it is preferable to recognise the typical economic development agreement (such as an oil concession) of today, with the detailed terms which the exigencies of the trade and the needs of the two contracting parties commonly dictate, as *sui generis*'. And in turning to the modern international corporation: '. . . a phenomenon of the modern world for which there is no adequate precedent in the experience of the past. This conclusion is reinforced by the consideration that the foreign corporation concerned will, in the vast majority of cases, be entirely non-Muslim in its national and cultural origin, for it is of the nature of the *Shari'a* that it should be regarded as addressed, in its technicalities, to Muslims alone.'[6]

The Anderson-Coulson article to which I have referred deals expressly with the liability of the Muslim ruler, who is equally liable in contract as are his subjects. However, express reference is made to 'the absence in Islamic legal theory and practice of the notion of an independent judiciary', as also that 'Islamic political theory is not based upon the principle of the separation of powers'.

Now, the learned authors suggest that the *lacunae* in the *Shari'a* in the world of modern commercial contracts might be dealt with by treating such contracts as *sui generis*. This might well have validity in international arbitration; indeed, this approach has virtually been adopted in the three arbitrations to which I have referred. It must be stressed, however, that such an approach would have no place whatever before a tribunal, be it court or arbitral, in an Arab jurisdiction where such tribunal found itself directed to apply the *Shari'a*. In those circumstances, the *Shari'a* would have to be applied, and there is no baulking the fact that its application would occasion grave difficulties, even impossibilities, in considering a modern international commercial contract.

May I now turn and, at risk of dangerous over-simplification, indulge in some generalities concerning the differences between the

Shari'a and the occidental systems. In so doing, may I dare to say this: occidental laws assume a fair degree of immorality and try to counteract it; the *Shari'a, par excellence*, having its roots in religion, assumes a high degree of religious rectitude, and legislates accordingly. The main sanction is, after all, hell-fire in the hereafter. In an extreme case, the oath may be administered, but jurisprudentially the possibility of perjury is really unthinkable.

Well, that is all very well; but it makes the *Shari'a* really inconsistent with what modern man has made of commerce. We cannot here enter into philosophical discussion as to which theory is right, although a glance at the existing Western banking system would seem to provide an immediate argument in favour of the *Shari'a*!

One of the great difficulties of the *Shari'a* is that in the field of contract, adapted to the circumstances at the time, it did not deal with general principles, but rather with specific instances, case by case, and with a series of nominate contracts. This obviously makes it very difficult to extract principles appropriate in the modern context. I will, if I may, quote a passage of great authority which gives emphasis to this situation: great authority because it came from the pen of Al-Sanhouri, to whom I have referred, in his '*Masaadir al-Haqq*':

> "*Attempt to extract a theory of contractual liability in the Shari'a*
> It cannot be said that there is a theory of contractual liability in the Islamic jurisprudence akin to that which we have seen in Western jurisprudence. It is only possible to extract from the provisions laid down in the Islamic jurisprudence the counterpart of the theory of contractual liability in Western jurisprudence. Such will be our task in the comparisons which we make between the two systems."

On the same question of the lack of general principles, the learned author went on to deal in the same work with the question of *imprévision, or unforeseen circumstances*:

> "It is difficult to say that the Islamic jurisprudence constructed a theory relating to 'unforeseen circumstances' equivalent to the theory in modern Western jurisprudence. Two reasons prevented that: the first is that the Islamic jurisprudence does not, whether in the theory of unforeseen events or in any other theory, subscribe to general principles. We have stated previously that the Islamic jurisprudence and all other early systems, only treats with matters case by case, and propounds

therefor just practical solutions, creating therein a hidden current of legal reasoning, and the researcher must uncover such current and must construct an appropriate theory supported by sound legal principles, from the various solutions established by various cases; thus is constructed a building with sound cornerstones. The second reason is that the Western jurisprudence was compelled to propound a general theory for unforeseen circumstances, because the force of the binding contract in such jurisprudence has been exaggerated, calling for the establishment of methods to alleviate the same in accordance with the requirements of justice: such exaggeration (i.e., in the sanctity of contract) being subject to the influence of individual authority, and such alleviation being under the influence of social or collective security. As for the Islamic jurisprudence, where the requirements of justice always rule when coming into conflict with the binding force of contract, it has managed in the light of such requirement to open various gaps in the binding force of the contract without the jurists seeing any need to propound a theory in justification thereof, as long as the requirements of justice can customarily be invoked to provide for any such justification."[7]

The learned work to which I have referred provides, in my view, the best potential bridge on a comparative basis known to me between Western principles and those of the *Shari'a*. Its essential value lies in the fact that it does almost bridge an unbridgeable situation. Many of the concepts of the *Shari'a* are extremely difficult even to explain outside the context of the Arabic language. Unfortunately, there is no English translation known to me of *Masaadir al-Haqq*.

The foregoing passage should not, of course, lead one to believe that the binding force of contract is not a basic precept of the *Shari'a*. On the contrary, it is enjoined by the highest authority. The principle of *pacta sunt servanda* is a basic rule. It is supported by the first verse of *Sura V* of the *Qur'an*: 'Oh ye who believe, fulfil all your contracts'. Another verse equally implores the Muslim to observe his obligations: 'Nay but (the Chosen of Allah) is he who fulfils his covenant' (*Qur'an* III, 76). In the *Qur'an*, there are countless references to the necessity of fulfilling one's obligations. The Prophet Muhammad also commented on the *Qur'anic* injunctions: 'Muslims are bound by their stipulations/agreements'.[8] All authority emphasises that 'a party to an agreement cannot free himself from his obligations thereunder by his will alone, even if he had resolved such faculty for himself at the time the contract was concluded, unless such stipulation is specifically authorised by the Divine Legislator'.[9]

That great *Hanbali* jurist, Ibn Taimiyya, in propounding the theory of the sanctity of contract, opined that transactions not expressly forbidden at the *Shari'a* are permissible:

> "The following rule shall be obeyed: men shall be permitted to make all the transactions they need, unless these transactions are forbidden by the Book or by the *Sunna*."[10]

To quote again from the Aramco Award:

> "Muslim law does not distinguish between a treaty, a contract of public or administration law and a contract of civil or commercial law. All these types are viewed by Muslim jurists as agreements or pacts which must be observed, since God is a witness to any contract entered into by individual or collectivities; under Muslim law, any valid contract is obligatory, in accordance with the principles of Islam and the law of God as expressed in the *Qur'an* . . ."[11]

The principle was further and more recently recorded by Professor René-Jean Dupuy:

> "The observance of contracts, generally speaking, is proclaimed by the *Qur'an* (see in particular *Sura V*, 1) the practice of the Prophet, which is the second source of law in Islam (*Bukhari*, III, 187). The writings of Muslim jurists uphold the same principle, in particular Ibn Qudama, a jurist of considerable authority of the *Hanbali* school, which is predominant in Saudi Arabia . . . This principle applies not only to agreements concluded by private persons, but also to agreements entered into by the sovereign. Thus, under the *Shari'a*, nobody, neither the sovereign nor any official is exempt as a matter of privilege."[12]

Thus far, we are on sound ground: the *Shari'a* recognises *par excellence* the principle of *pacta sunt servanda*. What then is the difficulty? Well, the difficulty is that this undoubted validity of the maxim *pacta sunt servanda* must be viewed in the light not only of the restrictions inherent in the system of nominative contracts to which I have referred, but the flexibility inherent in the adversion to changing circumstances. This flexibility is greater than in the Western systems with their more restricted doctrines of frustration (common law) and *impreévision* (civil law). Further, and more basically, it is almost trite to say that the *Shari'a*, while emphasising the sanctity of contract, is referring to a contract which is legal and enforceable at the *Shari'a* itself. Here, we begin to appreciate the differences.

I believe that it helps further to understand the difficulty by comprehending that there are three things which are absolutely repugnant to the *Shari'a*. One is *gharar*, which is almost impossible to translate, but may be roughly rendered as risk or uncertainty; the second is *riba*, which represents any unjustified one-sided accretion and upsetting of the equivalence of contract – the obvious topical example is the absolute ban on interest on monies lent; the third case is where you have a number of transactions within one contract: the precept is that each contract must be limited to one transaction. May I quote again from Al-Sanhouri's *Sources of Rights*:

> "You will observe that each of these three matters had a profound effect on detailed provisions to the extent that, in many such, the Islamic jurisprudence distanced itself from the requirements of the transaction. If it were possible to clarify our understanding of these three matters in accordance with the development of civilisation, then much of the reasoning which stops the Islamic jurisprudence from going along with the requirements of such development would disappear."[13]

Examples of prohibited dealings in this context are two sales in one contract; a sale plus an extraneous condition; a sale plus a loan; a sale of an ear of grain before it whitens or a grape before it blackens, etc., etc.

I trust that this very short analysis may have helped to point up some of the differences between the *Shari'a* and occidental jurisprudence. Not only is it necessary to allocate to a specific transaction a predetermined head of nominative contract; there are the constraints to which I have referred, to which must be added many other theories, not least that of equivalence *tamaathul* and the necessity to maintain the fair bargain between the parties.[14] A parallel may be drawn with the French *droit administratif*, where the financial equilibrium of the contract has been defined as 'the approximate relationship between the obligations and advantages that the contracting party has taken into consideration, as a calculation, at the time of concluding the contract, and which has induced such contracting party to make the deal'.[15]

In making a marked comparison between English law and the *Shari'a* in matters of changed circumstances, Professor Coulson writes with great clarity: 'For Islam, precisely the converse (i.e., to the absolute immutability of contract) is true. Circumstances dominate the promise'.[16]

The abhorrence at the *Shari'a* of transactions involving uncertainty (*gharar*), or *riba*, or going against the principle of equivalence, lead to other difficulties which may be anticipated. Not the least of these is that there can, in general, be no contract relating to a thing not in existence.

Let us develop further the concepts of *gharar* (uncertainty) and *riba* (unearned advantages) by reference to contract of sale. The weight attached to those principles may be emphasised by reference to occidental authorities writing on the *Shari'a* or quoting from the classical texts:

> "An eminent jurist of the *Hanbali* School has observed that the law has imposed equivalence (*tamaathul*) in sale, and has required that one of the two considerations shall not exceed the other.[17]
>
> 'The strict requirements of equivalence of the respective contributions (*apports*) in commutative contracts' is one of the general principles which have oriented the development of the law of obligations under Islamic law.[18]
>
> The fundamental idea which dominates contracts, i.e., the concept of the equivalence of prestations . . ."[19]

The abhorrence of the *Shari'a* of transactions involving *gharar* is well illustrated by the rule that the thing sold must be in existence at the time of contracting. The object or method of performance of the contract must be immediately possible. If the thing sold does not exist at the time of sale, even if it is probable that it will exist, the principle of *gharar* comes into it. Sanhouri refers to five possibilities:[20]

1 The thing exists in its entirety at the time of the contract.
2 The thing exists in essence, then comes to completion thereafter.
3 The thing does not exist but it is established that it will in the future.
4 The thing does not exist either in its entirety or in essence and it is not established that it will exist in the future.
5 The thing does not exist and will not exist in the future, i.e., the non-existence of the thing is established at the time of contracting.

There is no question of 'gharar' in either 1) or 5) above. As to 1) there can be a contract, as to 5) there cannot. This is the same in Western laws. As to the other three, there are shades of validity, and some confusion in the writings due perhaps to a departure from the basic principle of *gharar*, leading to a rigid acceptance of the idea, *per se*, that the thing sold must be in existence.

Let us advert to 2) above as an example: The element of *gharar* is almost extinct, thus there can be contracting on this basis. The main examples are fruits of the land which have sprung up but not come to fruition (literally a useful state: *salah*) and the sort of things which develop from agriculture successively one after the other – e.g., melons, egg plant, etc. In these cases it is certain that the fruit will appear (in the absence of *ja'iha* – *vide infra*). The *fiqh* in general accepts the above principles but there are many diverse writings in the traditional authors such as Sauhouri:[21]

> "The purchase or sale of fruits before they come to fruition (become beneficial) is not lawful because where there is no benefit (*lauslih*) to man or feed for animals, then this does not constitute *property having a counter-value (mal mutaqawim)*. If it becomes capable of benefit but its fruitfulness did not appear thereafter because of Act of God or rot and he (*sic*) bought it on condition of harvesting the same, that is lawful. If he bought it with the condition of leaving it *in situ*, that is not lawful. If he bought it absolutely (*mutlaqen*) then this is lawful according to our School, because the absolute contract envisages the delivery of the subject matter of the contract immediately, and this requirement and the condition of harvesting (cutting – *qat'*) are one [literally equal (*siwa*)]. However, according to Shaf'i this is not lawful because the Prophet decried the sale of fruits until their ripeness appeared or, as he said, until they came to fruition (flowered *zahar*) or, he said, until it be sure that there will be no intervening Act of God (*'aha*) . . ."

The general principle, with degrees of severity, is that a thing sold must be in existence and have an ascertainable counter-value and this is connected with *riba* and *gharar*. It will be noted that the unqualified absolute contract of sale and the contract with a condition to harvest both envisage *immediate* harvesting.

Again:[22]

> "If the buyer bought on condition of leaving (the fruits *in situ*), or on condition that they remain on the land of the seller until their fruitfulness appear, and then harvests and takes the benefit,

> then, despite the fact that this is the natural presumption, nonetheless the contract is voidable, firstly for uncertainty and then because the buyer thereby made it a condition that it remain in occupation of the land of the seller; and this – as Zi'ali says – is a condition not appropriate to the contract, i.e., occupational use of the land of another; or, as we say, bargain upon bargain (*safaqa'ala safaqa*), in that it is hire (engrafted) upon sale if the use of the land forms a share in the price; or it is sale (engrafted) upon loan if not part of the price and the Prophet of God forbade bargain upon bargain (i.e., double transaction)."

I trust that already the difficulties of the experts who were advising in the three major arbitrations to which I have referred above are becoming apparent. They rightly advised that at the strict *Shari'a*, a modern oil concession was full of irregularities and illegalities from end to end.

There are some differences between the Schools of Law where the leaving of fruits *in situ* is for a short time only, that is to say where the use of the land of the seller is negligible.

Again,[23]

> "If the buyer buys absolutely (i.e., without condition) and other fruits are produced, i.e., the matter is not confined to the development of the fruits or crop purchased but there is an addition thereto; then, if the increase occurs before taking possession, the sale is avoided for lack of delivery. Even if the increase occurs after possession, both seller and buyer share therein by reason of *admixtio* and the evidence of the buyer is accepted as to the amount thereof, because they are in his hand."

The *Hanbali* School subscribes to these principles. This is confirmed by the leading *Hanbali* authority, the Al-Mughni:

> The sale of fruits before their fruitfulness appears does not escape from three divisions:
>
> 1 That the buyer buys on condition of leaving them *in situ*; such a sale is by unanimity not valid because the Prophet forbade the sale of fruits before appearance of their fruitfulness that is as regards seller and buyer and this entails voidability.
> 2 Goes on to say that there is unanimity as to a *Hadith* that such sale on condition of harvesting is valid, because the

prohibition of that type of sale arose from the fear of damage to the fruits, an Act of God, before they are gathered – the Prophet again forbade the sale of fruits before they came to fruition. This is cured if there is a condition of harvesting – that is the equivalent to a sale after their fruitfulness appears.

3 An absolute sale with no condition of harvesting and no condition they have been left *in situ* – the sale is void (*Malik* and *Shafi'i*) but valid (*Abu Hanifa*) because the harvesting is implied in the contract.

As for the Imam Ahmad (i.e., Bin Hanbal) he considered that the tradition quoted envisages that the contract implies that they be left *in situ*, and is not a condition of harvesting (i.e., void).

> 'The sale of the fruits before their usefulness appears, without a condition, has the following aspects:
>
> 1 That the sale is isolated, made to other than the owner of the origin of the fruit (i.e., the tree, bush, etc.) – this is what we mentioned as void.
> 2 That the sale is made with such origin and this is lawful by virtue of the saying of the Prophet: 'Whoever buys a palm tree after it is pollinated, the fruits thereof are to him who sold it unless they are stipulated to the buyer, because if he sold them together with their origin (i.e., the palm tree) they are taken as an incident of the sale and there is no harm from the possibility of *ghatar* therein, as there is with ignorance in the sale of milk in the teat together with sale of the beast, and the date-stone with the date, and the foundations of the walls in the sale of the house'.

As I have said, this subject is developed at very great length by various authors. The vital importance accorded to the 'equivalence of prestations' is apparent.

The prohibition on selling something not in existence stems from the principle of *gharar* (uncertainty, risk, which is to be avoided at all costs) not from the non-existence of the thing itself. It is the degree of *gharar* which is important.[24]

The two contracts of *Istisna'* and *Salam* to the former of which we refer below are but examples of exceptions to the rule laid by the doctrine (*Qiyas*). The following quotations from Ibn Al-Qaiyyim point to the matter:

"Concerning that the sale of something not in existence is not lawful, what is said in that connection has two aspects. *Firstly*: to forbid the validity of such theory, in that there is nothing in the *Koran* nor in the teaching of the Prophet nor his companions to the effect that the sale of something non-existent is unlawful, neither by specific or general reference. There is merely a tradition, a ban on the sale of some things which are non-existent, just as there is a ban on some things which do exist. The key to the ban lies not in the non-existence or existence, but in the ban by tradition upon sale of an uncertainty; this is what cannot be estimated for delivery, whether existent or not: like the sale of a fugitive slave or a runaway camel, even if they exist. The essential element of sale is delivery of the thing sold; if the seller is unable to deliver it, then this is *gharar*, gambling and risk, and it cannot be sold save at a loss, and if the buyer can receive it, it is a gamble by the seller, and if he cannot then the seller has put him at risk. Such is the non-existent thing which is *gharar*, banned because of the *gharar*, not because of its non-existence. It is as if he sold 'what is in the belly of the slave-girl' or 'what may be borne by this tree' where the existence of the thing sold is not known nor is its *quantum* nor kind and this is gambling forbidden by God and His Prophet. The like of this in hire, is to hire out a beast not knowing at the time of hiring whether it exists or not! The same in marriage: if a man gives another in marriage a slave girl which he does not own or a daughter not born to him; likewise all commutative (*do ut des*) contracts (Contracts of *Mu'awadha*).

Secondly: We say that the legislator validated the sale of the non-existent thing in some cases: he legalised the sale of fruits after the appearance of their fruitfulness and grain after it is grown. The Prophet legalised the sale of fruit after the appearance of its fruitfulness, to be left until it comes to such state and did not make the essence of the contract the taking at once, but the ordinary gathering when it comes to fruition; thus what he permitted embraced the sale of something non-existent and not yet created."

The learned author goes on to comment and differentiate in great detail. I think it unnecessary to develop the subject further at this stage; the gist and possible rigidity of the principles involved are apparent.

As we have seen the precept against the sale of something not in existence goes to the element and degree of *gharar*. One of the exceptions to this principle is the contract of *Istisna'* which may be described as a contract to manufacture. Its principles are clearly relevant in the present context. Here again 'the contract of *Istisna'* is concluded on the thing, and not on the work of the manufacturer'.[25] *Istisna'* is allowed (*ja'iz*) by approval (*istihsan*) not by doctrine (*qiyas*). Such approval resulted from universal practice. The contract may be divided into two stages. 1 From time of contracting to sight by the buyer of the thing contracted for; 2 After such sight.

> "In the first stage the contract is not binding (*lazim*) upon either party: the maker may refrain from manufacture or may sell the thing made to a third party before the original buyer sees it. The buyer may resile from the contract before he sees the thing. This is because the doctrine is that it is not lawful basically, but *Istisna'* is only approved contrary to normal doctrine, because of the needs of the people, and he who buys a thing unseen has the option when he sees it. The maker who has sold the thing has no option at that stage. To obligate the buyer in terms of the contract would be damaging to him because it is legally possible that the manufactured article may not suit him and he may not consent thereto; if he were bound and he were to be demanded of the price he may need to purchase the same thing from a third party and not from the manufacturer at such a value and thereby he might be damaged. Whereas, there is no damage in obligating a manufacturer, because he, if the buyer does not accept the thing, could sell it to a third party for the like value and that is a risk he takes by virtue of his vocation."

Abu Yusuf is of a contrary view and states that neither has the option to avoid the contract. The seller may have spoiled his material, for example, making the thing to no purpose.

Imprévision, or Change of Circumstances

I have referred to the lack of any general theory of *imprévision* at the *Shari'a* and the reasons therefor. Apart from these reasons, which, as we have seen, proceed from an essential notion of equivalence and fairness and redound against unearned accretion or 'risk', there is much validity in this context in linking the foregoing principles to the theory of 'cause' and *Mahall* (the object or method of performance of the contract). There are examples in contracts of hire and again the sale of fruits which give point to this. In general the *Hanafis* take a wide view, the other three Schools a somewhat narrower view of change of circumstance. The *Hanbali* view is perhaps nearer to the Western theories. I quote again from the leading authority, Al-Mughni:

> "The fifth section is where there occurs a general apprehension which prevents the dwellers of that place wherein the thing hired is situated, or there is some impediment in the area to access to the land leased for agriculture, etc.; this gives the lessee the right to avoid (the contract), because it is a preponderating matter which precludes the lessee from benefiting from the use of the thing; this option is treated as deprivation of the thing. As if he hired a beast to be ridden, or to carry a load to an appointed place, and the road is cut by fear of some event, or he intends to go to Mecca and the people did not go on the pilgrimage that year by that road – in each of these cases the hiring is avoided. If (the hirer) likes to leave the matter until the use of the thing can be enjoyed, he may do so, because the right belongs to both (i.e., hiror and hirer), is not against them; so that if the fear is peculiar to the hirer, as, for example, that he alone fears the nearness of his enemies to the place leased, or their presence on the road, then he has no right to avoid (the contract) because this is an excuse peculiar to him, which does not prevent enjoyment of the use totally (i.e., in general). An example is his illness: if he is confined or ill or loses his money or his goods are damaged, this does not give the right to avoid the hiring, because he has abandoned the enjoyment of the use of the thing for a reason peculiar to him, which does not absolve him from the necessity of paying the hire, just as if he had abandoned the same voluntarily."

Again, Al-Mughni:[26]

> "If the agricultural holding is flooded or perishes by fire or locusts for frost or other cause, then the hiror is not liable in damages nor is there any option in the hirer – this was provided by Ahmad (bin Hanbal) and we know of no dispute therein, it is also according to the School of *Shaf'i*. Because the damage is outside the contract, and the property of the hirer is damaged thereby, it is as if one hires a shop and his goods catch fire therein . . .

> If one is precluded from cultivating the land or the water is cut off therefrom, then the hirer has the option because this is of the thing (hired) itself . . . and if the water is so deficient as not to suffice for the cultivation, then he has the right to avoid, because this is a defect."

The foregoing short extracts illustrate that the principles of the *Hanbali* School approximate more to those of *imprévision* in Western civil and administrative law.

It is useful to pursue the example of the sale of fruits on the tree again in this context. There is much writing on the occurrence of *ja'iha* which is damage occurring to the fruits by such as rot, storm, etc., before they are harvested.

Both the *Maleki*s and the *Hanbali*s take a wide view of *ja'iha*; the other two Schools have not established the theory as such. According to them if the fruit has been sold or on the tree and thereafter perishes, the risk is on the buyer. The *Hanbali*s and *Maleki*s take the contrary view – the risk of *ja'iha* remains with the seller; however where appropriate there is a reduction in the price and here again we find the emphasis upon the buyer.

Where the damage is due to the acts of third parties then according to the *Hanbali* School the buyer has the option to rescind the contract and ask the seller to return the price; or stay with the contract and demand the value from the faulty party. In *ja'iha* at *Hanbali* law if the fruits perish completely then the price may be demanded back from the seller and be in *pro rata* to the loss.

I appreciate that the foregoing short examples do little more, at this stage, than point to the complications involved. If they do so, however, then one of my main purposes will have been achieved. It would be foolhardy indeed to pretend that the application of a fourteen-hundred-year-old religious system of jurisprudence to a complex of modern contracts was simple, or even appropriate.

It will, I hope, be apparent from what I have said that the keynote in all this for the Western lawyer is the uncertainty: the *Shari'a* as a sword of Damocles which may be hanging over his head in any jurisdiction, in greater or less degree, where the *Shari'a* might be applied. That uncertainty goes not only to whether the *Shari'a* might be applied at all, but the degree of severity if it is. In the absence of express provisions, the *Qadhi* or judge has great flexibility at his disposal.

Can anything be done to relieve this uncertainty? I would submit that it can, to a limited extent, by a new process of *ijtihad* but really, as far as the basic issues are concerned, incisive legislation would be necessary, and in some cases such legislation would have to go against express provisions of *Qur'an* or *Sunna* – I have already referred to the Kuwaiti Commercial Code of 1981, which expressly permits the levying of interest on commercial loans (even so, the Code places a statutory ceiling upon the rate of interest chargeable). I am not therefore referring to such 'codification' as is represented by the Ottoman *Majallat al-Ahkam al-'Adliya*, or, much more recently, the *Majallat al-Ahkam ash-Shar'iya* published in Saudi Arabia to codify the Hanbali law, stemming from the able pens of Abd al-Wahab Ibrahim Abu Sulaiman and Muhammad Ibrahim Ahmed Ali. These codifications (if I may so call them) record the principles of the *Shari'a* as such; they do not seek to change it. They, of course, make no attempt to fit *Shari'a* concepts into a modern commercial code.

It seems to me that when we talk about a new *ijtihad*, a new development of the *Shari'a* by deductive processes, by consensus, by analogy, etc., we are really begging the question. No doubt by *ijtihad* much can be attained, even to the extent of upsetting previous writings of the *'Ulama*, the doctors of law. However, even accepting flexibility in that respect, such flexibility cannot extend to express *nussus*, express provisions of the *Qur'an* and *Sunna*.

It will be better to illustrate by way of express example, and what better example is there, once again, than that of *riba*, a concept readily understandable to the western mind in its limited application of interest on monies. Here we find express provisions in the *Qur'an*:

> Allah permitted sale (trade) and forbade usury (*riba*) (III, 275); Oh ye who believe, devour not usury, doubling and quadrupling the sum lent. (III, 130); And of their taking usury when they were forbidden it and devouring people's wealth by false pretences. We have prepared for those of them who disbelieve a painful doom. (IV, 161); That which ye give in usury in order that it may increase on other people's property, hath no increase with Allah. (XXX, 39).

Here, then, we have express provisions at the highest level, and the only flexibility here lies not in legalising *riba per se* – that is, in accordance with the *Shari'a*, impossible; but possibly in defining it restrictively. Such restrictive definition might limit the concept, for example, to usurious rates of interest, not all interest: indeed, this is a solution which has been suggested by many writers. Be that as it may, any such legislation, even in this restricted sense, would require to be common to the Muslim States, based perhaps on a common *maslaha*, or benefit. However, is that a view which would find acceptance at the present time? In the absence of such legislation, doubts must remain.

Writing in 1980, I said that:

> "The problem is that the Arabs have, to a greater or less degree, in wishing to adopt the existing international world of commerce, come face to face with the classic situation: an irresistible force against an irremovable object. As is not uncommon in these circumstances (not by any means only in the Arab world), the question has been begged on all sides. It will be, to say the least, interesting to see for how long and to what extent this apparent anomaly can continue."[27]

In his Foreword to the same book, Professor Norman Anderson wrote in October 1979:[28]

> "The present position in this regard is that (the *Shari'a*) still – officially, at least – reigns supreme in Saudi Arabia; that it constitutes only one among several mutually conflicting sources from which the comprehensive and progressive Kuwaiti codes have been derived; that it still prevails throughout the whole area, largely unchanged, in so far as the 'personal' or family law of Muslims is concerned; and that it is difficult to say whether (the Arab States) will continue to pursue their present line of policy. In all probability, they will; but it is far more difficult to foresee whether the references to the *Shari'a* which are included in almost all the constitutional enactments in the other States in the peninsula will prove to have been pointers to the law which will actually be applied in matters which are still wholly uncovered by legislation – or, indeed, to the way in which the courts will interpret, or fill in the *lacunae*, in those enactments which have already been, or will soon be, promulgated – or whether, instead, they will turn out to have been little more than pious acknowledgements of an undoubted religious allegiance."

Well, the anomaly did continue and still does.

In the present climate, is there likely to be any increase in secular legislation, in secular codes, to the increasing displacement of *Shari'a* principles? I would say that on the contrary, recent trends in that direction are being reversed, and there will be a reversion to the *Shari'a*. There is a strong trend of thought among Arab jurists that, in basing their modern legislation upon Western codes, they were mistaken, and that they would have done better to endeavour to interpret the *Shari'a* and embody such interpretation into the Codes needed to meet their fast-changing circumstances. Be that as it may, the whole matter is, as I stated previously, under urgent consideration by the Islamic Conference and its ancillary bodies. As a topical example, the new Civil Code of the UAE is based firmly upon *Shari'a* principles and, unlike Kuwait, there is no Commercial Code to dilute it. Furthermore, although that new Code contains for the first time articles on Private International Law (conflict) and provides for the principle of *autonomie de la volonteé*, i.e., the right of the parties to a contract to choose the substantive law they wish to govern it – yet that device is immediately severely qualified by a stipulation that *Shari'a* principles must not be offended.[29]

I note from a recent issue of the Saudi Official Gazette,[30] that the draft of a Saudi Civil Affairs Regulation has been approved by the Council of Ministers, but efforts to obtain this have not yet succeeded. One might apprehend, however, that it will be based upon undiluted *Shari'a* principles.

To end on a more philosophical, even practical, note – do the Arab States really wish, would they even be advised, to tamper with the existing concepts of *riba al-fadhl* and *riba nasi'a*? When they look at the world banking system, which is based essentially upon interest, and which may seem to them at times to be tottering on its base; when they see the most powerful nations preferring to be in debt rather than in credit – may this not provide, apart from basic beliefs which exist anyway, a powerful argument that what the Prophet uttered so long ago was entirely right, and that the principle of profit-sharing and partnership is better not only from the religious point of view, but in practice? Is not Islamic banking true merchant banking? Why then erode the principles of *riba* as they exist when, it may be contended, they provide the only solution to impending chaos? I am not saying that I subscribe to such an extreme view – I am not an economist – but it is a solemn thought.

Notes

1 *Legal Development in Arabia*. Graham & Trotman, London, 1980, p. 109.
2 My translation from 'The Muslims on the Map of the Future'. *Al-Arabi Magazine*, February 1987, at pp. 18 *et seq*. See also in the previous issue of

this excellent Kuwaiti cultural magazine, Dr M A Khalaf Allah on 'Islam and the Islamic Heritage' (p. 30, and esp. pp. 32 *et seq.*)

3 [1951] ILR Case No. 37; (1951) 1 ICLQ.
4 (1953) 20 ILR 534.
5 (1958) 27 ILR 117.
6 'The Muslim Ruler and Contractual Obligations', *N.Y. University Law Review* (1958).
7 Sanhouri, *Masaadir al-Haqq*, 'Sources of Rights in Islamic Jurisprudence', my translation from the Arabic.
8 Schacht, 'Islamic Law in Contemporary States', *American Journal of Comparative Law* (1959) 139; Habachy, 'Property, Right and Contract in Muslim Law', *Columbia Law Review* (1962) 459 *et seq.*
9 Aminoil Arbitration, Opinion filed by Professors Habachy and Morcos: see also Abu Zahra, *Property and Contract in Muslim Law*, 1938, p. 218; Sanhouri, *op. cit.* 1968, p. 50. Articles in English on the binding nature of contracts in Islamic law include: Mahmasani, 'Transactions in the *Shari'a*' in *Law in the Middle East*, eds. Khaddouri and Liebesny, Washington, 1955, p. 191; Mousa, 'The Liberty of the Individual in Contract and Conditions According to Islamic Law', *Islamic Quarterly* II, 1955, pp. 79 *et seq.*; Kourides, 'The Influence of Islamic Law on Contemporary Middle Eastern Legal Systems: the Formation and Binding Force of Contracts', *Columbia Journal of Transnational Law* IX, 1970, pp. 394 *et seq.*; 'Arawi, 'Principles of the Islamic Law on Contracts', *George Washington Law Review* (Symposium on Muslim Law), 1953, p. 32. See also in Arabic: '*Al-Majallat al-Ahkam ash-Shar'iya*' – Definitions, Articles 162–165.
10 Laoust, *Le Traiteé de Droit Publique d'ibn Taimiyya*, translation of *Siyaasa Shan'iya*. Beirut 1918. p. 167.
11 Aramco Arbitral Award as quoted at p. 56; Laoust, *Essai sur les Doctrines Sociales et Politiques de Taqi an-Din Ahmed bin Taimiyya*, Cairo 1939, p. 445, para. 1; see again also Anderson & Coulson, *The Muslim Ruler and Contractual Obligations.*
12 Libya Texaco Award, 19 Jan. 1977.
13 Sanhouri, *op. cit.*, Vol. III at p. 14.
14 Cattan, *The Law of Oil Concessions in the Middle East*, quoting Ibn Jawziya, *I'lam al-Waaqi'in*, Vol. III p. 167 in Arabic; *ibid.* & Milliot, *Droit Musulman* at p. 205; Bousquet, *Principes de Droit Musulman*, 2nd edn. p. 247.
15 Cattan, *op. cit.* quoting Laubadaire, *Contrats Administratifs* at p. 34.
16 Coulson, *Commercial Law in the Gulf States: The Islamic Legal Tradition*, Graham & Trotman, London, 1984.
17 Cattan, quoting Ibn Jawziya, *op. cit., loc. cit.*
18 *Ibid.* and Milliot, *Droit Musulman*, p. 205.
19 Bousquet, *Principes de Droit Musulman*, 2nd edn., p. 247.
20 Sanhouri, *op. cit.* Vol. III at pp. 14 *et seq.*
21 *Op. cit.*
22 *Op. cit.*
23 Zi'ali 4, p. 12.
24 Sanhouri, *op. cit.*
25 Sanhouri, *op. cit.*

26 V 445–446.
27 Ballantyne, *Legal Development in Arabia*, Graham & Trotman, London, 1980, p. 121.
28 *Op. cit.* p. vii.
29 See my article in (1986) 1 ALQ at p. 257.
30 Umm Al-Qura No. 3127, dated 19 Sept. 1986.

VII

Representation in Contracting: Agency

General

In law, the agent has power to commit his principal within the limits of his authority. Agency is:

> 'The relation which exists where one person has an authority or capacity to create legal relations between a person occupying the position of principal and third parties.' (International Harvester Co. of Australia v. Carrigans, 1958/100 CLR).

Often the facts of each transaction must be analysed to see whether 'agency' exists. The agency relationship arises with great frequency in commercial transactions, and is, accordingly, of vast importance:

> *qui facit per alium facit per se.*

We are here concerned not with the principles of agency as they affect family relationships (parents, guardians, *etc.*) but with their commercial contractual aspect. However, to appreciate that aspect, and before going on to specifics, we must first have a background of the general principles. We consider these general principles under the Codes, at secular law, and at the Shari'a.

First, an important caveat: popular use of the word 'agent' has many misunderstood meanings. It should only be used sparingly in legal documents and with full comprehension of what is intended. The unwary fall into the common trap of appointing 'our Bahraini Agent', 'our Kuwaiti Agent', *etc.*, without adverting to this danger. The Arabic word 'wakil' has similar, or even more dangerous connotations.

The Kuwaiti Civil Code

Agency is dealt with in the Kuwaiti Civil Code, our model Code,[1] in Articles 54 through 64 (General Principles of Representation), and in Articles 698 through 719 (Strict Contractual Agency; Powers of Attorney), which we may summarise as follows:

General Principles of Representation

54. 1. Authority is limited by the appointing document.
 2. Yet, if there is an Agreement and the principal announces generally other terms, even if additional, the third party may adopt these (C.p. 'Warranty of Authority'.)

55. The appointing document need not be in the form of the contract to be concluded.

56. 1. In contracting the person of the representative counts not that of the principal.
 2. 'Yet, if the representation arises out of an Agreement and the representative acted in accordance with limited instructions received from the principal, the latter may not, within the limits of the execution of his instructions, take advantage of the ignorance of his representative of matters known to him (the principal) or which he is presumed to have known. In such case defects in the consent of the principal are taken into account.'

57. Where the representative concludes a contract in the name of the principal, all the effects of the contract enure to the principal.

58. Where the representative does not disclose that he is acting on behalf of a principal, the party contracting with the representative is not obligated to consider the contract as being between him and the principal unless he knows, or must be presumed to know, that the contracting was by way of representation, or where it is of equal account to him whether the contracting be with the representative or the principal. (C.p. the general position that the agent must name the principal in order for the latter to become involved at law, and also the Shari'a *infra.*)

59. If the party contracting with the representative is not obligated to consider the contracting as being between him and the principal and he has not so consented, then the contracting is considered to be between him and the

representative personally without the representative being entitled to take advantage of his consensus going to contracting in the name of the principal.

60. In representation by Agreement, if the representative contracts in the name of the principal after the termination of his representation, the party contracting with the representative may consider the contracting nonetheless duly based (thereon), if he and the representative, at the time of contracting did not know of the determination of the representation, nor could they have so known, had they expended the care of a reasonable person in the circumstances.

61. 1. If the representative exceeds his authority or has no authority, the principal is not liable unless he ratifies.
2. If there is no ratification a third party may go against the person with no, or exceeding his, authority for damages – unless the third party knew or is presumed to have known.

62. The representative may not contract with himself in the name of the principal, *etc. etc.*

63. There shall be no sub-delegation unless the law or the Agreement allows.

64. . . .

Powers of Attorney – Agency (Wakalat)

698. 'A contract whereby the appointor (principal) appoints a person in his place to carry out a legal act.'

Characteristics

699. The Agent must have the capacity to carry out the act.

700. Power of Attorney must be in a form required for the contract or other transaction.

701. General Power only gives an administrative right. General Power suffices for:
hiring, not exceeding three years;
maintenance and custody;
getting in rights and satisfaction of debts; and all activities coming within the scope of 'administration'.

702. All other matters require special power, *e.g.*, sale, conciliation, mortgage or pledge, admission (*iqrar*), arbitration, the oath, pleading before the Courts.

703. Agent's authority is limited to the terms of the Power of Attorney.

Liabilities of Agent

704. To carry out the terms of the Power of Attorney *but* may exceed those if necessary if of preponderant opinion that principal would agree. Must inform principal.

705. 1. Where the Power is gratuitous – care which the Attorney would exercise in his own affairs, not exceeding the care of an ordinary person.
2. If for consideration the care of an ordinary person.

706. Must keep the principal informed and render account.

707. Not without consent use the principal's assets for his own account – liable in damages to be assessed by the Judge.

708.)
709.) Multiplicity of agents – joint and several liability.

710. 1. No sub-delegation unless authorised by the principal or by law.
2. Agent not liable for sub-agent except for agent's mistake in choosing him or in instructing him. In such case, the principal and sub-agent may both have recourse directly against the other.

Liability of Principal

711. 1. The agency is gratuitous, unless contrary is agreed expressly or is implied from the profession of the agent or other circumstances of the case.
2. If consideration is agreed for the agency, such is subject to estimation by the Judge unless it be paid willingly after the execution of the agency.

712. 1. Principal must reimburse expenses whether agent successful or not.
2. Must supply agent with funds.

713. Principal to indemnify the agent against harm by virtue of his carrying out the agency, unless due to his fault.

714. Where there is a multiplicity of agents: joint and several liability to the principal unless otherwise agreed.

715. Provisions of Articles 56 to 61 (*supra*) apply as to the relationship of the principal with the third party.

Termination

716. By completion of work or expiry of period specified: also by death of principal or agent, or lack of capacity of either.

717. 1. Principal may dismiss agent at any time or limit his agency even if there is agreement to the contrary.
 2. But, if agent or third party has some interest in the agency, principal may not terminate except with agreement of whomsoever has the interest.
 3. In any case, the principal must compensate the agent for damage suffered by virtue of dismissal at an unsuitable time or without reasonable excuse.

718. 1. The agent may at any time resign the agency, agreement to the contrary notwithstanding, by notification to the principal; but similar provisions for compensation.
 2. Limitation on agent where third party has an interest unless serious justification and sufficient notice.

719. 1. If the agency terminates before work is completed the agent must complete the work sufficiently to avoid damage to the principal.
 2. If it terminates by the death of the principal, the heirs must notify the agent and take steps to safeguard the principal's interests.

In relation to the doctrine of the undisclosed principal (as to which, at the Shari'a, at the Common Law, and at the secular Codes, *vide infra*), the Kuwaiti Code again takes a secular view: see Articles 58 and 59, summarised *supra*. The Commentary says that the other party's intention to contract with the person of the agent should be respected, where to do otherwise would harm him, while the hidden intention of the agent or representative cannot be considered at law. This principle is enshrined in Article 38, which allows a party to rely upon an expression of will if he has acted upon it and would suffer damage if the true intention was then introduced.

The Secular Approach Compared

In both secular and Islamic jurisprudence, representation or agency may be legal, judicial or consensual (that is, by operation of law, by order of the court, or by agreement). In secular jurisprudence, the conditions for establishment of agency may be summarised as follows:

1 the representative's will is to be substituted for that of a principal,
2 within the designated limits of his representation,
3 with the representative dealing in the name of the principal.

Condition 1 is shared with Islamic *fiqh*, with both the consequence (burden), and even in some cases the rights of the contract, going to the principal, even though the representative or agent is the contracting party (this is what distinguishes the *na'ib* from the *rasuul*). The two jurisprudences also agree that the principal must have legal capacity (the agent must be of the age of discernment: *lahu at-tamyiz*). The requirements of Islamic jurisprudence are more rigorous: the principal must have legal capacity both at the time of creation of the agency, and throughout.

Condition 2 is also agreed between secular and Shari'a jurisprudence, although the Shari'a does not agree that the representative or agent's transaction ensures to the principal if the agent does not know, for example, that he has been dismissed or that his principal is dead, so that he is technically exceeding his authority. The Kuwaiti Civil Code takes the secular view: see Article 60, summarised *supra*.

Condition 3 at the Shari'a, is a perfect agency (*niaba kaamila*), as it is under the secular legal systems; however, the Shari'a also allows a representative to contract in his own name, with the agency persisting: indeed this is the normal way for an agent to contract. Contrast the secular system, where the 'assumed name' régime comes into play, with the need for a new contract between agent and principal in order to transfer the effects of the transaction to the principal; the agency in fact disappears if the principal's name/existence is not disclosed to the other contracting party ('the agency is void of representation').

The Shari'a

The Shari'a law (*fiqh*) contains well-defined principles of agency. In particular, a clear distinction is made between the position where the obligation incurred by the agent vis-à-vis the third party is ascribed by the agent to the principal, that is to say, the principal is made known to the third party, and where the principal is undisclosed. In the first place, that is to say where the agent ascribes the contract to the principal, the *fiqh* is in accord with modern concepts of secular law. In this all four schools adopt the same doctrine: in such case, both the burden of the contract and its rights adhere to the principal directly, in their entirety, to the exclusion of the agent. In this situation the *fiqh* is even more stringent in the effect of this relationship than secular law: it makes the relationship between the principal and the third party direct in all respects, so that the agent disappears from between them (*yukhfa alwakil*). The *fiqh* based its doctrine in this respect on Roman law, although Roman law never went as far in principle as the *fiqh*. The *fiqh* of the Shari'a in this case (*i.e.*, where the contract is ascribed by the agent to his principal) draws an analogy with a 'messenger' or 'ambassador' (*rusul* or *safir*).

As a general principle, the Shari'a accords with the Common Law in recognising the theory of the undisclosed principal – indeed this is almost the rule at the Shari'a, not an exception. Thus, in the *fiqh* in the majority of cases the agent does not ascribe the contract to his principal, but contracts ostensibly on his own behalf. Generally, in this case, the agent contracts in his own name, not that of his principal, and does not disclose the fact that he is acting for a principal. At the Shari'a, then, the general position is the reverse of that in secular systems of law: if the agent ascribes the contract to himself, the contract enures to the principal despite this fact even though the third party has no knowledge of him, and all four schools are unanimous in this. There are essential anomalies which result from the fact that the Shari'a does not proceed by reference to general principles of law, but by analogy with set examples. Thus, if an agent buys a house, ascribing the contract to himself, but in fact acting for a principal, the principal rather than the agent becomes directly the owner of the house. It is all the same in *fiqh* whether the seller knows of the agency or not, or whether or not he believes that the agent is a principal acting for his own account. Here we have a prime example of the way in which the Shari'a, being a religious law, repeatedly goes to morals, to intent:[2]

> "The agent who ascribes the contract to himself in the Islamic *fiqh*, if he is in a personal situation where his intent must go to his acting for the account of the principal, then at the same time he is in a material situation where the knowledge or ignorance of the person contracting with him as to the existence of the agency has no effect on such situation. He is in a *personal* situation as regards his own intention: and a *material* situation as regards the intention of the party contracting with him. (I have translated this passage as best I may, but it is not easy to convey the concept in western thought.)"

The texts go on to give express examples based on contracts of sale and purchase, and also contracts of leasing. It is appreciated that a vendor might well object to selling to an undisclosed purchaser, and *a fortiori* to leasing to him. Be that as it may, in the Shari'a the contract enures immediately to the principal:[3]

> "If it be contended that this principle constitutes a danger to the party who contracts with the agent, in ignorance of the agency, and in the belief that he is contracting with a principal, not an agent, in reliance upon his suitability, such objection can be met in that the rights of the contract – which are what concern us as regards such suitability – go to the agent not to the principal in the Hanafi School, as we shall see, so that the party contracting with the agent does not lose anything upon which he is relying as to the suitability of the agent. This is because it is from the agent in the sale of the house that the purchaser may demand its delivery, and the agent whom he may sue as to warranting its fitness against defects destruction *etc.* In the purchase of a house, it is from the agent that the vendor may demand the price."

I have quoted the preceding passage at length, because it represents the position in the Hanafi School of thought, and it is that School which provides the basis for the Majella, the 'codification' of Islamic Law made in the Ottoman Empire in the nineteenth century, and the book usually relied upon in the first instance by persons seeking guidance in this system of law: it is the most generally available, and it is furthermore available in English.

However, this is not the position in the three other Schools of Law, *i.e.*, the Shafi'i, the Maliki, and in particular the Hanbali School, which is the School generally applied in Saudi Arabia and, with the Maliki, the Gulf States. As to the Maliki School, the position is as the Hanafi, unless either the agent has stipulated otherwise, or the other party knows that he is an agent. In the Hanbali School, the incidents of the contract, including rights thereunder, enure *ab initio* to the principal. In the case, for example, of a contract for purchase, it is the principal who may demand that the seller deliver the thing sold and receive the same, although the agent has a similar right on behalf of his principal. The principal may also have a direct right of recourse against the seller for defect, although there is valid opinion to the effect that the agent also may have recourse against the seller. Further, it is against the principal that the seller may demand the price, although the agent is guarantor therefor, that is to say the price falls within the primary responsibility of the principal, and the ancillary responsibility of the agent. The seller may demand from which of the two he sees fit; if he discharges the agent he does not thereby discharge the principal, but if he discharges the principal the agent is also discharged, by analogy with guarantee. It is also of importance to note that anything which the agent receives for the account of his principal (property, price, as the case may be) is in trust for the principal.[4]

Sanhouri is critical of this approach, which he says is going to unreliable limits.

The Secular Codes

Under the secular Codes, and thus the Arab Codes generally, the agent must name his principal in order for the latter to become involved at law. (This is a generality, and there are shades of this). There is no theory of the undisclosed principal, in contrast to the position at the Shari'a, and, similarly, at the common law.

Article 1984, alinéa 1, of the French Civil Code provides for:

> . . . a deed whereby one person gives to another the power to do something for the appointer *and in his name*.

At French law, where the agent is undisclosed, the contract is made between the agent and the third party, and all rights and obligations enure to the agent. A particular example of this is the *contrat de commission* (dealt with in the French Commercial Code): the third party knows that he is dealing with an agent, but does not know the identity of the principal: still the rights and obligations enure to the agent.

Similarly, article 1388 of the Italian Civil Code provides that a contract may be entered into:

> . . . *in the name* and for the interest of the party represented.

Again, if the agent acts in his own name, the contract enures to him even if the third party knows that he is acting on behalf of a principal (whose identity is unknown): article 1705.

As is not uncommon, the German Civil Code takes a similarly strict view: if the agency is not disclosed, and the contract is concluded in the name of the agent, then only the agent may be treated as a contracting party, even if (sometimes) the agency relationship is known.

In the civil jurisdictions there is often another alleviating provision, that the agency may be recognised if the third party suffers no detriment: compare the Commentary to Articles 58 and 59 of the

Kuwaiti Civil Code, and Article 38 thereof. This is similar to the position at the Common Law, although the emphasis is slightly different: the contract enures to the principal, but not to the prejudice of the third party (*vide infra*).

The Common Law Jurisdictions

As we have seen, the basic principle is *contra* the above, and in general accords with the Shari'a: if an agent acts within the scope of his authority, the principal acquires rights and duties even if undisclosed. However, there are provisos: the principal may not acquire rights and duties to the prejudice of the third party (for example, in respect of rights of set-off available vis-à-vis the agent but not the principal, or defences available to the third party to legal proceedings brought by the agent which would not otherwise be available against the principal), and the third party may perform to the agent. Interestingly, and as is not uncommon, the Common Law and Continental systems work towards the same end, although starting at opposite ends of the scale. Sometimes the practical results are very similar.

Thus, at Common Law, the third party may sue the principal once he has discovered his identity, unless he stated at the moment of concluding the contract that he would only look to the agent whatever might happen. For obvious reasons, this situation is rare. That apart, if the third party knows of the principal's identity as such, does he lose the right to go against the principal by suing the agent? and, especially, to judgment? Or do they remain jointly and severally liable? The general Common Law view is that the third party loses the right in these circumstances; but there are many exceptions (see, for example, the U.S. jurisdictions: particularly the New York Statute of 1939).

In our Arab jurisdictions, a good comparison may be made between our model Kuwaiti Code (see my translated extracts and summary *supra*), and the Bahraini Contracts Law (the Section on Agency) (as to which, see my book, 'Commercial Law in the Arab Middle East: The Gulf States,' (1986) London, Appendix XVII).

Commercial Agency

Virtually all the Arab jurisdictions have special Commercial Agency Laws amplifying the foregoing principles and controlling the conduct of business by foreigners in their jurisdictions, notably limiting commercial agency to nationals. Specific provisions governing commercial agency agreements are also found in the Commercial Codes, where those exist. The basic principles of agency discussed *supra* apply, whether deriving from a Civil Code or from the Shari'a, and are simply supplemented by these specific provisions. Thus, the Commercial Code of Kuwait provides, at the commencement of Book II: Commercial Obligations and Contracts (Article 96):

> With the exception of what is provided in this Book, there shall apply to commercial obligations and contracts the provisions set out in the Civil Code.

The relationship between the Kuwaiti Civil and Commercial Codes will be familiar to the civil lawyer: a similar division is to be found in the secular Codes (for example, specific aspects of commercial agency agreements, to which the basic provisions of the German Civil Code apply, are dealt with in Article 48*ff* of the German Commercial Code).

The provisions of the Commercial Code dealing with agency agreements may be summarised, as follows:

Section 1: Commercial Agency: General Provisions

260. Commercial agency limited to commercial business unless otherwise agreed, even where general Power of Attorney.

261. 1. Remuneration unless otherwise agreed,
 2. and unless amount agreed, tariff or usage applies.
 3. Remuneration due only on execution of transaction, unless execution impossible (in which case, remuneration for work done).

262. 1. Agent to act in accordance with principal's instructions.
 2. Agent may delay carrying out principal's instructions to consult with principal if sure would otherwise cause serious damage to principal.
 3. Agent may delay carrying out principal's instructions where not express, unless urgent or agent has wide general instructions.

263. 1. Agent liable for damage to articles he keeps for principal: except where damage unavoidable, *force majeure*, inherent vice, *etc.*
 2. No obligation to insure goods of principal unless principal so requires or usage deems compulsory.

264. 1. Agent to safeguard goods which have suffered damage in transit.

2. Agent to seek permission from President of *Al Kulliya* Court to sell goods where unable to consult principal and goods likely to be damaged or perish or fall in value.

265. 1. Agent to keep principal informed, and give account of agency.
2. Account shall be truthful; otherwise, principal entitled to reject transaction and claim damages, and agent not entitled to remuneration.

266. 1. to 4. Agent to have special rights over goods, or proceeds if sold, to secure remuneration, and other amounts due, with interest;

267. 1. provides that goods remain in agent's custody.
2. Situations in which goods deemed to be in agent's custody.

268. 1. Agent's special rights over goods or proceeds have priority over all other interests, except legal costs and government levies.
2.&3. Methods of enforcement of agent's special rights.

269. Where principal not domiciled in Kuwait, principal's domicile deemed to be that of agent; address for service *etc.* in relation to business carried on by agent on principal's behalf.

270. Commercial agency business governed by the *ad hoc* laws.

The Code continues with provisions governing particular types of agency agreements, thus:

Section 2: Certain Kinds of Commercial Agency

271. to 286. 1. Contracts Agency and Distribution Agreements

287. to 296. 2. Commission Agency

Section 3: Commercial Representatives

297. to 305.

In addition, Law No. 36 of 1964 Regulating Commercial Agencies provides, in outline, as follows:

1. Commercial agency limited to Kuwaiti nationals (and see Article 10).

2. to 5.	Registration of commercial agency agreements.
6.	Extracts of register available to any person from Ministry of Trade.
7.	Fees payable for registration or extracts of register.
8. to 9.	Deletion of registration of agency and penalty for non-observance.
10.	Penalty for non-observance of Article 1.
11.	Penalties for submission of incorrect information with regard to registration, *etc.*
12.	Penalties for falsely asserting that one is a commercial agent.
13. to 15.	Implementation *etc.* of provisions.

The apparently ordered nature of the statutory framework belies the complexity of commercial agency agreements in the Arab jurisdictions, particularly with regard to termination. Grave social stigma attaches to the erstwhile agent when an agency agreement is terminated, and the essential rules governing agency (and not just those governing the formalities, such as registration of agency agreements) are regarded as going to *ordre public* (*nitham al-'am*), and therefore cannot be contracted out of. The principle of *pacta sunt servanda* is thus forced to yield its ground to competing principles, and in particular to two concepts which are of almost universal application in the Arab legal systems: firstly, that an agency agreement exists for the mutual benefit of the agent and principal; and, secondly, the principle of abuse of rights. These principles are embodied in the Codes and in the various special statutes regulating commercial agency agreements (for example, Articles 716 to 719 of the Kuwaiti Civil Code, summarised *supra*, regulating termination of agency agreements).

The former principle is, self-evidently, limited to agency situations. The latter, which is of general application, is an ancient Islamic principle of good faith, which is often assumed, wrongly, to have been absorbed from secular Codes. In the field of termination of agency agreements these principles have a great impact: their net effect is to make it extremely difficult for a principal to terminate a commercial agency agreement, whatever its terms, without compensating the agent.

Additionally, the legal complexities involved in terminating a commercial agency agreement are often compounded by administrative difficulties. A principal who purports to terminate such an agreement may find, even without judicial intervention, that he is forced to pay compensation to the agent: until such compensation is paid, deregistration of the agreement, and registration of an agreement with a new agent, mandatory under local law, may not be forthcoming from the appropriate government Registry.

A Practical Example of Contracting by Agent

Company AB, an English registered company entered into a contract for major construction works in Saudi Arabia. Unbeknown to the Saudi Government, AB entered into this contract as agent for CD, a Panamanian company.

The English Inspector of Taxes subsequently sought to make Company AB liable for profits arising out of the contract. The Inspector argued that the theory of undisclosed principal had no application in Saudi Arabia.

It appeared that the Inspector had based his argument upon the Hanafi School of law as represented in the Majella. The counter-argument against the Inspector was that the Hanbali School ruled in Saudi Arabia; that the theory of undisclosed principal in the Shari'a was the rule rather than the exception; and that in the Hanbali School, a strict view was taken, making the principal immediately the direct party the contract to the exclusion of the agent, even where the existence of the principal was unknown to the other contracting party. Therefore, the profits under the contract enured directly to the principal CD, not to the agent, AB. AB was not liable to tax on income it had not acquired.

Notes

1 The Kuwaiti Codes are taken as models for the LLM course of which this lecture forms part.
2 Al Mughni and the Sharah Alkabir Pt V 92–3.
3 Al Mughni and the Sharah Alkabir Pt V at bottom of page 211.
4 Al Mughni and the Sharah Alkabir Pt V 249.

Bibliography

Ballantyne, Commercial Law in the Arab Middle East: The Gulf States, 1986, London

Dannemann, German Civil and Commercial Law, 1993, London

David and Brierley, Major Legal Systems in the World Today, 3rd Edition (1985), London

Karam, Business Laws of Kuwait, Volume I (1987 Edition)
Saleh, Commercial Agency and Distributorship in the Arab Middle East, Volume I, 1989
Zweigert and Kötz, An Introduction to Comparative Law, 2nd Edition (1987), tr. Weir

VIII

The New Commercial Code of Bahrain

In order to appreciate the essential background to this new Code, it is perhaps useful to quote from the article which I wrote for the first issue of this Quarterly.[1]

Bahrain

"We recall the provisions of the Bahrain Constitution prescribing the *Shari'a* as a principal source of law.

Against that ever-present backdrop, we record that Bahrain has as yet little legislation on the civil model and no Civil Code as such and we therefore find that the sources of law are still prescribed in the Judicature Law of 1971. That Law provides:

> in the event the judge finds no provision of law capable of application, he shall deduce the basis of his judgment from the principles of the *Shari'a* and the provisions thereof, and in the absence of any such provision, Custom shall be applied. A particular Custom shall be preferred to a general Custom, and in the absence of Custom the tenets of natural law or the principles of equity and good conscience shall be applied.

Thus, in the event of a lacuna in enacted legislation, the judge is expressly directed firstly to the principles of the *Shari'a*. However, it is instructive to compare this formula with those of Kuwait and Qatar to which we have referred; it has some interesting features. First, the formula seems to envisage that secular legislation may be preferred to the *Shari'a*, the inference being that it may not be in accord with the *Shari'a*. Secondly, and very significantly, it is envisaged that the *Shari'a* may be deficient in supplying a solution to a particular problem – in that case Custom applies. We then revert to the ever-present question, as to whether such Custom would be applicable if contrary to the tenets of the *Shari'a*? Finally, the judge is directed to 'the tenets of natural justice or the principles of equity and good conscience'. Once again, are these tenets or principles to be applied in defiance of the *Shari'a* or only if in accord therewith?

These are difficult questions indeed. Bahrain is a modern State with a fully developed commercial community and an emancipated banking system on the modern occidental model both domestic and offshore. There is still a dearth of commercial legislation in Bahrain in view of which reference to commercial and in particular banking custom becomes increasingly relevant. If the principles of the *Shari'a* were to be applied strictly to these matters, then many aspects of such commerce and banking would be found to be illegal. Practically speaking, it is unlikely that this conflict would at the present time be allowed to develop but these anomalies must always be borne in mind.

With regard to the secular law and the principles which might be applied by a judge sitting in Bahrain we note that the law of contract and tort in Bahrain is still common law based and that consequently it would be relevant to adduce common law precedent although in many respects reliance may also be made and is made in practice upon Egyptian and other authorities on the civil side. It may be submitted that a comparative law argument should thus carry considerable weight. The position with regard to the common law will change when the new Civil and Commercial Code which has been so long awaited in Bahrain, and which is based upon Egyptian civil principle, is issued."

The last sentence of the above-quoted passage is now proved to have been too optimistic. In fact the new legislation which is the subject of this review is not a Civil and Commercial Code as anticipated, it is a Commercial Code. As such, while dealing, as would be expected, with the law applicable to merchants and commercial acts, it does not attempt to deal with the general Law of Obligations for Bahrain. The latter aspect continues to be covered by the Bahrain Contract Law of 1961 and the Bahrain Civil Wrongs Ordinance of 1970.[2]

Both of the last-named enactments are virtually codifications of English law, whereas the new Commercial Code, as anticipated, derives its provisions from the other Arab Codes, notably the Egyptian and Kuwaiti, behind which of course stand the Commercial Codes of the Continent of Europe, pre-eminently the French. Thus, we find in Bahrain a situation where the general Law of Obligations (Contract and Torts) is based upon principles of the Common Law, whereas the Commercial Code derives from the European system. It can hardly be hoped that this situation will not lead to difficulties – one can envisage the position of an Egyptian-trained judge grappling with the doctrine of consideration in a commercial contract governed by the new Code – and it is therefore to be hoped that a new Civil Code will be promulgated in Bahrain as soon as possible.

Be the foregoing as it may, the new Code must certainly be welcomed as resolving at least some of the anomalies at present in the Bahraini system, not least those caused by the uncertainty engendered by the role of the *Shari'a*. I shall refer later in this Note to the particular and important aspect of interest on money. The Bahraini Code has, perhaps surprisingly at the present time, at last firmly grasped this nettle, and has followed the example of Kuwait in permitting interest, thus defying the *Shari'a* doctrine of *riba*.[3]

Article 2 of the new Code is, as far as it goes, of value in clearly subscribing for the first time in legislation in Bahrain the principle of *autonomie de la volonté* of the parties to a commercial contract. Unlike Kuwait and now, to a certain extent, the UAE,[4] Bahrain possesses no Conflict Code. Such references as there are to matters containing a foreign element are to be found in the Bahraini Code for Civil and Commercial Procedure[5] and are largely concerned with jurisdiction.[6] Thus Article 2 of the new Code assumes an importance which warrants my translating it in full:

Article 2

"1 There shall apply to commercial matters that which the two contracting parties have agreed upon provided that such agreement does not conflict with mandatory legislative provisions.

2 If there is no special agreement the principles of commercial custom shall apply insofar as there is no relevant provision in this or any other law relating to commercial matters. Special custom shall be preferred over general custom.

3 If there is no commercial custom the laws relating to civil matters shall be applied in the absence of which the judge shall deduce the bases of his judgment from the principles of the Islamic *Shari'a* then the principles of natural law and justice."

Against the background which I have outlined above, against the general background of the *Sharia'* as a principal source of law in Bahrain and with the possible conflicts between common law and civil principles, it may perhaps be doubted whether in practice these provisions will be found to have clarified matters or merely created more confusion. However, the following tentative analysis may be made:

1 In a commercial contract the principle *pacta sunt servanda* is fully subscribed. There would appear to be the usual qualification to the effect that provisions of the law going to *ordre public* cannot be avoided by contract. However, while at first sight the Article might be taken to imply that the parties are free to choose the proper law of their contract, a closer look reveals that this is not stated expressly. Can parties to a commercial contract invoke this Article in support of the choice of a proper law or must they continue to rely as hitherto in Bahrain upon general principles of private international law in support of such a right? However, in the context of the following two sub-articles of Article 2 it may be submitted that sub-head 1 must be intended to mean that the parties are free to choose the law which they require to govern their contract.

2 In the absence of express agreement the hierarchy would appear to be:
   a) the Commercial Code,
   b) any other law relating to commercial matters,
   c) commercial custom, special custom being preferred over general.

3 Failing the above sources the judge is directed to:
   a) Bahraini Civil Law which, as indicated, means the Contracts Law and the Law of Civil Wrongs;
   b) in the absence of any such, the principles of the *Shari'a* followed by the principles of natural law and justice.

The interesting point that remains here is, of course, whether the *Shari'a* must be regarded as a mandatory legislative provision in a commercial matter which overrides everything else. It may be submitted with some confidence that such is not now the case in Bahrain having regard to the overall jurisprudential situation, and in particular, latterly, these provisions of the new Commercial Code. It remains to be said however that each case must be examined minutely in this respect.

The intent of this short Note is to assess immediately the overall impact of the new Code. To write a Commentary on the provisions of the Code would of course require a book in itself. It may, however, be useful to indicate its main provisions and this can perhaps best be done by translating the Index to the Code:

The new commercial code of Bahrain

Chapter I: Commerce in General Provisions
Section 1: Commercial acts.
Section 2: The merchant (*commerçant*).
Section 3: Commercial acts.
Section 4: The place of business, commercial address, illegal competition, and commercial statements (*bayanat*).
- (i) The place of business and carrying on business thereat.
- (ii) The commercial address.
- (iii) Illegal competition.
- (iv) Commercial statement (*bayanat*).
- (v) Commercial obligations – general provisions.

Chapter II: Nominate Commercial Contracts
Section 1: Commercial sale
- (i) General provisions
- (ii) Some types of commercial sale:
  1. Sale by instalments.
  2. Sale f.o.b.
  3. Sale c.i.f.
  4. Sales on delivery
  5. Other commercial sales

Section 2: The commercial mortgage.
Section 3: Deposit in public warehouses.
Section 4: Commercial agency:
- (i) Commercial agency in general
- (ii) Commission agency
- (iii) Commercial representation

Section 5: Commercial brokerage and exchanges:
- (i) Brokerage
- (ii) The commercial paper market (exchange)

Section 6: Carriage:
- (i) Carriage of goods
- (ii) Carriage of persons
- (iii) Carriage commission agency
- (iv) Limitation.

Chapter III: Commercial Banking Operations
Section 1: Deposit of monies
Section 2: Deposit of paper (bills)
Section 3: Leasing of depositories
Section 4: Banking transfer
Section 5: Simple credit
Section 6: Documentary credit
Section 7: Discounting
Section 8: Letter of Guarantee
Section 9: Current Account

Chapter IV: Commercial Paper
Section 1: A Bill of Exchange:
- (i) Creating of the bill
- (ii) Endorsement
- (iii) Value
- (iv) Acceptance
- (v) Reserve Guarantee
- (vi) Performance due
- (vii) Payment
- (viii) Recourse
- (ix) Accommodation
  1. General provisions
  2. Acceptance by intervention
  3. Payment by intervention
- (x) Bills in a set
- (xi) Copies
- (xii) Alterations
- (xiii) Limitation.

Section 2: The Promissory Note
Section 3: The cheque
Section 4: Pledge of banking documents or other commercial paper

Section 5: Joint provisions

It will be appreciated from the foregoing that the general format of the Code provides no surprises: it constitutes in fact a somewhat truncated version of the Commercial Codes normal in Arab jurisdictions. Provisions relating to commercial bankruptcy are notable by their absence, but these have appeared in a subsequent *Gazette* and will be dealt with in an ensuing article in *Quarterly*.

As stated either, the new Code appears firmly to have grasped the nettle constituted by the problem of interest on monies and I think it necessary to translate the relevant Articles in full:

Article 76

1. There shall be considered as a commercial loan every loan concluded by a merchant in matters relating to his commercial activities.
2. It shall be presumed that the contracting parties have stipulated for interest on such loan unless it be proved that they intended otherwise.
3. If the activity of the merchant required a granting of loans to his fellow merchants or otherwise or the payment of amounts or expenses for their account then he may require from them interest thereon from the day of payment unless it be agreed otherwise.
4. Interest shall be calculated at the legal rate unless another rate be agreed upon provided that the same shall not exceed the limit provided for by law.
5. The Bahrain Monetary Agency shall from time to time prescribe by notice the legal rate and the maximum limit for interest as provided in the preceding sub-article.
6. Interest shall be payable at the end of each year where the loan is deferred for more than a year, and on due date where the period is one year or less, unless it be agreed or custom dictates otherwise.

Article 275

1. A money deposit is a contract which grants to the bank possession of the monies deposited and the right to deal therein consistently with its professional practice with the obligation to return the equivalent to the depositor such return to be in the same currency as the deposit. Interest may be stipulated in a contract for the deposit of money and in such case the provisions of sub-paragraphs 4, 5 and 6 of Article 76 of this Law shall apply.

Notes

1 (1985) 1 ALQ 3, at page 10: and for a general and comparative survey see Ballantyne, *Commercial Law of the Arab Middle East: The Gulf States*, Lloyd's of London Press, 1986.
2 The text of these is set out in Ballantyne, *op. cit.*, Appendices XVII and XVIII at pages 279 *et seq.* and 313 *et seq.*
3 For general survey see Ballantyne, *op. cit.*, pages 111 *et seq.*
4 (1985) 1 ALQ 245 *et seq.*
5 Law 12/1971, *Gazette* 926/1971.
6 Ballantyne, *op. cit.*, pages 161 *et seq.*

IX

The New Civil Code of the United Arab Emirates: A Further Reassertion of the Shari'a

The extent to which the *Shari'a* must be regarded as paramount in the jurisprudence of the United Arab Emirates (U.A.E.) has been dealt with at some length in the first issue of the *Arab Law Quarterly*.[1] The long-awaited Civil Code[2] provides a topical and important example of the increasing trend towards a reassertion of Islam in legislation and jurisprudence[3] in the Islamic countries, and gives further emphasis, if such were needed, of the essentiality in all cases of an analysis of the extent to which the *Shari'a* may apply in any particular case.[4]

In anticipation of the detailed analysis which follows, it may be said that the new Civil Code of the U.A.E. is firmly based on *Shari'a* principles.

Before turning to a detailed analysis of the Civil Code it is relevant to consider shortly the recent history of the Gulf area as a whole. It is particularly relevant to recall that the British Crown exercised extraterritorial jurisdiction over, broadly, all non-Muslim foreigners in Kuwait, Bahrain, Qatar, and The Trucial States (now the U.A.E.). To a lesser extent such jurisdiction also operated in Oman, although this was a special case and need not concern us here. No such jurisdiction operated in Saudi Arabia where there has remained throughout a virtually unalloyed adherence to the *Shari'a*, modified only by secular 'regulations'. The extraterritorial jurisdiction ended in Kuwait in 1961; and in the rest of the area in 1971.[5] During the currency of the extraterritorial jurisdiction, the local or indigenous courts operated, of course, in parallel with British extraterritorial courts. In the former courts there was little written law. It is not surprising that the one book to be found at the right hand of, perhaps, every judge of such courts in the area was the *Majella*, the nineteenth century Ottoman 'codification' of the *Shari'a* in the Hanafi School.[6] The *Majella* was never promulgated expressly as law in any of the Gulf jurisdictions but in practice became the *ad hoc* civil code in those jurisdictions. The apparent imminence of the cessation of British extraterritorial jurisdiction in Kuwait in the late 1950s gave an immediate and urgent impetus to the necessity for legislation in Kuwait to fill the vacuum left by that cessation. It is perhaps strange that at that time in Kuwait only two choices were really considered: the continued use of the *Majella* or the adoption of occidental codes based upon the Egyptian model behind which lie, of course, the French and other great continental codes of Europe. In the event, Kuwait opted for the latter course and in its Commercial Code of 1961 took the bold step of recording the inapplicability of the *Majella* to modern commercial transactions and virtually the rejection of *Shari'a* principles to such transactions. This set the pattern for ensuing legislation in the rest of the area. The middle way was not considered: namely whether *Shari'a* principles might be adapted and newly codified to suit the modern needs of the State. In fairness it must be said that the latter solution presents immeasurable difficulties: firstly, certainly in Kuwait, time did not permit such an immense undertaking; secondly, it would have envisaged the facing, four-square, of what has been described elsewhere as the situation of an irresistible force against an immovable object;[7] thirdly, it would have involved equally a consideration of whether the *Shari'a* can in fact be adapted to what the world has made of modern commerce.[8] This embarrassing issue was similarly begged on the cessation of extraterritorial jurisdiction in the other Gulf States in 1971, and has continued to be so until recently. Now the realisation has dawned upon the Arab legislator that in avoiding the issue or, in particular, opting for occidental legislation in defiance of the *Shari'a*, he has been moving too far and too fast in the wrong direction in States which all have as their basic concept the constitutional principle of the *Shari'a* as a, or sometimes, *the*, principle source of legislation.[9] Pressures for a reversion to *Shari'a* principles in legislation are increasingly apparent. In Kuwait in 1980 the device was adopted of maintaining those principles largely in a Civil Code, while promulgating at the same time a Commercial Code which diluted the *Shari'a* in matters of Commerce.[10] As will be apparent from the following analysis, the new U.A.E. Civil Code hardly begs the question at all: it came down four-square on the basis of the *Shari'a*.

There can be little doubt that the pressures to which reference has been made owe their origin in no small measure to increasing discontent in the Islamic countries at the imposition of laws which are regarded as 'foreign' in concept, as distinct from the *Shari'a* which is, of course, a part of their innermost faith. There is a feeling that society, having 'outgrown' the *Majella* in its present form, made the mistake of imposing law which the citizen feels to be alien, thus causing a split between society and the law and making the law a 'burden rather than a source of confidence and respect'.[11] Legal scholars who make and expound the law found the gap ever widening, not only because of the people's coolness towards it, but because some of it was in direct conflict with the prevailing view of society, particularly in the field of penal law. The First Convention of Law School Deans of Arab Universities was held in Beirut in 1973. It recommended (a) that the *Shari'a* should be studied in the Law Schools as it was an official source of law in the Arab countries and an historic source in all of them and (b) that Arab legislators in most Arab countries should take the *Shari'a* as a principle source of the substantive law.

The Second Convention held in Baghdad in 1974 recommended (a) the necessity for a careful study of Islamic jurisprudence because a return to the *Shari'a* as a basic source of uniform Arab law is essential to the fulfilment of the Arab personality, (b) the establishment of an academy for the *Shari'a* and the law covering the whole Arab world, to prepare studies in both fields for the benefit of the substantive legislator and to give opinions and advice upon matters submitted by Arab governments and official bodies. The decision to set up the learned Academy of Islamic Jurisprudence was taken at the Taif Islamic Conference. The general principle involved must be taken to be a rejection of the adoption of the principles of substantive law in preference to *Shari'a* principles: that basis of legislation is to be totally rejected in favour of a reorganisation and reshaping of the provisions of the *fiqh* in a modern legal mould so as to facilitate recourse thereto.[12]

Against this background, we may turn to as detailed an analysis of the Code as is possible within an article of reasonable length. The Code consists of 1,528 Articles of often difficult Arabic. The Code owes the overwhelming majority of its provisions to the *fiqh*; thus, conveniently, the *Majella*, with undertones of civil law gleaned from the Jordanian, Egyptian, and other Arab Codes, behind which stand, of course, the French and other great civil codes of Europe. Yet a comparison with the Kuwait Civil Code of 1980 (also largely *Shari'a*-based[13]), reveals many differences, and, in the U.A.E. Code, a stronger *Shari'a* emphasis. The U.A.E. Code owes much to the Civil Code of

Jordan and accords in many respects with the new Code of the Sudan.[14]

The plan of the Code is illustrated by the Index, which is published with it, and which it will be useful to translate in full. Here, a note of warning must be sounded: as stated, the Arabic of the Code is difficult – often, as with *Shari'a* terms, archaic and virtually impossible to translate without explanation; thus the translation which follows can only be used as a guide, to give an overall picture of the Code's content. In particular, some *Shari'a* words are not matched by a single word equivalent in English. In some instances, therefore, a transliteration of the Arabic is given, to assist the Arab or Arabist lawyer who will readily appreciate the true meaning. That apart, the English lawyer may follow up the matter by reference to various text books in English,[15] where the incidents of the various *Shari'a* terms are explained. It is not very helpful, for example, to know that a '*salam*' contract, listed simply as such in the Index, is 'a contract for delivery with prepayment' (Schacht's definition) without further comment.

With these reservations, the Index to the Code may be reproduced in translation as follows:

Introductory Chapter: General Provisions

Section 1: Provisions relating to the application of the law and its applicability as to time and place
- Sub-section 1: The law and its application
- Sub-section 2: Application of the law as to time
- Sub-section 3: Application of the law as to place

Section 2: Some basic principles of legal interpretation

Section 3: Persons
- Sub-section 1: The natural person
- Sub-section 2: Juridical persons

Section 4: Things and property

Section 5: Rights
- Sub-section 1: The extent of the use of the right
- Sub-section 2: Abuse of rights
- Sub-section 3: Classes of right
- Sub-section 4: Proof of the right
  - (1) Indications of proof
  - (2) General principles of proof
  - (3) The application of the principles of proof

The New Civil Code of the United Arab Emirates

Book I: Personal obligations and rights

Chapter I: Sources of obligation or personal rights

Section 1: Contract

Sub-section 1: General provisions

Sub-section 2: The elements of contract, its validity and effectiveness, and the options

1. Concluding the contract
2. Representation in contracting
3. Capacity in contracting
4. Defects in consent
   - (a) Duress
   - (b) Inducement and deceit
   - (c) Mistake
5. The object of the contract and its cause
   - (a) The object of the contract
   - (b) The cause of the contract
6. The valid contract, the void contract and the voidable contract
   - (a) The valid contract
   - (b) The void contract
   - (c) The voidable contract
7. The suspended contract and the contract which is not binding
   - (a) The suspended contract
   - (b) The contract which is not binding
8. The options affecting the binding nature of the contract
   - (a) The option of condition
   - (b) The option of sight
   - (c) The option of appointment
   - (d) The option of defect

Sub-section 3: The effects of contract

(1) In relation to the contracting parties

(2) In relation to third parties

Sub-section 4: The interpretation of contracts

Sub-section 5: Determination of the contract and discharge

Section 2: Individual volition

Section 3: The injurious act

Sub-section 1: General provisions

Sub-section 2: Liability for personal acts
(1) Damage to the person
(2) Damage to property
(3) Dispossession and treepass
Sub-section 3: Liability for the act of another
Sub-section 4: Liability for animals and things and use of the public highway
1. Offences by animals
2. Collapse of buildings
3. Things and machinery
4. Use of the public highway

Section 4: The beneficial act
Sub-section 1: Enrichment without cause
Sub-section 2: Receipt of that which is not due/owing
Sub-section 3: Interference
Sub-section 4: Discharge of the debt of another
Sub-section 5: Extinctive prescription

Section 5: The Law

Chapter 2: The effects of rights

Section 1: General provisions

Section 2: Means of execution
Sub-section 1: Voluntary execution
(1) Performance
(a) The two parties to performance
(b) The person to whom performance is made
(c) Refusal of performance
(d) The means of performance, and the time, place, cost and proof thereof
(2) Execution by the equivalent of performance:
(a) Performance by substitute
(b) Set-off
(c) Consolidation of liabilities
Sub-section 2: Compulsory execution
(1) By specific performance
(2) By way of damages
Sub-section 3: Legal means of securing execution:
(1) Security over the property of the debtor
(2) The indirect action (*action paulienne*)
(3) The action upon an apparent or fictional contract

(4) The action as to non-effect of actions of the obligor upon rights of the obligee
(5) Attachment upon the bankrupt obligor
(6) The right of detention

Section 3: Dispositions affected by condition and delay
Sub-section 1: Condition
Sub-section 2: Delay

Section 4: Multiplicity of ways of discharge
Sub-section 1: Choice of discharge
Sub-section 2: Substitution of discharge

Section 5: Multiplicity of parties
Sub-section 1: Joint and several creditors (obligees)
Sub-section 2: The joint debt
Sub-section 3: Joint and several debtors (obligors)
Sub-section 4: Non-divisibility

Section 6: Determination of the Right
Sub-section 1: Release
Sub-section 2: Impossibility of performance
Sub-section 3: Extinctive prescription

Book II: Contracts

Chapter 1: Contracts vesting ownership

Section 1: Sale and barter
Sub-section 1: Sale
(1) The definition and elements of sale
(2) Effects of sale
(a) Obligations of the seller:
(i) Transfer of ownership
(ii) Delivery of the thing sold
(iii) Warranty against hidden defects
(b) Obligations of the buyer
(i) Payment of the price and taking delivery of the thing sold
(ii) Expenses of sale

Sub-section 2: Various kinds of sale
(1) The '*salam* sale
(2) Sale of airspace
(3) Sale of a certain amount of quantity (*juzaaf*)
(4) Sale at a deferred price (*al aajaal*)

(5) Sale of goods acquired at the behest of the purchaser (*al ayina*)
(6) Sale of food, etc., before obtaining the same
(7) Sale of fruits
(8) Sale of cultivated (planted) and sown land
(9) Example of sale of palms and trees
(10) Sale of foods of which the edible part is hidden (*fi jaufihi*)
(11) Sale of a share in an inheritance
(12) Sale during terminal illness
(13) Sale by an agent to himself
(14) Sale of the property of a third party

Sub-section 3: Barter for exchange
Sub-section 4: Prohibited sale and barter

Section 2: Gift

Sub-section 1: The elements of gift and conditions of its effectiveness
Sub-section 2: Effects of gift
(1) in relation to the donor
(2) in relation to the donee
Sub-section 3: Revocation of gift

Section 3: Partnership

Sub-section 1: Partnership in general
(1) General provisions
(2) Elements of partnership
(3) Administration of partnership
(4) Effects of partnership
(5) Determination of partnership
(6) Liquidation of partnership and distribution
Sub-section 2: Certain kinds of partnership
(1) Partnership of works
(2) Partnership of creditworthiness (*shirka al-wujuh*)
(3) Partnership between capital and labour (*mudharaba*)

Section 4: Loan of a fungible (*qarḍ*)
Section 5: Compromise (*sulh*)

Chapter 2: Contracts for beneficial use
Section 1: hire

Sub-section 1: Hire in general
(1) Definition of hire

Sub-section 1: The conclusion and conditions thereof
Sub-section 2: Effects of the contract for labour
(1) Obligations of the workman
(2) Obligations of the employer
Sub-section 3: Determination of the contract for labour

Section 3: Contracts of agency
Sub-section 1: General provisions
Sub-section 2: Effects of agency
(1) Obligations of the agent
(2) Obligations of the principal
Sub-section 3: Determination of agency

Section 4: Contract of deposit or bailment
Sub-section 1: General provisions
Sub-section 2: Effects of the contract
(1) Obligations of the bailee
(2) Obligations of the bailor
Sub-section 3: Special provisions relating to some bailments

Section 5: Custodianship
Sub-section 1: General Provisions
Sub-section 2: Obligations and rights of the custodian
Sub-section 3: Determination of custodianship

Chapter 4: Contracts of hazard

Section 1: Competition (for a prize) and gambling

Section 2: Payment for life

Section 3: Insurance contracts
Sub-section 1: General Provisions
Sub-section 2: Effects of the contract
(1) Obligations of the insured
(2) Obligations of the insurer
Sub-section 3: Provisions specific to some kinds of insurance
(1) Fire insurance
(2) Life insurance

Chapter 5: Contracts of personal surety

Section 1: Guarantee
Sub-section 1: Elements of guarantee
Sub-section 2: Some types of guarantee
(1) Surety for the person
(2) Surety for default
Sub-section 3: Effects of guarantee

(1) Between the guarantor and the obligee (creditor)
(2) Between the guarantor and the obligor (debtor)
Sub-section 4: Determination of guarantee
Section 2: Assignment (of debt or liability)
Sub-section 1: Making the assignment
Sub-section 2: Effects of the assignment
(1) As between the creditor (obligee) and the assignee (of the obligation)
(2) As between the assignor and the assignee
(3) As between the creditor (obligee) and the assignor
(4) As between the creditor (obligee) and third parties
Sub-section 3: Determination of assignment

Book III: Original real rights

Chapter 1: The right of ownership
Section 1: The right of ownership in general
Sub-section 1: The scope and methods of protection thereof
Sub-section 2: Restrictions upon ownership
(1) General provisions
(2) Restrictions in favour of neighbours
(3) Restrictions on the transferee of rights
(4) Right of passage
Sub-section 3: Joint ownership
(1) General provisions
(2) Determination of joint ownership
(3) Division of benefits of joint ownership
(4) Mandatory joint ownership
(5) Family property
(6) Ownership of flats and apartments
(7) Federations/associations of owners of flats (residents associations and condominiums)
(8) Walls jointly owned
Section 2: Causes of acquisition of ownership
Sub-section 1: Acquisition of ownerless ('Permitted') things
(1) Movables
(2) Immovables
Sub-section 2: Guarantee
Sub-section 3: Inheritance and the winding up of estates
(1) General provisions

(2) The estate
- (a) General provisions
- (b) Liquidation of debts of the estate
- (c) Delivery of the assets of the estate and the division thereof
- (d) Provisions relating to estates not liquidated

Sub-section 4: Wills

Sub-section 5: Acquisition by accretion

(1) Accretion to realty:
- (a) by operation of nature
- (b) by act of persons
- (c) Accretion to movables

Sub-section 6: Contract

Sub-section 7: Pre-emption

(1) General Provisions

(2) Incidents of pre-emption

(3) Effects of pre-emption

Sub-section 8: Possession

(1) General Provisions

(2) Effects of possession
- (a) Passage of time in prescription
- (b) Possession of movables
- (c) Acquisition of fruits by possession
- (d) Reclaiming expenses
- (e) Liability for destruction

Chapter 2: Rights stemming from ownership

Section 1: Rights of user, use, residence, and user of the land of another (*musaataha*)

Sub-section 1: Rights of user

(1) General provisions

(2) Effects of right of user

(3) Determination of rights of user

Sub-section 2: Rights of use and the right of residence

Sub-section 3: Rights of use of the land of another (*musaataha*)

Section 2: Charitable trust (*waqf*)

Section 3: Real rights over the land of another (*irtifaaq*) (easements)

Sub-section 1: Creation of rights of *irtifaaq*

Sub-section 2: The scope thereof

Sub-section 3: Determination thereof

Sub-section 4: Certain of such rights:
(1) Right of passage
(2) Right to drink
(3) Right to bring water across another's land for irrigation
(4) Right to free flow

Book IV: Real securities

Chapter 1: Mortgage
Section 1: Definition of mortgage and the creation thereof
Section 2: Effects of Mortgage
Sub-section 1: Effects of mortgage as between the contracting parties
(1) As regards the mortgagor
(2) As regards the creditor mortgagee
Sub-section 2: Effects of the mortgage as regards third parties
(1) General Provisions
(2) Rights of priority
(3) Rights to follow
Section 3: Determination of the mortgage

Chapter 2: Pledge
Section 1: Definition of pledge and the creation thereof
Section 2: Effects of pledge
Sub-section 1: Effect as between the contracting parties
(1) As regards the pledgor
(2) As regards the creditor pledgee
Sub-section 2: Effects of pledge as regards third parties
Section 3: Special provisions relating to some pledges
Sub-section 1: Possessory pledge over land
Sub-section 2: Pledge of movables
Sub-section 3: Pledge of debts
Section 4: Determination of pledge

Chapter 3: Priority rights
Section 1: General provisions
Section 2: Categories of priority rights
Sub-section 1: General provision
Sub-section 2: Public and private priority rights over movables
Sub-section 3: Private priority rights over realty.

A glance at the index set out above will be sufficient to demonstrate immediately to the lawyer schooled in the *Shari'a* that the code is solidly *Shari'a* based.

This solid base in the *Shari'a* caused immediate practical commercial problems, which led to an amendment to the Code in 1987, which must be considered.

The 1987 Amendment: 'Civil' and 'commercial'

An Amendment to the Civil Code in 1987 provided[16]

> "The attached law shall apply in respect of civil transactions in the State of the U.A.E., but commercial transactions shall continue to be governed by the laws and regulations in force in that regard until the Union Commercial Code is enacted."

It may be pertinent in this context to consider also the history of the Amendment. When the Civil Code was promulgated, it was quickly realised by commercial interests in the U.A.E., in particular by the banks, that its provisions struck a possibly lethal blow at conventional banking activities, in that interest on monies lent was proscribed in accordance with generally recognised principles of the Shari'a. His Excellency Sheikh Suroor attempted to regularise this position with a letter, but it was clear that a letter could not vary the law constitutionally; thus the Amendment was passed. The philosophy behind it was no doubt that a 'commercial loan' would continue to be governed by existing banking practice, without the necessity for actually saying so.

A Commercial Code was enacted in 1993.[17] In the 'civil' or 'continental' system generally and thus in the Arab systems based upon it, a differentiation is made between 'civil' and 'commercial' matters which are regulated by 'civil' and 'commercial' codes respectively. Thus, in contract, the Civil Code lays down the general principles; the Commercial Code rules in specific commercial matters. Matters involving commercial companies and commercial contracts are 'commercial. In the U.A.E., the injunction that the Civil Code was not to apply to commercial matters raised the question as to whether even the general principles in the Code were to apply to such matters. This question is still of importance even after the coming into force of the Commercial Code, because the answer to it affects commercial contracts entered into between the date of the amendment and the coming into force of that code, that is to say during a period of some six years.

The respective roles of Civil and Commercial Codes are well summed up by a leading Egyptian author:[18]

> "To sum up, the Commercial Code is not just an exceptional code by comparison with the Civil Code, but is a code having special rules and principles which accord to it an independent existence from the Civil Code.
>
> This is not to say that the Commercial Code and the Civil code are completely separate, but there is between them a solid connection which calls for the application of the Civil Code in many cases. The basis for that is that the Civil Code is the home of the general principles which govern all branches of private law, and contains in particular the general theory of obligations which transcends the scope of the Civil Code and regulates in general all legal relations between persons of private law."

Another leading author puts the matter with great clarity:[19]

> "The Commercial Code – as one of the branches of private law – is not the original branch, if this expression may be permitted. The original is the Civil Code. The Civil Code is in fact considered the broad basis for all branches of private law, in that it lays down the general principles which regulate the relationships of individuals without regard to the nature of the activity, or the calling practised by them, and it is the 'common law' for links between individuals. Indeed, the provisions of the Civil Code contain the common basic provisions upon which the logic of the law relies in any field wherein we need the logic of law.
>
> Thus, the study of the principles of the Commercial Code depends in the first place upon a broad knowledge of the essential nature of the principles of the Civil Code, in particular in the matter of obligations, which are the corner stone not only of the provisions of the Civil Code, but also of the provisions of the Commercial Code . . .
>
> Thus, also, the nature of commercial contracts does not differ from that of civil contracts. How often do the commercial courts rely upon the provisions of the Civil Code directly in deciding disputes arising from commercial contracts. The provisions of the Civil Code are the comprehensive background to the shape of the Commercial Code, in that they are a direct origin of its provisions in the absence of a written commercial provision and established commercial custom."

As to what is 'commercial', the Commercial Code follows expected lines. Article 1 provides:

> "This Code shall apply to merchants (commerçants) and to all commercial acts engaged in by any person even if not a merchant."

The normal umbrella effect of a Civil Code in commercial matters is reflected in the new Commercial Code. Article 2.2 provides:

> "If there is no commercial custom, the principles relating to civil matters shall apply which do not conflict with the general principles of commercial activity."

A typical list of activities considered 'commercial' per se is contained in Article 5 of the U.A.E. Commercial Code.

In view of the overall position between civil and commercial codes to which I have referred, *supra*, it is necessary to construe the Amendment itself carefully to ascertain its true meaning. The Amendment itself is limited to 'commercial transactions'. It thus adopts the 'material' test which is related to the character of 'merchant' (commerçant – tajir), *i.e.*, of the parties carrying out the transaction.[20]

The Dubai Court of Cassation has held, in a case concerning an arbitration agreement contained in a charterparty, that the effect of the Amendment was to withdraw entirely from the scope of application of the Civil Code all commercial transactions, so that even those general provisions of the Civil Code (for example, those governing the formation and validity of contracts) should not apply.[21] The Court in that case applied instead to a commercial contract the provisions of the Dubai Contracts Law of 1971 (a survival from the British extra-territorial jurisdiction and which was therefore based upon common law principles), which law was the general law of contract in Dubai, applicable to both civil and commercial matters, prior to the entry into force of the Civil Code.

With respect, and in particular having regard to the history of the Amendment, I am unable to accept the Court's interpretation of the Amendment. I do not consider it to be a proper interpretation that all the principles of the Civil Code were to be excluded from a contract merely because it was 'commercial'. What was meant by the Amendment, in my opinion, on its proper construction, was that those incidents of the law particularised in a Commercial Code should continue to be governed by the principles already existing in U.A.E. law until the promulgation of such a Code.

Private international law: Conflict

Articles 1 to 28 inclusive of the Code set out, for the first time in the U.A.E. or any of the Emirates, provisions of private international law. While these must be welcome as obviating the uncertainty which has hitherto existed on this topic, they provide no comfort for those who might have hoped that some of the more embarrassing attributes of the *Shari'a* (e.g. interest, prohibited consumables such as alcohol) might be eliminated by the choice in the contract of foreign law. Be that as it may, this is the first conflict code to be published in the Gulf States since the Kuwaiti code of 1961,[22] and thus merits analysis in some detail. Before proceeding to such analysis, however, we may advert briefly to the overriding and important consideration to which I have referred, namely, in the light of the new Code, will the Courts of the U.A.E. or the Emirates give effect to appropriate provisions of foreign law where such provisions are not in accord with the *Shari'a; a fortiori*, where such provisions are in conflict with the *Shari'a*[23]? Must the provisions of the *Shari'a* be regarded as basically going to the *Nitham al-'am* (public policy: *ordre public*)? To take the ever-recurring problem of interest on loans, illegal at the *Shari'a* – could interest provisions be 'legalised' by the choice by the parties of a foreign law to govern their contract of loan? Would the courts enforce a contract expressed to be subject to English law, for the sale of alcohol or pork meat? To anticipate the study which follows, the matter would appear to have been put beyond doubt by Article 27 of the Code. Although Article 19 respects the principle of *autonomie de la volonté*, that is to say the right of the parties to choose the proper law of the contract, Article 27 provides: 'It shall not be lawful to apply principles of law designated by the foregoing provisions if such principles are contrary to the Islamic *Shari'a* or public policy or morals in the U.A.E.'.

We turn now to a detailed review of these new conflict Articles.

Articles 1 to 3 inclusive of the Code deal with the scope of application of the law and its interpretation.

Article 1 provides that legislative provisions shall apply to all matters contained therein either expressly or by implication; that there shall be no place for construction or interpretation where a provision is clear; and that if the judge does not find any provision in the law, then he must adjudicate in accordance with the Islamic *Shari'a*. In so doing, he adverts to the two schools, Maliki and Hanbali: if he finds no answer therein, then he adverts to the Shafi'i and Hanafi schools as the matter may require.[24] If the judge still does not find the guidance which he requires, then he gives judgment in accordance with custom, which custom must not, however, be contrary to public policy or morals, and if the custom is peculiar to a particular Emirate, then his judgment applies to such Emirate.

Article 2 provides definitively that in the comprehension and interpretation of a provision, reference shall be made to the principles of the Islamic *fiqh*.

Article 3 further defines public policy as embracing in particular matters of personal status such as marriage and inheritance, etc., the matters relating to the regulation of judgments and freedom of trade and the circulation of wealth, the principles of individual ownership and the other basic principles upon which society rests; but, once again, we find the dictate that all of this is not to be contrary to the mandatory provisions and basic principles of the Islamic *Shari'a*.

All in all, it may be submitted that the paramountcy of the *Shari'a* in the jurisprudence of the U.A.E. could hardly be more strongly stated.

Articles 4 to 9 of the Code provide for the application of the law in time. Article 4 deals with the effect of subsequent legislation upon prior legislation; Article 5 deals with capacity and changes therein; Articles 6 and 7 with extinctive prescription and changes therein (limitation); Article 8 covers the timing of the application of rules of evidence; while Article 9 applies the 'sun' calendar unless the law otherwise provides.

Articles 10 *et seq.* of this section contain the provisions relating to the application of the law as to 'place', and specify the law which is to apply to procedural and substantive matters. In view of their obvious importance, I propose to translate these provisions in detail while necessarily making the usual reservations as to reference thereto in the ultimate analysis in any language other than the original Arabic.

Article 10: The law of the U.A.E. shall be referred to in classifying relationships when it is required to identify the kind of such relationships in a case where there is a conflict of laws, in order to determine which of such laws must be applied.

Article 11: (1) There shall be applied to the civil status of persons and their capacity the law of the state to which they belong by way of nationality, provided that in financial transactions concluded in the U.A.E. resulting in effects therein, and where one of the parties is foreign of defective capacity and where such lack of capacity goes to an obscure reason where it is difficult for the other party to define the same: in such case, such reason shall not affect his capacity.

(2) The legal order of foreign juridical persons, companies, societies, and corporations, etc., shall be governed by the law of the state wherein such persons have taken *de facto* their principal place of management, provided that where they conduct an activity within the U.A.E. then the national law shall apply.

Article 12: (1) In matters of substance concerning the validity of marriage reference shall be made to the law of each of the two parties at the time of conclusion of the marriage.

(2) As to form, a marriage between two foreigners, or between a foreigner and a national, shall be considered valid if it was concluded in accordance with the principles of the country wherein it was finalised or if there were observed therein the principles laid down by the law of each of the two spouses.

Article 13: (1) The law of the state to which the husband belongs at the time of conclusion of the marriage shall apply to the personal consequences and consequences relating to the property resulting from the marriage contract.

(2) Divorce shall be governed by the law of the state to which the husband belongs at the time of the divorce, and the action for divorce and separation shall be governed by the law of the state to which the husband belongs at the time of filing the case.

Article 14: In the circumstances set out in the two preceding Articles, where one of the two spouses is a national at the time of conclusion of the marriage, the law of the U.A.E. alone shall apply with the exception of the condition relating to capacity to marry.

Article 15: The obligation to defray expenses as between persons in propinquity shall be governed by the law of the party charged therewith.

Article 16: Substantive matters relating to guardianship, trusteeship, and other substantive rules relating to the protection of those of no or insufficient capacity or absent persons, shall be governed by the law of the person who must be protected.

Article 17: (1) There shall apply to inheritance the law of the deceased at the time of his death.

(2) There shall inure to the state property rights situate in its territory and relating to a foreigner who has no heir.

(3) There shall apply to the substantive provisions of the will and all additional transactions subsequent to death the law of the state to which belonged by nationality at the time of his death the person originating such transaction.

(4) There shall apply to the form of the will and all additional transactions subsequent to the death the law of the state to which belonged by nationality at the time of issue thereof the person from whom issued such transaction, or the law of the state wherein the transaction was completed.

(5) Provided that the law of the U.A.E. shall be the law to be applied in the case of a will issuing from a foreigner in respect of real property situate in the state.

Article 18: (1) There shall apply to possession and ownership and rights in kind, insofar as the same relate to realty the *lex situs* thereof, and so far as the same relate to movables the law of the *situs* of the moveable at the time of realisation of the cause from which resulted the acquisition or loss of the possession or ownership or other rights in kind.

(2) Whether property be realty or *movable* shall be defined by the law of the state wherein such property is situate.

Article 19: (1) There shall apply to contractual obligations both as to form and substance, the law of the state of the joint domicile of the contracting parties where they have joint domicile, and if of different domicile there shall apply the law of the state wherein the contract was concluded (*lex loci contractus*) unless the contracting parties agree or it appears from the circumstances that some other law was intended to be applied.

(2) Provided that the law of the *situs* of real property shall be applied to contracts concluded in respect thereof.

Here we find the generally recognised principle of private international law of *autonomie de la volonté*, that the parties are in general entitled to choose the law which they wish to apply to their contractual relations. However, in the case of the U.A.E. Code, as we have seen, this choice is severely restricted by the necessity for compliance with the *Shari'a*.

Article 20: (1) There shall apply to obligations other than contractual the law of the state wherein occurred the event giving rise to the obligation.

(2) The provisions of the foregoing sub-Article shall not apply to obligations arising out of an illegal act (civil wrong, delict, 'tort') in relation to events happening abroad and being legal in the U.A.E., even if the same be considered illegal in the country wherein it occurred.

That is to say, a civil wrong committed outside the U.A.E. is not actionable in the U.A.E. unless it constitutes a civil wrong in that jurisdiction also.[25]

Article 21: There shall apply to the principles of jurisdiction and all procedural matters the law of the state wherein the case is filed or the proceedings are conducted.

This records the well-known principle that it is the *lex fori* which governs these matters.

Article 22: The provisions of the foregoing Articles shall not apply if there be any provision in a special law or in an international treaty in force in the country contrary thereto.

Article 23: The principles of private international law shall be followed in any matter in respect of which there does not appear in the foregoing a provision of conflict of laws.

Article 24: The Law of the U.A.E. shall apply to those of unknown nationality or to whom is proved several nationalities at the same time: provided that in the case of persons to whom is proved at the same time nationality of the U.A.E. and the nationality of another state, the law of the U.A.E. shall be applied.

Article 25: If it appears from the provisions set out in the preceding Articles that the law to be applied is the law of a prescribed state wherein there is a multiplicity of laws, then the internal law of such state shall prescribe any law thereof to be applied. If no such provision is to be found, the predominant law shall be applied or the law of domicile, in accordance with the circumstances.

Article 26: (1) If it be established that foreign law must be applied, where the provisions of private international law relating to the law to be applied remit (the matter) to its rules (ie the rules of the UAE).

(2) Provided that the law of the U.A.E. shall be applied where it remits to its principles the provisions of international law relating to the law which must be applied.

Article 27: Has been translated above.

Article 28: the law of the U.A.E. shall be applied where the existence of the foreign law to be applied is not proved or its effect established.

This Article gives effect to the well-known principle that unless the foreign law and its incidents be proved, then the law of the U.A.E. is applied; to put this another way, in English legal parlance, foreign law must be proved, otherwise it will be assumed to be the same as the law of the forum.

Section 2, of this Introductory Chapter of the Code contains various legal maxims, most deriving from the *Shari'a*. These are extremely abstruse, and in some cases impossible of translation. A comparison may be made with the similar list of maxims in the *Majella*.[26]

Section 3 of the preliminary Chapter deals with persons natural and judicial. Natural persons are covered by Articles 71 to 91 inclusive. Article 81 in particular deals with the attribute which I have translated here as 'domicile' (*mawtan*),[27] and in view of the importance of this concept in the context of this Code, as indeed in continental law generally, I translate this Article as follows:

Article 81: (1) Domicile is the place wherein a person ordinarily resides.

(2) A person may have at the same time more than one domicile.

(3) If a person does not have a place wherein he ordinarily resides, he shall be considered without domicile.

Article 82: The place wherein a person carries on business or a profession or trade shall be considered a domicile in relation to the carrying on of the activities relating to such business, profession or trade.

Article 83: (1) Domicile in a minor and restricted person, person of lost capacity and absentee, is the domicile of the person representing the same at law.

(2) The minor permitted to engage in business shall have a special domicile in relation to the acts and activities which the law considers that he has capacity to carry on.

Article 84: (1) A domicile of choice may be adopted for the carrying out of a specific legal act.

(2) Proof of the existence of a domicile of choice shall only be by writing.

(3) Domicile of choice for the execution of a legal act shall be the domicile in relation to everything which concerns such act, including the procedures of mandatory execution, unless it be stipulated expressly that such domicile is limited exclusively to certain acts.

Juridical persons are dealt with in Articles 92 to 94. These short provisions merely set out general principles, and Article 94 subjects juridical persons to the special Laws which govern them. The main Law in this respect is the U.A.E. Law of Commercial Companies, Law No. 8 of 1984.

Section 4 of the preliminary chapter deals with property and things generally (Articles 95 to 103 inclusive) and covers in general terms both personalty and realty; while Section 5 deals with rights. In the matter of rights, the exercise and infringement thereof, it is important to note that Article 106 expressly records the principle of abuse of rights and lays down the circumstances which constitute such an abuse. This, with its concomitant principle of good faith, is a provision which would be expected to be found in a Code of this nature, whether based on the *Shari'a* or on continental principles generally.[28] Article 107 to 111 inclusive subdivide the classes of right; while Articles 112 to 123 inclusive cover methods of proof and evidence. Once again, these follow *Shari'a* principles.[29]

Book I

The Articles to which brief reference has been made conclude the preliminary chapter of the Code, which then passes on to *Book 1*, which deals with personal rights and liabilities, commencing with the sources thereof, set out as 1. contract; 2. individual conduct; 3. the harmful act; 4. the beneficial act; 5. the law. These heads are then dealt with in turn.

Contract

'Commercial law is, strictly speaking, merely one aspect of the law of contract . . .'.[30] The importance of contract to the business man and commercial lawyer does not need to be stressed. Thus, not only the overall indications of the applicability of the *Shari'a* to which reference has already been made, but the incidence of the Law of Contract in the new Code expressly attributable to that source, must be a matter for close consideration and, perhaps, concern.

It comes as no surprise to a lawyer of any persuasion, common, civil, or *Shari'a*, to find that the basic principle of contract in the Code consists in the linking of offer and acceptance linked in such a way as to reflect the subject-matter of the contract resulting in mutually binding legal obligations.[31] The contract may concern various incidents, and in general 'anything not forbidden by a provision of the law or contrary to public policy or morals'.[32] It is perhaps hardly necessary to note that these exceptions would embrace any contractual provisions contrary to the *Shari'a*.

Article 128 of the Code envisages the system of nominate contracts and provides that the principles of the Code should apply to both nominate and non-nominate contracts;[33] sub-section 2 of this Article may be significant: 'as for the principles peculiar to certain contracts these shall be established by special provisions regulating the same in this law or in other laws'.

Article 129 further establishes the corner-stones of contract as being essentially the following:

a) that the mutality of consent must be achieved on the essential elements;
b) that the object of the contract should be a thing possible and prescribed or which can be prescribed, and which may lawfully be dealt in;
c) that the obligation stemming from the contract shall constitute a legal cause and it is also provided that the contract shall be formed by the mere joinder of offer and acceptance, subject to what the law otherwise provides.

Apart from the more normal incidence of defective consent, the Code contains in this respect the 'options' (*Khiyaraat*) peculiar, in the form in which they are here spelt out, to the *Shari'a* system.[34]

Articles 131 to 135 inclusive deal with the ways in which intention and consensus may be expressed.

Article 136 deals with the principle of *Khiyar al majlis*, the option of the *majlis*.[35]

The Code continues[36] to deal with the various incidents of offer and acceptance including the necessary elements which must be agreed; contracting between absent parties; contracting by telephone etc.; auctions; contracts of adhesion (*ith'aan*); contracts for future performance; payment of advance or deposit.

Agency

Articles 149 to 156 inclusive of the Code deal with contract through a representative or agent (*niyabat* not *wakaalat*).

Agency may be by express contract or by operation of law. Where the agent contracts in the name of the principal, the rights and liabilities accruing under the contract adhere to the principal. Where the party entering into the contract has not announced at the time his role as agent then the effect of the contract does not go to the principal whether he be debtor or creditor unless there be a conclusive implication that the other contracting party knew of the existence of the agency or whether it made no difference to him whether he was transacting with the principal or the agent. Perhaps surprisingly, these provisions appear to conflict with the teaching in some Schools of the *Shari'a*.

Articles 157 to 175 inclusive of the Code deal with capacity.

Defective consent

Defective consent Defective consent is dealt with in Articles 176 to 198 of the Code under principles which may be translated as duress, deceit or misrepresentation, and mistake.

Object and 'cause'

Article 200 of the Code makes the overall provision that the subject-matter of the contract must be something known and capable of valuation; this accords with the overall *Shari'a* requirements of certainty and consequently avoidance of *riba* (see also Article 96). A future consideration may however be the subject of a valid contract provided that uncertainty is absolutely avoided. The estate of a person still alive is not a permitted subject for contract. Article 204 is of particular significance in the *Shari'a* context: 'If the object for consideration for the transaction consists of money the amount and kind thereof must be specified without any effect being accorded to increase or decrease in the value of such money at the time of payment'. This would appear to confirm that the concept of *riba* within the ambit of this Code recognises no exception which might otherwise be made due to modern inflationary circumstances.[37]

If the object of the contract is contrary to the tenor of the contract, contrary to law, or in particular to public policy or morals, then the contract is void.

The *Shari'a* restriction as to the insertion of conditions is reflected in Article 206: such conditions must be in accordance with the tenor of the contract or sanctioned by custom or usage or beneficial to one of the two contracting parties – with the usual saving for public policy or morals. In this Article however the principle of severance is recognised; the condition only is avoided unless it constituted the motive for contracting in which case the whole contract is avoided.

Article 207 defines cause as 'the direct purpose intended by the contract'. It must be in existence, valid and permitted (as at the *Shari'a*) and not contrary to public policy or morals. The contract is not valid unless there be a legal benefit therein for the parties, and the existence of such benefit is presumed unless there are indications to the contrary.[38]

Valid, void and 'voidable'

Valid, void and 'voidable' contracts are defined in Article 200 to 212 of the Code. 'Voidable' is put in inverted commas here in order to indicate the interchangeability of the two Arabic terms *baatil* and *faasid* in some of the Schools of the *Shari'a*. It is clearly not possible in an article of this length to go into a dissertation on the precise meanings of the *Shari'a* terms.

Articles 213 to 218 inclusive of the Code deal with the two other forms of qualified contract, namely those which are 'suspended' (*mawqūf*) and not binding (*ghair lazim*).

The Khiyaraat or Options

These are the options to rescind. The option of the *majlis* has already been referred to in another part of the Code: the remaining options may be rendered in English by the terms: 'option by stipulation or express condition' that is to say, an option to rescind given by an express provision in the contract; the 'option of sight', i.e., of the thing dealt in; the 'option of designation' that is to say, where the contract consists of more than one thing in the alternative a contracting party having the right to choose; the 'option of defect', i.e., to rescind the contract from the discovery of a latent defect or fault.[39]

The effects of contract

The effects of contract, as regards the contracting parties and third parties are dealt with in Articles 243 to 256 inclusive. It is interesting to note that Article 246 provides expressly for execution of the contract in accordance with its terms and expressly lays down the principle of good faith. It also provides that the contract is not limited always to the express provisions of the contract but includes necessary implied terms and ancillary matters dictated by law and custom and the nature of the transaction.

The general provisions on Contract are followed by those governing Individual Volition, to which the general provisions relating to contract apply. There follows a much longer section, on injurious acts.

Injurious acts ('torts')

Articles 282 to 286 contain general provisions governing liability for injurious acts and the consequences thereof. Provision is then made in Articles 288 and 289 for the recognition of certain defences (self-defence, and the defence of others (defence of person, honour, property), and physical duress). The Judge may apportion loss between the doer of an injurious act and a person suffering harm as a result thereof in circumstances in which that person's actions partially caused, or increased, the damage suffered. The Judge has a discretion, where several persons are responsible for an injurious act, to apportion liability to compensate between the actors.[40] Articles 292 to 295 set out the principles of compensation for injurious acts: compensation is to be assessed by reference to harm suffered by the victim, including loss of profit naturally resulting from the harmful act, and may include moral damage; it is payable in money terms, but the Judge may, on the application of the victim, make an order that the victim be put in the position he had been in prior to the injury, or that a particular act be done to make good the injury. The Judge may order payment by instalments, and may order the obligator to provide a guarantee or security. The measure of damages prescribed is thus in general more generous than would be awarded at strict Shari'a.

Articles 296 to 297 deal with the interplay between the provisions governing injurious acts, and those governing contracts and criminal offences. Article 296 provides that any condition purporting to exempt the doer of an injury from liability shall fall void, and Article 297 that a criminal penalty may be imposed in relation to an act for which the doer has already been made liable in civil terms under this section, or vice versa. These provisions enact the general civil law principle that there can be no contract out of liability in 'tort', and go to public order.

Limitation (Extinctive Prescription)

Limitation periods are dealt with in Article 298, which provides for a three-year limitation period unless criminal proceedings relating to the same act are on foot, in which case time does not run until the conclusion of such proceedings. There is in all cases a fifteen-year long-stop. Time starts to run for the purposes of Article 298 only when the victim becomes aware both that he has suffered harm and of the identity of the wrongdoer. The provisions governing limitation of actions are virtually standard throughout the Code.[41]

Liability for personal acts

There follow specific provisions governing liability for personal acts, divided into injury to the person, damage to property, and dispossession and trespass to goods. The provisions on injury to the person are contained in Article 299, which provides that compensation shall be payable for such injury. The Shari'a remedies of blood money (*diya*) or damages for personal injury (*arsh*) are an alternative to compensation at the Code. Damage to property is also dealt with shortly. The basic position is that compensation is payable for damage to or destruction of property.[42] Similar principles apply in relation to dispossession and trespass.[43]

Liability for the acts of others, for animals and objects and the use of public roads[44]

These succinct articles follow the French and general civil line that the basic principles are contained in the Code, leaving their development to the Courts.[45] Again, a single Article deals with liability for the acts of others.[46] The basic principle is that a person is not liable for the acts of others, but there are exceptions: a Judge may, on the application of the victim, and in his discretion, hold liable for the acts of another any person who is charged with supervising or directing that other, if either he has actual control over that person, or if that person is an infant or is mentally or physically incapacitated. In the latter case, it shall be a defence to show that the duty of supervision had been carried out with all due care. Sub-section 4 treats liability for animals and things and use of the public highway; it is divided into offences by animals, collapse of buildings, things and machinery, and use of the public highway.

The beneficial act

Under the heading 'The beneficial act' are grouped a variety of circumstances in which, to use current legal phraseology, one party may be said to have been unjustly enriched at the expense of another, and is therefore obliged to make restitution (to return a thing or to repay money). Situations in which this obligation may arise include property transfers under a mistake of fact ('Receipt of that which is not due/owing'[47]), agency of necessity ('Interference'[48]), discharge of the debt of another.[49] As with the French Civil Code[50], there is no attempt in the U.A.E. Civil Code to make any statement of general principle. A contrast may be made with the German Civil Code, Article 812(1), which is at the commencement of a special chapter on rights arising from beneficial acts:[51]

> "A person who without legal justification (*ohne rechtlichen Grund*) obtains anything from a person at his expense, whether by transfer or otherwise, is bound to give it up to him. This obligation also arises if the legal justification subsequently ceases to exist or if the transfer does not have the effect envisaged in the transaction."

The Swiss Code of Obligations, which is similarly structured, provides, under the heading 'Obligations resulting from unjust enrichment':[52]

> "A person who is unjustly enriched at the expense of another must make restitution to that other.
>
> Restitution must be made, in particular, by a person who has received a benefit without cause, by virtue of a cause which did not come into being, or of a cause which has ceased to exist."

As noted *supra*, the limitation period in respect of beneficial acts is three years from the date on which the obligee became aware of his right to restitution, with the usual fifteen-year longstop.[53]

The effects of rights. Under the heading 'The effects of rights' are grouped together provisions governing the enforcement and discharge of obligations. Article 338 provides, by way of introduction:[54]

> "A right must be satisfied when the legal conditions rendering it due for performance exist, and if an obligor fails to perform an obligation, he shall be compelled to do so either by way of specific performance or by way of compensation in accordance with the provisions of the law."

Under this heading are to be found, *inter alia*, provisions governing set-off, specific performance and damages, and (under the sub-heading 'Legal means of securing execution') security over the property of the debtor, the *action paulienne*, attachment of the bankrupt obligor, and the right of detention.[55]

Dispositions affected by condition and delay

'Condition' is defined in Article 420 as 'a future matter upon the existence or absence of which the full effectiveness (of a disposition) depends'.[56]

Multiplicity of parties

Article 450 provides that joint liability between debtors may not arise except by agreement or by operation of law. The characteristics of joint liability are as follows: discharge by a single debtor discharges all;[57] the obligee(s) may claim against any debtor or debtors.[58]

Determination of the Right

Rights may be determined in three ways: Release, Impossibility of performance, and Extinctive prescription.

Contracts/Pacta Sunt Servanda

Before we turn to consider in detail Book II of the Civil Code, on Contracts, it is pertinent to consider the nature of the contractual obligation in Islamic law. This was discussed at length in the course of the Arbitration *American Independent Oil Company (Aminoil)* v. *State of Kuwait*, (in which the author was of Counsel for Aminoil), and in which the agreed 'compromis' provided for the application of general principles of law. Opinions were filed by leading jurists, whereby the principles were dealt with on a comparative basis. The Opinion on the law of Kuwait was filed by Professor Suleman Morqos and Dr Saba Habachy. The eminent jurist Professor Berthold Goldman was asked to prepare a synthesis of the Opinions given (on English law, French law, German and Swiss law, and U.S. law, in addition to Kuwaiti law). In dealing with the universality of the principle that *pacta sunt servanda*, Professor Goldman stated:[59]

> "The answer here is unanimous: the principle *pacta sunt servanda*, which means that parties who freely and legally entered into a contract are bound to fulfil the obligations undertaken through it, is one of the basic principles of the six legislations."

Again:[60]

> "It thus appears that *pacta sunt servanda* is a fundamental principle under the six municipal laws – hence at common law, civil law and Muslim law – and that the conditions under which, by virtue of this principle, contracts are binding for the parties are identical or close one to each other under these laws." (underlining added)

That is not to say, however, that the rationale behind the adherence of each system of law to the principle that *pacta sunt servanda* is identical, or even similar. This is illustrated by the following excerpt from the Opinion on Kuwaiti law filed by Morqos and Habachy in the *Aminoil* proceedings;[61] the 'sacred Muslim law' referred to is the sacred law of al Islam – the Shari'a – and the principles involved are the same in the U.A.E. as in Kuwait:

> "The principle Pacta Sunt Servanda is one of the important foundations of any developed legal system, such as the system of law of Kuwait. It simply means that a contract is binding on the parties who entered into it, and that such contract obligates each party to fulfil his undertakings towards the other party who is vested with the rights which correspond to his obligations. The rights which the contract creates in favour of one party must be respected by the other party. Any modifications or changes in the contract can only be made by mutual agreement of the parties. . . .
>
> The principle Pacta Sunt Servanda is a basic rule of Kuwait Law. This is true both of the recent secular legislation contained in the Commercial Code promulgated in 1961 and of the Sacred Muslim Law as formulated in the Mejalla which was in force in commercial matters up till the date on which the Code became effective. The Mejalla is still in force in Kuwait in non-commercial transactions which do not fall within the domain of the Code of Commerce.[62]
>
> In Muslim Law, the principle Pacta Sunt Servanda rests on the first verse of Surah 5 of the Qur'an which reads:
>
> 'O ye who have believed, fulfil your contracts'.
>
> The Prophet made this comment on the Qur'anic precept;
>
> 'al Muslimuna inda shurutihim', which means:
>
> 'Muslims are bound by the stipulations of their contracts'.
>
> The Qur'anic text and the commentaries of Muslim jurists emphasise that a party to an agreement cannot free himself from his obligations thereunder by his own will alone, even if he had reserved such facility for himself at the time the contract was concluded, unless such stipulation is specifically authorised by the Divine Legislator.

Commenting on the Qur'anic commandment, the late Professor Abu Zahra, formerly head of the Department of Islamic Law, University of Cairo, wrote the following:

'The Legislator has ascribed to each lawful contract an effect which follows from it *ipso jure* when the terms and conditions, as well as the fundamental elements for its validity, are present. Once this is realised, a contracting party has no way out of the rules laid down in the contract as concluded, unless his co-contracting party waives his right to insist on its implementation, and both parties agree to cancel the contract and liberate themselves from their reciprocal obligations thereunder . . . to each contract is attached the legal effect attributed to it by the Legislator, irrespective of whether this effect is deemed desirable or undesirable by either contracting party. Consequently, such contracting party cannot free himself from the obligations imposed on him by the Legislator by stipulating in the contract a clause to this effect. This rule of law applies whether such clause is stipulated at the time the contract is concluded or afterwards when it is being implemented, unless he is authorised to do so by virtue of a dispensation on the part of the Legislator'. (Abu Zahra, 'Property and Contract in Muslin Law', 1939, p. 218).

Expressed in modern legal terminology, Prof. Abu Zahra's statement leads to the conclusion that when a contract is lawfully entered into, it has a legal status which is determined by Divine Law. The mutual agreement of the parties is merely the instrumentality through which a legal situation is created. However, the role of the parties ends here, and from this point onwards, the Divine Law takes over and defines the status of the contract, the position of the parties and their reciprocal rights and obligations."

This, then, is the background against which Book II of the U.A.E. Civil Code, on Contracts, must be viewed. It may be noted that the phrase often used in English as the equivalent of *pacta sunt servanda*, 'the sanctity of contract', assumes even greater relevance when used in the light of the Shari'a. A contract is indeed 'sacred' and must be performed in good faith and in accordance with its true intent and the spirit underlying it: the injunction so to do stems from the Qur'an.

Another remark preliminary to any study of the provisions governing Contracts in the U.A.E. Civil code must be that, although there is no general theory of contract at the Shari'a, as we have already seen, the Code itself contains a general section on Contract with Book I, Personal obligations and rights. The provisions contained in Book II of the Code are specific, relating to particular 'Contracts' (and not to 'Contract' in the singular), amongst which feature the four basic nominate contracts: sale (*bay'*), gift (*hiba*), hire (*ijara*) and loan (*'ariyya*). Professor Coulson has said:[63]

> "With their zeal for tidy and systematic classification, Muslim jurists often state that the system of *'uqud* rests upon a quartet of basic contracts which cover the two primary issues of whether the transfer is of the corpus or of the usufruct and whether it is for a consideration or not."

Sale and gift, along with loan of a fungible, are treated under Chapter 1, 'Contracts vesting ownership'. Hire and loan of non-fungibles are dealt with in Chapter 2, 'Contracts for beneficial use'. It should be noted that the basic characteristic of a loan is that it is, to adopt Professor Coulson's description, a transfer of the usufruct without consideration (contrast hire).

Partnership

Next comes partnership (note that the Arabic does not distinguish between partnerships and companies).[64] Partnership, which is defined in Article 654, denotes 'a contract whereby two or more persons are bound each to participate in a financial project by providing a share of property or work for the exploitation of that project and the division of any profit or loss which may arise thereout'.[65] A partnership thus defined has legal personality.[66] Detailed provisions extending over more than fifty Articles of the Code follow, regulating *inter alia* the workings of the partnership, the attendant formalities, and methods of termination. Certain types of partnership (partnerships of work, of creditworthiness (*shirka al-wujuh*), and between capital and labour (*mudharaba*)) are specifically dealt with.

Loan of a Fungible (Qard)

Loans of fungibles are dealt with in Articles 710–721 inclusive of the Code; they are defined as (710):

> "... The transfer of a fungible property or thing to another on condition of return of the equivalent thereof in amount and kind

> and nature to the lender on determination of the period of the loan."

This section of the Code is taken substantially from, *inter alia*, Articles 462–479 of the Majella, and accordingly follows Shari's principles as adopted by, in particular, the Hanafi school. Those principles include the abhorrence of RIBA, which includes interest upon monies lent, which constitutes the most topical incident today of the loan of fungibles. Thus, Article 714 of the Code states that where the contract provides for any increase in the fungible lent, that provision shall be severed from the contract; while Article 719 provides for the exact return of the equivalent without adverting to change of value during the period of the loan.

The concept of RIBA, particularly with regard to interest on monies lent does, of course, form a huge and complicated subject, which cannot be covered in this short survey.

Compromise

Compromise (*sulh*) is expressly provided for.[67]

Contracts for beneficial use

As we have seen, encompassed within the Chapter on Contracts for beneficial use are the provisions regulating Contracts of hire (which includes both movables and immovables: no separate provision is made in the Code for leasing of movables); and Loan of non-fungibles (*i'ara, 'ariya*).

The contract of hire is defined in Article 742:[68]

> "A hire shall be the conferring by the lessor on the lessee of the right of use intended for the thing hired for a specified period in consideration of an ascertained rent."

There follow approximately 100 Articles regulating in detail Contracts of hire, with specific provision being made for certain kinds of hire, such as the lease of agricultural lands, (*muyatala*), the contract for agricultural labour against a share of produce (*musaaqaa*), the contract for tree-planting and sharing of produce of trees (*mughaarasa*), and the lease of charitable trust (*waqf*).

Contracts for work

Within the general area of contracts for work, different rules apply depending on whether the contract is classified as a contract for works (muqaawala), a contract for labour, a contract of agency, a contract of deposit or bailment, or a contract of custodianship.

The contract for works (*muqaawala*: the example par excellence is the construction contract) is defined in Article 872 of the Civil Code:[69]

> "Muqawala is a contract whereby one of two parties undertakes to make something or perform a work against a consideration undertaken by the other party."

Such a contract may be 'civil' or 'commercial'. Sanhouri has this to say about a contract of *muqaawala*:[70]

> "**Muqaawala**
> Contrary to that is the contract with the architect for this contract also relates to a mixture of material and legal acts such that it combines the rules of contracting and the rules of agency. However, the contracting element prevails; so if there were a contradiction between the two rules the rules of contracting shall apply
> . . .
> The contracting agreement – from the contractor's side – is sometimes civil and sometimes commercial. It is civil if it is not considered a commercial activity. Liberal professions are considered civil activities. So, if the physician contracted with the patient to treat him, or the solicitor contracted with his client to defend him or the architect contracted with a person to prepare a design requested by the latter or the sculptor contracted with a client to make a painting or a statue, the contract in all these cases is a civil one, even from the side of the contractor who is a professional. We have seen also that the contract is considered also civil from the employer's side.
>
> However, the professional may perform commercial activities that consume much of his effort like the architect who prepares the design and bill of quantities, supervises the work and carries out the construction works by supplying material, machinery and the required labour. In this case the contract cannot be divided and shall be deemed commercial with respect to the architect."

The importance of distinguishing between a contract of muqaawala which is 'civil' and one which is 'commercial' is self-evident: not so perhaps, or not to the same extent, the importance of deciding whether the muqaawala is an 'agency'. We have already had occasion to consider very briefly the fundamental principles of agency, which are set out within the general provisions on contract under the heading of Personal Rights and Liabilities in Book I.[71] A feature of agency agreements in the Arabian Gulf, including the U.A.E., which often surprises both Western businessmen and common lawyers is the fact that, whatever the terms of an agency agreement (commercial or otherwise, but of particular importance in the field of commercial agencies), it is virtually impossible to terminate the agreement without paying compensation to the agent. For example, Article 956 of the Civil Code of the U.A.E. provides:

> "The principal must indemnify the agent against any loss suffered by him arising out of his being dismissed at an inappropriate time or without acceptable justification."

This (and similar provisions) must be viewed in particular against the background of commercial agency agreements in the U.A.E. as elsewhere in the Arabian Gulf:[72] foreigners may not act as commercial agents, and such agreements are thus the preserve of nationals within their own territory; further, social stigma attaches to an agent whose appointment is terminated by his principal. Finally, the legal provisions on agency cannot in general be contracted out of, and so many standard terms of business or seemingly appropriately drafted agreements are to no effect.

The standard of care with which an agent must comply depends on whether the agency is gratuitous or remunerated. If gratuitous, the standard of care is that which the agent would exercise in his own affairs;[73] if remunerated, it is the standard of the reasonable man.[74]

The Contract of deposit or bailment

The Contract of deposit or bailment is dealt with in Articles 962 to 996. The bailee holds the property bailed in 'trust' for the bailor, and, unless otherwise agreed, is liable for it if it perishes as a result of his wrongful act or default.[75] The standard of care with which the bailee must comply is that of the reasonable man in relation to his own property: an interesting amalgam of the dual standards of care imposed upon an agent by Article 932.[76] Custodianship, where a third party holds property on behalf of two others who are in dispute, is dealt with in Articles 997 to 1001.

Contracts of hazard

Contracts of hazard are: competition for a prize; gambling; payment (of income) for life; and insurance contracts. Of these, all are permitted except gambling.[77] Contracts of insurance are defined in Article 1026, thus:[78]

> "Insurance is a contract whereby the assured and the insurer cooperate in facing the insured risks or events, and whereby the assured pays to the insurer a specified sum or periodical instalments, and if the risk or the event set out in the contract materialises, the insurer pays to the assured or the person stipulated as the beneficiary a sum of money or a regular income or any other pecuniary right."

Those risks in relation to which contracts of insurance may be entered into are listed in Article 1027, and include personal injury, accidents at work, theft, breach of trust, the use of motor vehicles, civil liability, and any other risks against which by custom and special laws one may insure. Provision is made for more detailed legislation governing contracts of insurance not covered by the Code.[79] The Code treats fire and life insurance separately.

Article 1028 provides that certain clauses shall be void if included in a contract of insurance; these include:[80]

> (b) a provision whereby the right of the assured shall lapse by reason of his delay in giving notice of the incident insured against to the parties which should be notified or to provide documents in the event that it appears that there is a reasonable excuse for the delay;
>
> (c) any printed clause not shown conspicuously, if it relates to any circumstance leading to the avoidance of the contract or the lapse of the right of the assured;
>
> (d) an arbitration clause unless contained in a special agreement separate from the general printed conditions in the policy of insurance;
>
> (e) any arbitrary clause breach of which it appears would have no effect on the occurrence of the incident insured against.[81]

Article 1030 allows for the insurer to be subrogated to the rights of the insured, on payment to the insured of an indemnity, with certain limited exceptions. Further provisions govern the obligations of the insured and of the insurer (for example, to pay the premium on time and to disclose material facts when the contract is entered into (the insured), and to pay the indemnity when the risk materialises (the insurer)). The limitation period for claims arising out of contracts of insurance is three years, and time starts to run from the occurrence of the incident out of which the claim arose, or knowledge thereof on the part of the person entitled to make the claim.[82]

Contracts of personal surety are then dealt with: first Guarantee, and then Assignment. Guarantee is the joining of the liability of the guarantor with that of the obligor in the performance of his obligations.[83] Assignment is 'the transfer of a debt and claim from the liability of the transferor to the transferee'.[84] The provisions governing assignment seem peculiar to Western eyes, because they envisage an assignor debtor rather than an assignor creditor (contrast the common law doctrine of assignment): they are based upon the Shari'a concepts, which do not recognise assignment in the sense accorded to it in secular law. Not surprisingly, in these circumstances, for an assignment to be valid, not only must the assignor (debtor) and assignee consent, but the creditor must also consent.[85] The Code makes detailed provision for the making of an assignment, for its effects (as between creditor and assignee, assignor (debtor) and assignee, creditor and assignor (debtor), creditor and third parties) and for its termination.[86] These provisions follow the Shari'a.

Original real rights

The Code turns its attentions in Book III to the law of property, or Original real rights. The Book is divided into two Chapters, the first dealing with The right of ownership, including the scope and methods of protection thereof, restrictions upon ownership, joint ownership, and the various Causes of acquisition of ownership. These latter include, in turn, Acquisition of ownerless ('permitted') things, Guarantee, Inheritance and the winding up of estates, Wills, Acquisition by accretion, Contract, Pre-emption and Possession. The Second Chapter of Book III covers Rights stemming from ownership, which include Rights of user, use, residence, and user of the land of another (*musaataha*), Charitable trust (*waqf*), and Real rights over the land of another (*irtifaaq*: easements).

The Code defines the right of ownership as:[87]

> the power of the owner to dispose absolutely of his property, whether of the property itself, or of the benefit or exploitation of it.

Article 1133 is situated at the head of a short section of general provisions within a section entitled, 'Restrictions upon ownership'; more specific sections follow, namely 'Restrictions in favour of neighbours', 'Restrictions on the transferee of rights', and 'Right of passage'. Given the nature of the right of ownership in Islamic law, and the definition in Article 1133, it is an interesting question to what extent the right, and its derivative rights, are absolute under the Code. In other words, does the principle of the abuse of rights,[88] or anything akin to it, restrict the exercise of such rights? Articles 104 and 106 provide:[89]

> **Article 104**
> The doing of what is permitted by law negates liability, and no person who lawfully exercises his rights shall be liable for any harm arising thereout.
>
> **Article 106**
> 1) A person shall be held liable for an unlawful exercise of his rights.
> 2) The exercise of a right shall be unlawful:
>   a) if there is an intentional infringement (of another's rights);
>   b) if the interests which such exercise of right is designed to bring about are contrary to the rules of the Islamic Shari'ah, the law, public order, or morals;
>   c) if the interests desired are disproportionate to the harm that will be suffered by others; or
>   d) if it exceeds the bounds of usage and custom.

Dr Saba Habachy suggests that the *fiqh* does not embrace the theory of abuse of rights:

> "Following the Roman law tradition, Article 544 of the French Civil code defines ownership as 'the right to enjoy and dispose of things in the most absolute manner, provided such use is not prohibited by the laws or by the regulations.'
>
> Modern jurists, however, criticize this definition. They point out that, rather than being an absolute right over a thing, ownership

> is *the most absolute right in respect of a thing*. In addition to the explicit legal and regulatory restrictions referred to in the article, there developed the theory of misuse of rights. According to the most reliable authorities, such as Santillana, Schacht, Professor Emile Tyan of the University of Beirut, and Professor Chehata of the University of Cairo, the concept of misuse of rights was not part of Muslim law."[90]

The Official Commentary in Arabic to Article 106 of the U.A.E. Civil Code is *contra* the view expressed by Dr Habachy; it reads as follows:

> "This Article deals with abuse of right, and the jurisprudents of Islam defined this condition of old and legislated therefor, whereafter Westerners followed them as a result of development in sentiments and thinking required by social advance in the West, in that their old individual thinking which was prominent at the end of the 18th Century declined before their current thinking, which has at its aim the consideration of right as only granted to individuals in realisation of a social purpose, and thus representing a true social function (duty). Based upon such thinking, they said that if the exercise of the right deviated from its purport (*maqsud*), then that enjoined a penalty.
>
> The principle of abuse of right is not limited to rights arising from obligations, but extends to rights in rem and the ties of personal affairs and commercial law and the law of procedure; indeed, it includes also public law (or common law) in that it can be said that there is there abuse of the right of freedom or right of assembly, wherefor the legislator was free to accord to the provision relating to abuse of right a prominent place among the introductory provisions [*i.e.*, of the Code] in order that it may spread over all aspects of the Law in its various branches, not merely be applied to the principle (*fikrat*) of civil wrong constrained to personal rights: the Islamic Shari'a so laid down, describing it as a general theory and the Islamic jurisprudence designated its formulation as resembling (if not agreeing exactly and textually with) the most modern propositions in that respect of the contemporary jurisprudents of the West. Thus, the draft [*i.e.* of the Code] was intent upon taking the essence of the principles established in the Islamic jurisprudence (*fiqh*) in this field, such as 'No harm or causing of harm' – 'Harm must be put an end to' – 'Harm is not terminated by equivalent harm' – 'The

greater harm is not terminated by lesser harm' – 'To ward off ill is more worthy than to obtain benefit'.

The legislator sacrificed any general formulation such as deliberate intent and malice by reason of its obscurity and lack of precision and extrapolated from the Islamic jurisprudence and the principles laid down therein, some of them being for precepts contained in the Article, and elaboration of such percepts in this respect prepares for the Judge useful elements for guidance."

Thus, the writer of the Official Commentary was clearly of the view that not only was the principle an ancient Islamic principle, but it extended to all aspects of the exercise of a right, including real property rights.

Fortified by the opinion expressed by the writer of the Official Commentary, I take the view that the provisions of the Code on abuse of rights were intended to be of general application within the Code, and not limited to any particular area or areas. This view is perhaps supported by the fact that those provisions are contained near the beginning of the Code, in the section on Rights in the Introductory Chapter of General Provisions.

In order fully to understand the operation of the principle of abuse of rights, it is necessary to consider also the principle of good faith in contracting, which is codified in Article 246:

Article 246

1) The contract must be performed in accordance with its contents, and in a manner consistent with the requirements of good faith.
2) The contract shall not be restricted to an obligation upon the contracting party to do that which is (expressly) contained in it, but shall also embrace that which is appurtenant to it by virtue of the law, custom, and the nature of the transaction.

The principle of good faith is a general principle of law, common to virtually all civilised systems, including municipal systems, the Islamic Shari'a and International Law. It is one of the general principles of law recognised by civilised nations, hence a prescribed source of international law.[91] The close relationship between the principles of good faith and abuse of right will be apparent: good faith is in particular the foundation of the concept of abuse of rights (and, in the common law system, of estoppel). Each is a necessary consequence of good faith and fair dealing:[92]

"Such jural postulates of civilised society – to use Roscoe Pound's celebrated formula – as good faith and equity in the interpretation of legal obligations, or the prohibition of an abuse of rights are standards; they are excellent tools in the hands of international Courts and arbitration tribunals which can apply them to specific factual situations."

The principle is well-established in both national and international jurisprudence, despite differences among legal systems on matters of terminology and approach.[93]

These provisions relating to good faith, and the concomitant theory of abuse of right, however they are expressed, are general principles of law which apply overall, and which are endorsed by the Shari'a; they are now expressly codified in the Civil Code, the Commentary thereof expressly confirming that the Shari'a agrees.

Morqos[94] points out the great antiquity of the principle and that it is essentially the courts which have developed it, in advance of the legislators or the commentators. 'The right ceases where the abuse begins.[95]

The Courts have not adopted any particular theory, but have sought to meet each case on its facts and merits in arriving at a just decision:[96]

". . . the behaviour of the ordinary man in exercising his right, that behaviour to which he is authorised by general principles of law and what is imposed upon him by such principles by way of the tenets of justice and morals."

The theory developed to embrace consideration of motive in the exercise of a right. In referring to judgments which have restricted the exercise of a right where the motive therefor was not 'legitimate', 'just', 'legitimate reason', 'legitimate case', the Courts have so decided because:[97]

". . . the motive was not considered lawful unless consonant with the economic or social purpose for which the right was established.

Thus the Plaintiff who brings a case by way of stratagem, merely to punish or oppress his opponent by the procedures of litigation, is liable for all damage caused to such opponent, even those damages for which he would not be liable unless he used his right without intent to damage the same because of the right

> of recourse to justice even if one of the general rights enabled to all, is not available to he who exercises such right to deviate therefrom and use it in a vexatious manner in the desire to harm another . . ."

The principle similarly applies where the exercise of the right is to obtain an advantage out of proportion to the damage caused to another party.

Again:[98]

> **"263–the requirement to perform contracts in good faith**
> The admission that the contract is the law of the contracting parties and that all its effects have to be performed leads sometimes the contracting party to adhere to the contract and to try to go to the extreme in benefiting from it at the expense of the other contracting party by choosing in performing it the route which is most unfair to that other party. For instance, if the taxi driver, having agreed to transport the passenger to a specific destination, chooses the longest way there or intentionally takes the longest route by driving through roads needlessly in order to increase the fare; or if a contractor undertakes to connect power (lines) from one point to another on a cost-plus-fee basis, then he uses expensive materials or unnecessary materials to get rid of his stock. there is no doubt that such conduct violates the rules of ethics and justice.
>
> For this reason, the Code provided in Article 148(1) that, 'The contract has to be performed in accordance with its provisions and in a manner compatible with the requirements of good faith' (67).
>
> What is meant by the necessity of performing a contract with good faith is that it is necessary to abide by honesty and faithfulness and to seek economy and moderation in performance so that it does not become disastrous to the other contracting party. So, in the preceding instances, the contract requires the driver to take the shortest route to his destination and the contractor to select the best and most suitable materials; otherwise, he would be in breach of the *bona fide* performance of the contract and he would be accountable for that."

Footnote 67 is as follows:

> The Supreme court decided that the meaning of Articles 147 and 148 of the Civil Code is that a contract does not create a right

nor an obligation unless it is provided for therein. An obligor shall perform his obligation as provided in the contract, not more or less, unless it is a requisite of the performance. The performance of the contract in accordance with its provisions has to take place *bona fide*; and good faith is a matter of fact left to the discretion of the court which decides on the merits (Civil Supreme Court, 16 May 1977 . . .); also, to the same effect, Civil Supreme Court, 27 December 1984 in Supreme Court Appeal No. 1148, year 51.

Real securities

Book IV regulates Real securities, which are Mortgage, Pledge and Priority Rights. Article 1399 states:[99]

> "A [mortgage] is a contract whereby an obligee acquires, over real property allocated for the satisfaction of his debt, a right in rem whereby he shall take precedence over ordinary obligees and obligees subsequent in rank to him in the satisfaction of his right out of the proceeds of such land, in the possession of whomsoever it may be."

Detailed provisions governing all aspects of the formalities required for a valid mortgage, the circumstances in which a mortgage may be made, and its effects, are set out in the Articles which follow.

Pledges may be made of any property, real or personal (including fruit,[100,101] other perishable goods[102] and debts[103]), with the pledgee having possession of the property.[104] Some of the provisions of the Code regarding mortgages apply also to pledges.[105]

The concluding provisions of the Code are those dealing with priority or concessionary rights:[106]

> "A priority right is a specific right over property following (such property), conferring upon the obligee priority status in obtaining his right in accordance with his bargain and as acknowledged by law."

As with pledges, a priority right may exist in relation to all types of property, both real and personal. Many of the provisions of the Code relating to pledges apply also to priority rights.[107]

Mortgages and priority rights over real property must be registered in order to be valid, even as between the parties to the transaction.[108]

There is, consistent with their possessory nature, no registration requirement for pledges.

The Code has the advantage of being now accompanied by a massive official Commentary or 'explanatory memorandum' from which I have on occasion quoted in this article. The main value perhaps of this Commentary lies in its identifying and explaining the Shari'a sources of those articles which are Shari'a based – and they are many. The commercial lawyer must, of course, study in detail the new U.A.E. Commercial Code to which I have referred briefly in this article. The extent to which the Commercial Code, subsumed as it is by the general principles in the Civil Code, overrides the latter as a 'special law' is of course of paramount importance in commercial transactions: but that requires a separate and detailed study.

Notes

1 See the article by the author 'The States of the GCC: sources of Law' in (1985) 1 ALQ 3; and at pp. 58 et seq. in this volume.

2 Union Law No. 5/1985 issuing the Code of Civil Transaction for The United Arab Emirates, Gazette 158, December 1985. The Law was dated 15 December 1985 to come into force *three months after its publication*. In the absence of a precise publication date, it must be presumed that the Law came into effect at the latest, at the end of March 1986. The Code will be referred to in this article simply as 'The Civil Code'.

3 I use the words here in the French sense of court practice rather than the English sense.

4 See generally the article in 1 ALQ above cited: *ibid.* at p. 109; Ballantyne, *Legal Development in Arabia*, 1980, foreword by Professor Sir Norma Anderson at p. viii; and at pp. 109 *et seq.*; 121.

5 For a detailed account see Ballantyne, *Commercial Law in the Arab Middle East: The Gulf States*, Lloyd's of London Press, 1986.

6 The Majellat Al Ahkam Al'Adiya issued in 1295 AH: see the excellent translation by Judge C A Hooper, *Civil Law of Palestine and Transjordan*, Vol. 1, Sweet & Maxwell, 1938.

7 Ballantyne *Legal Development in Arabia, op. cit*, p. 121.

8 Ballantyne, *op cit.*, p. 109.

9 Ballantyne, *Commercial Law in the Arab Middle East: The Gulf States*, Lloyd's of London Press Ltd., 1986, pp. 48 *et seq.*

10 Ballantyne, *Commercial Law, op. cit.*, at pp. 82, 107.

11 See the article by Mohammad Farouk Al Nabhaan in *El Araby* magazine, No. 299, October 1983 (Arabic).

12 The article by Al Nabhaan in *El Araby* quoted above.

13 The Kuwait Civil Code has, however, a contemporaneous Commercial Code which dilutes many of the strict *Shari'a* principles in matters of commerce.

14 Which, unfortunately, the author does not have to hand at the time of writing, and is thus unable to give a reference.

15 e.g., Schacht, *Introduction to Islamic Law*, Oxford, 1964; Coulson, *Commercial Law in the Gulf States: The Islamic Legal Tradition*, Graham & Trotman, 1984. In general, Schacht's translation of the various forms of contract has been used for the sake of uniformity and reference; there are no standard translations of these terms.

16 Enabling Law 5/1985, as amended by Law I/1987.

17 Law 18/1993 dated 7 September 1993; Gazette 255.

18 Mustafa Kemal Taha, 'Commercial Law', Alexandria, 1962, at page 5 (Arabic).

19 Dr Ali Barudy, 'The Commercial Code', Alexandria, pages 5 and 6 (Arabic); see also *ibid.* at page 35.

For a modern authority on commercial law, see Dr Mahmood Sharqawi, 'Commercial Law', 1986 (Arabic). Dr Sharqawi, in dealing with the overall effect of the Civil Code, states (page 6 *in fine*, paragraph 5):

'The Commercial Code in accordance with traditional division of the branches of law is considered to be one of the branches of private law at the head of which is the Civil Code which is considered the general law for transactions.

We have seen that the traditional view of the Commercial Law is that it is a collection of exceptional principles engrafted upon the provisions of the Civil Law: the existence of such exceptional principles engendered the nature of the creation of the Commercial Law (as a law of merchants, as we have seen *supra*), and the majority of jurisprudents justify the independence of the Commercial Law having regard to its special nature in the commercial environment.

But having regard to the firm link between the Commercial Code and the Civil Code, many commentators have called for their unification and inclusion in one compilation.'

The learned author goes on to discuss in detail the essential link between the two Codes. The two Codes were in fact united in Kuwait in 1961, by Sanhouri; the experiment was not a success, and they were later separated (1981).

20 Ali Al Barudy, *op. cit.*, at page 16.

21 Dubai Cassation Case 230/1990. See also Dubai Cassation Case 323/1991. The Dubai Courts have not yet opted into the Union court system; they are however, under the Constitution, bound to apply Union laws.

22 See Ballantyen, *Commercial Law, op cit.*, pp. 157 *et seq.* and Kuwaiti Law 5/1961 regulating legal relations containing a foreign element.

23 See Ballantyne *op. cit.*, for the distinction. It may be submitted that in the U.A.E. jurisdiction, in view of the directive as to legal schools to be preferred, the view of Ibn Taimiyya should consequently be preferred, i.e., that a provisoin is acceptable unless it be expressly forbidden by the *Shari'a*.

24 Hanafi is the school upon which the Ottoman *Majella* was based.

25 See Ballantyne, *op. cit.*, at p. 160, fn. 4; see *Boys* v *Chaplin* [1971] AC 356 (HL): Hoyle, *Private International Law Cases and Materials*, Laureate Press, London, 1982, at p. 250.
26 Hooper translation, *op. cit.*: *Majella*, Articles 1 to 100 inclusive.
27 It need hardly be stressed that this is not the same as the Anglo/Saxon 'domicile': in the latter context, '*mawtan*' would be better translated here 'ordinary residence'.
28 These principles, and their relationship, are considered in more detail at pp. 162, *infra*.
29 But, as to the principle of good faith and abuse of rights see further *infra* at p. 162 *et seq*.
30 Gutteridge, *Comparative Law*, Cambridge, 1949, at p. 34.
31 Article 125.
32 Article 126d.
33 As to the system of nominate contracts in the *Shari'a*, see Coulson *op. cit.* at pp. 18 *et seq*.
34 See Coulson, *op. cit.*, at pp. 58 *et seq*.
35 Coulson, *op. cit.*
36 Articles 138 to 148.
37 C.f. Ballantyne, *Commercial Law, op. cit.* at pp. 125 *et seq*.
38 Article 208.
39 For a general description of these *Shari'a* options see Coulson, *op. cit.*, Chapter 5 'Voidable Contracts at pp. 56 *et seq*., and see Rayner, *op. cit.* 93 *et seq*.
40 Articles 290–291.
41 See, for example, the provisions on limitation with regard to unjust enrichment (the making of restitution for beneficial acts): Article 336, *infra*.
42 Articles 300 to 303.
43 Articles 304 to 312.
44 Articles 313 to 317.
45 See further Zweigert and Kötz, An Introduction to Comparative Law, 2nd edition, 1987, at pp. 91 to 95.
46 Article 313.
47 Article 320: *répétition de l'indu*.
48 Article 325.
49 Articles 333 to 335.
50 Articles 1371 to 1381 on 'Quasi-contracts', more often referred to as 'enrichissement sans cause'.
51 Tr. Weir, in Zweigert and Kötz, *op. cit.*, page 578.
52 Article 62.
53 Article 336.
54 Tr. Whelan and Hall.
55 Articles 338 to 419.
56 Tr. Whelan and Hall.
57 Article 450.
58 Article 452.
59 Proceedings, Vol. V, Goldman at page 17. The Proceedings, including the legal Opinions, have been filed in leading law libraries, including Cambridge, Oxford and Harvard, and are available to genuine researchers.

60 At page 23.
61 Proceedings, Vol. IV.
62 Since Morqos and Habachy filed the Opinion, the position has changed: in 1980, the 1961 Commercial Code was replaced by a Civil Code and a Commercial Code, and the Majella was repealed.
63 'Commercial Law in the Gulf States', London, 1984, page 19.
64 For Commercial Companies in the U.A.E., however, see Law 8/1984 referred to *supra* at page 146.
65 Tr. Whelan and Hall.
66 Article 655: with regard to *commercial* companies however, see Law 8/1984.
67 Articles 722 to 741.
68 Tr. Whelan and Hall.
69 Tr. Whelan and Hall.
70 Al Sanhoury, 'Al Waseet', Vol. VII, pages 21 and 45, Arabic.
71 See pp. 148, *supra*.
72 As to which see, generally, Saleh, 'Commercial Agency and Distributorship in the Arab Middle East – a Study in Shari'a and Statute Law' (1989) Vol. I, Chapter 6.
73 Article 932.
74 *Ibid.*
75 Article 966.
76 Article 967.
77 Article 1021.
78 Tr. Whelan and Hall.
79 Article 1031.
80 Tr. Whelan and Hall.
81 Article 1036.
82 Article 1056.
83 Article 1106; tr. Whelan and Hall.
84 Article 1109.
85 Articles 1077 to 1132.
86 Article 1133 (1).
87 Codified in Articles 104 and 106 of the Civil Code of the U.A.E., which are set out in full *infra*, together with Article 246 which codifies the principle of good faith in contracting. The link between this principle and the principle of abuse of right is explored *infra*.
88 Tr Whelan and Hall. Provisions equivalent to Articles 104, 106 and 246 (as to which *vide infra*) are to be found in the codes of Egypt (Articles 4, 6 and 148), Syria (Article 149(2)), Libya (Article 148(2)), Iraq (Article 150(2)), Lebanon (Articles 370 and 371) and Jordan (Article 202): Sanhouri, 'Al Waseet,' 1981 edition, p. 835 and n. 1. Among the Western codes, examples of provisions to broadly similar effect may be found in Articles 1134(3) and 1135 of the French Civil Code (good faith in contracting), Articles 157 and 242 of the German Civil Code (the 'BGB'), and Article 2(2) of the Swiss Civil Code, which provides that: '[l]'abus manifeste d'un droit n'est pas protégé par la loi'. While the French Civil Code does not contain an express provision regarding the principle of abuse of right, its existence, and its application in all fields, is beyond question: see, for example, David,

'English Law and French Law', 1980, at page 154. While there are no equivalent provisions in the common law systems, it will be readily apparent to a common lawyer that the expression and particular theory of estoppel, may be bracketed with the basic theory described in these Articles, and that similar results will often be arrived at by a different route, *viz.*, the implication of terms into the contract.

89 In his influential article, 'Property, Right and Contract in Muslim Law', (1962) 62 Columbia Law Review 450, at pages 455 to 456.

90 Article 38, Statute I.C.J.: for a thorough survey see Bin Cheng, 'General Principles of Law', 1953 at page 141 *et seq.*

91 Friedmann, 'The Changing Structure of International Law', 1964, page 199; see also Lauterpacht, 'The Function of Law in the International Community', pages 286 to 306; The Free Zone Case, P.C.I.J., Series A, no. 24 at page 12 (1930).

92 Lauterpacht, *op. cit.*

93 Al Wafi-II-2, Cairo, 1988, at page 324 *et seq.* (Arabic).

94 *Ibid.* at page 338.

95 *Ibid.* at pages 342 and 369.

96 *Ibid.* at pages 349 and at pages 369 *et seq.*

97 *Ibid.* at page 371.

98 *Ibid.*

99 Tr Whelan and Hall. I prefer the term 'mortgage' to Whelan and Hall's 'pledge by way of security'.

100 Article 1450.

101 Article 1451.

102 Articles 1491 *et seq.*

103 Article 1448; see also Article 1453 *et seq.*

104 See, for example, Articles 1459 and 1460.

105 Tr Whelan and Hall.

106 See Articles 1508 to 1510.

107 Mortgages: Article 1400; priority rights: Articles 1508 and 1528 *et seq.*

X

Islamic Law and Financial Transactions in Contemporary Perspective

I would like to refer briefly to the subject-matter of the papers in order to establish in advance the structure and context of the conference.* The first paper is 'Financial Transactions and the Islamic Theory of Obligations and Contracts', by Nabil Salih.

Now, nobody who has read or heard anything which I have uttered over the past few years will be in any doubt of my strong views as to the practical importance of an understanding of the *Shari'a* law at the present time in the context of the undoubted reassertion of Islam, and thus the Shari'a, which we are witnessing. I do not believe that anybody who knows the Arab world will doubt this: I do not have time to go into the justifications for this belief; I deal with the subject at some length in the Coulson Memorial Lecture, which I delivered here a couple of weeks ago. However, commercial law overall is really basically a matter of contract, and an understanding of the legal background is of increasing and vital importance. Thus this paper of Nabil's is itself of great importance. Nabil will forgive me for quoting a phrase which you will hear from him in the course of his paper: 'inevitable clash or mutual tolerance'. And he links this with a warning to those who may tend to view the possible collapse of Islamic banking with eagerness: as I say, I hope I may be forgiven for anticipating this, because it is a subject so close to my own heart. I am not of course summing up this conference, and, as there may be no further chance for me to do so, I would like directly to identify myself with the sentiments which he will express. An earnest plea must be made for an attempt to co-ordinate the two systems of Islam and the West. Once again, time simply does not permit me to analyze how this might be done – I have tried to do so in previous papers, but it does seem to me that the least that is required is:

1 An international Arab Code of the Shari'a – a new *Majalla*? – to remove the uncertainty surrounding the true, immutable precepts of the Shari'a in basic *Nusus*, so that at least we can all know where we are; and so that above all we can ascertain where there exists in the Shari'a sufficient flexibility to make it adaptable to modern economic circumstances; and at the same time:
2 Flexibility on the part of the occidental systems of law and finance in considering how far the Islamic concepts really do constitute anathema, in so far as their interests are concerned. If I may, I will come on to this later.

It is not surprising that, given the title of this conference, the main preoccupation should be with Islamic banking, although the title could take the matter further than that. Thus Munir Murad's paper on taxation, with its learned analyses, is very welcome. It is, of course, easy for a lawyer who has spent the whole of his professional life practising in and with the Arab world to become obsessed solely with the Arab jurisdictions. In assessing the importance of our subject today, we must not forget that there are between 700 and 1,000 million Muslims, encompassing a vast area of the world. This is in part evidenced at our conference here today by the fact that Jane Connors will speak on the system in Malaysia, Abbas Mirakhor on Iran and Pakistan, and David Baldwin and Rodney Wilson make special reference to Turkey. Finally, Volker Nienhaus, in dealing with the comparative performance of Islamic banks, makes specific reference to several jurisdictions, and – and I found this extremely interesting and significant – points up the importance of the agricultural sector and the tendency to neglect the rural areas. I would hope that this aspect might be a particular subject for discussion.

That brings me finally to Chibli Mallat's paper on *riba* – the great debate on riba. This points out, as always in studying this eternal subject, that the key element is *doubt*. There is still not even unanimity on what riba really means, on a proper definition, on the extent of its application. It is while such doubts remain that there can be no constancy in financial negotiations where there is any question of the Shari'a law being applicable. This doubt, of course, extends beyond riba to the concept of *gharar*, and into the third hobgoblin highlighted by Al-Sanhouri, the ban on multiplicity of transactions, etc, etc. It is for these considerations that in my opinion a unified codification of

Shari'a principles is of the utmost urgency, wherein those precepts of the Shari'a which are by common consent deemed to be immutable, that is to say as stemming from the Qur'an or the Sunna, from the Qur'an itself or from the traditions of the Prophet – wherein such precepts can be defined by common consent between the Islamic jurisdictions – an international convention to that effect. The Learned Academy of Islamic Jurisprudence is presumably engaged in some such exercise, but since its formation little has emerged. On the other side, as I have said, Western lawyers and economists should be urgently considering the extent to which flexibility exists in the Western system, whereby the two systems, Western and Islamic, may be brought closer together. May I briefly try to point out the importance and practical application of these difficulties by stating three propositions:

1 that in a jurisdiction where the Shari'a applies, contracts not in accordance with its precepts are quite simply illegal: in our present context, banking transactions based upon the conventional Western system of interest;
2 that in Muslim eyes, not only is a system of economics which is not based on Shari'a principles anti-religious, illegal, and sinful, but that in the world today, the Islamic system is better;
3 that, as I have said, the alternative to some co-operation is a clash, a confrontation.

I The Basic Illegality

Let me take a topical example – I always find that practical examples point the thing out better than theory – a syndicated loan agreement. You are all familiar with these – let us suppose several liability in a syndicate of banks for a period loan to an Arab State, probably with guarantees via ECGD, COFAS, EXIM, as the case may be. Interest is defined by a rate above an inter-bank rate, and in case of default there is interest upon interest. Let us suppose that in our example, it is a sterling loan, with payments to be made in London, and that there is a proper law clause which defines English law as the proper law of the agreement; and there is a jurisdiction clause giving non-exclusive jurisdiction to the English courts, but vesting jurisdiction also in the courts of the borrowing State and indeed any other courts which may properly have jurisdiction according to their own laws. There is usually also, in the case of the State, express waiver of sovereign immunity.

Now, as you all know, such agreements invariably contain a number of conditions precedent, not the least of them being the necessity for the opinion of a lawyer qualified in the law of the borrowing State to the effect that the agreement is legal according to the law of that State. Why is this necessary in view of the choice of law clause and the jurisdiction clause? There are, of course, a number of reasons, but not the least are that it may be necessary to sue upon the contract in the courts of the borrowing State, either directly or by way of enforcing a foreign judgment obtained on the contract, and it is also not inconceivable that an English court or other appropriate foreign forum may, despite the choice of law clause in the contract, take cognizance of public policy provisions in the law of the borrowing State. Thus an expert or 'clearing' opinion is sought. The lawyer giving such opinion must of course be fully cognizant of the Laws of the borrowing State, but where it is an Islamic State, the first question he must ask himself is, does the Shari'a have any application? In dealing with the Arab States, as I am accustomed to do, the answer to this depends upon the jurisdiction: to take examples at one end of the scale, in Kuwait and Bahrain (since its new Commercial Code of 1987) the answer would be 'no', but with a caveat that interest rates are pegged by the Central Banks. At the other end of the Scale, Saudi Arabia, the answer would be 'yes', the Shari'a is most certainly relevant, and the whole contract is illegal. In various other jurisdictions, there are varying shades. Whether such contract would in any case be denied as being illegal in present circumstances is another matter; what the lawyer has to advise is on the position of that contract at law. If, despite such caveats as may have to be entered, the bankers take, nonetheless, a commercial risk (and this has happened in many cases), that is entirely another matter. Hardly satisfactory! It is one thing where a State is obliged from a position of weakness to reschedule or renegotiate its loans; it is entirely another where that State has a valid legal or constitutional argument on which to base its renegotiation.

In the simplest terms, the Shari'a forbids interest on monies. Western economies are structured upon it. With the onset of oil wealth, the Arab world has entered the Western system, and in the majority of cases the conflict has simply not been allowed to arise. However, for a lawyer this is hardly satisfactory when he has to advise his clients on the possible legal risks involved in such a transaction as we have been considering. As to the generality of the prohibition of interest qua riba, we may refer to that great Hanbali jurist, Ibn Al-Qayyim, who, following Shafi'i's view, writes in *I'lam al-Muwaqqi'in*,

> "Dirhams and dinars are the prices of articles sold, and the price is the standard by which the evaluation of property is recognized. It must therefore be fixed and regulated so that it does not go up and down, since were the price to go up or down like commodities we would not have a price with which to value the articles sold. Indeed, everything is commodity, and the people's need for a price by which to value articles sold is a general and compelling one. Such valuing is not possible, save on the basis of which things are assessed, which continues upon one state of affairs, and which is not itself assessed by reference to anything else. If it becomes a commodity which goes up and down, then the transactions of people will be impaired . . ."

II

The second, and no doubt controversial, issue to which I direct your attention for discussion, is the extent not only to which the Arabs may now be largely committed to a system of Islamic financing, but the extent to which they may be justified in regarding this system as better than the conventional Western system. May I quote from what I said at the Coulson Memorial Lecture:

> "Do the Arab States really wish, would they even be advised, to tamper with the existing concepts of riba at the present time? When they look at the world banking system, which is based essentially upon interest, and which may seem to them at times to be tottering on its base; when they see the most powerful nations in debt rather than in credit – may this not provide, apart from basic beliefs which exist anyway, a powerful argument that what the Prophet uttered so long ago was entirely right, and that the principle of profit-sharing and partnership is better not only from the religious point of view but in practice? Is Islamic banking not true merchant banking? Why then, they may say, erode the principles of riba as they exist, when it may be contended that they provide the only solution to impending chaos? I am not saying that I subscribe to such an extreme view – I am simply not sufficient of an economist – but it is a solemn thought. I hope that some of these issues will be discussed at our conference on Islamic finance which takes place here on 15th April."

Well, I hope indeed that we may discuss this aspect seriatim. In order to give further background for such a discussion, I would like to refer very briefly to the main incidents in the economic history of the Gulf States, since they provide, after all, the prime example of the sudden onset of vast wealth, and the necessity for its absorption in to the world economic scene. Those who heard my Coulson Lecture will forgive my repetition of basic facts in the first part of what now follows.

When I first went to the Gulf in 1948, it was common form for the oil concessions of the time to provide for a fixed royalty on the oil produced by the oil companies of 3 rupees 8 annas per ton! The rupee was then valued at 1s. 6d., and a ton of oil is seven barrels. Even these munificent terms were of largely academic interest over much of the area because virtually no oil was being produced, because it did not suit the international oil cartel to fit it into the existing international marketing pattern. When I advised on the first 50/50 sharing agreement in Bahrain in 1952, the 50% tax payable to the Ruler of Bahrain was calculated upon an inter-company price of $1.40 per barrel (the posted price at that time of comparable crude was, as far as I recall, $1.75). The average annual rent for a concession was 100,000 rupees, or £7,500. These undoubted exploitations of the early years were, of course, gradually redressed by the increasing power of OPEC and the demands of that organization, together with the increasing demands for energy, until in the latter 1970s the spot price for a barrel of oil in the Gulf reached $41–$42, of which the OPEC countries were taking the major share. This led, of course, to astronomical increases in income. The current scene reveals an average price of $15 per barrel, and it has been lower. As we know, in all the producing countries there have been drastic cut-backs, and recently Saudi Arabia went to the length of restoring personal income tax, not to control inflation or for any other like economic reason, but because the income was needed. This measure was almost immediately withdrawn, but it tells its own story.

Against this background, the Arabs, looking at the contemporary scene, and having subscribed to the Western economic system in large measure, may perhaps be forgiven for wondering where on earth they have got to!

The *Observer* Business Section only last Sunday, 3rd April, contained a heading 'The U.S. Bank Bust'. 'Some 184 American banks failed last year, the largest number in a single year since the Great Depression. In the first three months of this year, another 44 have gone under. In 1987, America's 200 largest banks suffered a combined deficit of $21 billion, while the top 25 lost more than $7.2 billion. The major cause related to the necessity to raise provisions against Third World debt'.

If I may quote further from the World Debt Crisis and Its Resolution, a recent publication by the United States Department of Agriculture:

> "Debt rescheduling has become increasingly common since 1982. Such a move, however, only superficially improves the immediate payment structure. The long term effect of rescheduling will probably be to make the total cost of the debt even more expensive, and to make overcoming the debt problem even more difficult. Developed countries and their lending institutions may find that the benefits of forgiving some portion of the debts outweigh the costs that will result. Forgiving some of the indebtedness of the developing countries may stimulate the world marketplace, leading to mutually beneficial trade among nations."

The report to which I have just referred indicates the commencement of the debt crisis as beginning ostensibly with the international debt repayment problems of Poland in 1981, followed by those of Mexico, Brazil and Argentina in 1982. The report accentuates the circular effect of the various forces which go to make up the problem into which we do not have time to go here, except perhaps in discussions afterwards. Briefly, for our present purposes, we might sum up the progression as follows:

1 Rapid growth in development in the 1960s and early 70s, when credit was readily available and inexpensive.
2 Excessive demand for resources, notably petroleum, resulting in a virtual monopoly position for OPEC.
3 Fourfold increase in petroleum prices initiated by OPEC in 1973–74.
4 A resulting vast liquidity in the OPEC countries recycled by international bankers in the form of 'petrodollar' deposits by a massive lending program to developing countries. To quote from the report, 'these bankers anticipated high returns on investments, and assumed that a country guarantee was adequate provision against repayment defaults. The bankers did not ask if the funds were being invested in such a way that a stream of foreign exchange earnings would be forthcoming to repay the loan'.

Pausing there for a moment, might not an Arab banker say that the attitude of the international banks would have been far different if Islamic principles had been adhered to, and if the banks themselves had had equity interests in the projects in which these vast amounts of money were to be invested? Would such a contention be a valid one? Personally I would very much like to hear a discussion on this from the floor.

Well, as we all know, the 1973–74 oil price rise set the stage for the large debt accumulation, and then there came the second oil shock of 1979–80. This was too much, and the major industrial countries restricted available credit.

It must be salutary surely to reflect that the guarantee of a sovereign State to pay a debt, regarded historically as sacrosanct, rapidly loses that status in circumstances where the State simply cannot repay. It would appear that of the 25 countries rescheduling between 1981 and 1985, only two, Morocco and Sudan, were Arab States, and of these only one, the Sudan, may be regarded as having essentially an Islamic regime. It is, however, sobering to reflect that in many Arab Islamic jurisdictions, should difficulties arise, there might be a legal, even constitutional, argument at the Shari'a with which to bolster up renegotiation or rescheduling.

III

I must end my scene setting exercise because I shall run out of time and you all want to get on with the business of the meeting. However, may I just refer briefly to my third proposition, which is in effect – can anything be done by cooperation between the two ideologies to regularize all this? Because I believe that with the undoubted reassertion of Islam and the Shari'a which is upon us, the alternative is a clash. I gave my views on this situation at the Coulson Lecture two weeks go, and as those views have not changed since then, perhaps I may restate them here.

> "What, if anything, can be done by the Western lawyer, other than to sit back and wait for an inevitable crash application of the Shari'a? First of all, realize the existence of the problem, and problem it is! Secondly, Western lawyers must show a great sympathy and understanding for this powerful religious and cultural background, and we have to devise where necessary (not as yet in all jurisdictions) our bridges – if indeed these can be

> built. There are many ifs. The Shari'a is a sacred subject, and apart from understanding on the Western side, any dialogue must require the cooperation of the Muslim side in what in many quarters is regarded as a forbidden subject. Certainly, let us never underestimate the importance of this subject at this time – a classical and rigid application of the Shari'a to modern economic agreements could be catastrophic, and it is sobering to reflect that this could occur in most of the Arab jurisdictions with no need for prior legislation. Let it not be thought either that such application is relevant only within a Muslim jurisdiction – what of the situation in a Western court directed by its conflict rules to apply to a contract the Shari'a law, proved by expert evidence to be the law applicable as the proper law of contract? Also, what of the enforcement of foreign judgments in the Muslim jurisdictions? These are grave matters."

Perhaps what is required in today's climate is not just a restructuring of the Shari'a to fit Western economic concepts, but some restructuring of those concepts in order to meet the Shari'a: a study of just how far Western and Shari'a concepts are incompatible in the light of a new ijtihad. In so far as dialogue is possible, let us pursue it. The need for it is the reason that I insisted upon 'The Shari'a in Transnational Transactions' as the leading subject of the first conference of the International Bar Association to be held in an Arab country – Cairo, February 1987. The Arab Regional Committee of the IBA formed as a result of the outstanding success of the conference (of which I have the honour to be the first chairman) will, I hope, provide an opportunity for such dialogue. Another hopeful initiative with which I am concerned is that of the Euro-Arab Chambers of Commerce in the field of arbitration. We must take the opportunity for discussion while wise and moderate men are available to participate in it. Really, this can be done by lawyers, and, in the final analysis Muslim lawyers at that – such is the difficulty where the law is identified with religion. The political implications are, of course, obvious; but for the issue to become an international political issue, or to be overtly treated as such, is, I hope, unthinkable – to say that that would be counterproductive is to understate the obvious. We are too apt to write learned memoranda based upon the material pros and cons of a situation. Our Arab friends can be supreme materialists; but also supreme romantic idealists, and, of course, religionists. Despite the obvious difficulties, I am optimistic enough to believe that something may be achieved.

XI

Back to the Shari'a?

There was, of course, only one person who could possibly have been asked to give the first Coulson Memorial Lecture, and that was Sir Norman Anderson. There must have been several possible choices for the second, and I am very honoured that the choice has fallen upon me; but pity me – Sir Norman is really an impossible act to follow. The next hour could well be spent defending myself against the very kind things he has said about me rather than trying to live up to them! Not only do I have to follow him now, I also have to follow his lecture of last year, the erudition of which I simply cannot emulate.

II In his lecture last year, Sir Norman, in paying tribute to Noel Coulson, gave us a short history of the early years of SOAS, and in particular his association with Noel, which dated from 1954. Noel had clearly been a brilliant scholar (double First in Classical Mods. and Oriental Languages at Oxford), and that association had been a very close one. I myself first had experience of it when, in the late 1950s or early 60s, I think it was, I was advising on the international legal status of the Kuwait/Saudi Arab Neutral Zone, and, not surprisingly, I advised my clients that they should get a first-class Opinion on that status at the Sharī'a. This brought me into contact with Sir Norman, I believe, for the first time, and certainly for the first time with Noel Coulson. Thereafter, I met Noel at only rare intervals – as I shall explain in a moment, my own career has been very far from academia and essentially that of a practising lawyer in Arabia – until in 1983 he asked me to devise and deliver a series of lectures in Arab comparative commercial law based as far as possible on my practical experience in the region. That course has this year been re-devised and expanded, and will, I hope, serve as another memorial to Noel as its originator.

Thus, I knew Noel only in the last few years of his life. Like so many of us, I feel as a result deprived. Above all, perhaps, do I feel deprived in never having heard Noel teach, though he was, by common acclaim, a brilliant teacher. I continue to benefit, however, from his writings. In the written word, few have been gifted with a greater art of simplification and lucidity.

III It is always with temerity that the practising lawyer ventures to stand up and speak in the halls of academia. Prior to my present and recent essay into the academic world, I had had hardly any contact with it since my very brief experience at Cambridge in 1940 and 1946. In this context, may I make a general remark: there has been far too little contact in my opinion between the practitioners of this country and the academics. I believe that that position is now ameliorating, but there is a stark contrast with the position on the Continent, where, in any major case, in my experience, the first step is to nobble all the professors in sight before the other side gets them! Perhaps we, in this country, do not need to go that far.

Thus, it is essentially as a commercial lawyer with 40 years practice exclusively in and with the Arab world that I address you this evening. I want, if I may, to stress this, because I shall be referring to some of my early experiences and recollections, not merely as anecdotal, but as giving emphasis to that vast economic and social explosion which has occurred in the Arab world during my period of experience. I count myself indeed very fortunate to have lived through this fascinating period. I count myself doubly fortunate to have been able to absorb a little of the Arab language and culture (I stress *little* without any false humility) in order to enable me to reach perhaps just the periphery of Arab thinking. I stress these aspects, because in my opinion it is the very speed of development which, particularly in the context of law, now causes the Arab to consider seriously whether in the field of legal development he has not gone too far too fast: and that brings me directly to the title of this lecture.

IV My title comes in fact from Sir Norman's lecture of last year. That lecture gave what was for me an absorbing historical survey of the history of Islamic law as constituting the background to 'Islamic Fundamentalism'. I want to try to carry the torch forward from where he laid it. In order to do that, I would like to quote briefly from the concluding passages of his lecture. He asked the question: 'Is this picture of the Muslim world that I have been etching still valid today, in 1987?' The answer is I believe 'yes' – in most of that world. But the situation has changed to some extent in those countries which have espoused 'Islamic fundamentalism' – Iran, Pakistan, the Sudan and (in its own way) Libya, for example (while even Egypt and Turkey are under some degree of political challenge). For the fact is that Islamic fundamentalism is virtually epitomized in the demand 'Back to the Sharī'a!'

V Hence my title, but it will be noted that I have carefully placed after the quotation a question mark: is it to be back to the Sharī'a, and if so, what does that entail? We shall come to that in a moment; but first two more quotes:

First a quotation from a book which I wrote in 1980, and to which Sir Norman was kind enough to write a forward:

> "In confronting any legal problem, perhaps the first question to be asked is: 'To what extent, if at all, does the Sharī'a affect the matter?' The answer may vary from, 'not at all' in a problem falling within the Commercial Code of Kuwait, to 'basically' in a problem in Saudi Arabia, while in the other jurisdictions, the answer may be somewhere between these two extremes. Overall, we must record and always bear in mind the *uncertainty* engendered by the looming presence of the Sharī'a, which should be one of the factors to be borne in mind in weighing the benefits and risks of any commercial contract . . ."

As my last quote from last year's lecture (Sir Norman, in summing up):

> "Finally, we noted the contemporary emergence of Islamic fundamentalism, which seems to me to be a two-sided phenomenon: on the one hand a very understandable revolt against the dominance and (until recently) the colonialism of Western powers; on the other hand, a reaction against what might be termed the Western philosophy of life, which, although basically founded upon Christian faith and ethics, has become so engulfed in liberalism and agnosticism, that it has largely lost both its cutting edge and its persuasive power."

Well, as to Christianity, alas! Not so, however, with Islam, which has lost neither its cutting edge nor its persuasive power; and in talking of a reassertion or restatement of Islam, we are automatically talking of a reassertion or restatement of the Sharī'a. Thus the essence of our subject is: 1) is it to be back to the Sharī'a? 2) what would be the effect? To anticipate, my answers to these questions would be: 1) Yes, inevitably, in greater or lesser degree; 2) The effect depends on the degree. To some extent, order could be established by a joint effort not only by the Islamic nations to define and thereby remove the uncertainty from the Sharī'a: but also, there is required an effort by the Western lawyers to endeavour to join in such initiative, not only in the legislative field, but more importantly and practically in the economic field. Strangely, there are already signs that this latter may be happening, although brought about by economic forces, not by any volition engendered by the considerations to which I am referring in this lecture – not by reason of a wish to follow the Sharī'a! Although not acknowledged as such, the principles of Islamic banking, for example, appear to have been recently recommended by the IMF! Equity sharing over loans!

But if any of this is to come about, then the West must stop dismissing the Sharī'a as something unknown, to be feared, and thus resisted: while the Arabs must stop regarding the Sharī'a as a holy subject, with any incursion by the West resented. In that way only could a way perhaps be found of reconciling two systems which appear, at first assessment, to be wholly irreconcilable. There are, alas, few signs at the present time that even the Arabs themselves are obtaining cohesion in this respect.

VI Now of course Al-Islam today embraces a vast area of the world, and there are perhaps between 700 and 1000 million Muslims. The limitations of my personal knowledge restrict me to the Arab countries: this is, after all, sufficient for one brief – 18 jurisdictions, with the application of the Sharī'a ranging in severity from its paramountcy as the sole source of legislation (Saudi Arabia), to those countries with written Constitutions which prescribe it as *a* or *the* principal source of legislation. Within the constitutional framework, the degree of application of the Sharī'a in each jurisdiction varies, and, as I constantly point out, it is always the first duty of the practising lawyer to ascertain to what extent if at all the Sharī'a applies in the jurisdiction with which he is immediately concerned .

VII Now, I think that the best way to describe what is happening in the Arab world today, is by the phrase 'a reassertion of Al-Islam'. I was indebted for the word 'reassertion' to an article in *The Daily Telegraph* some years ago, and I think it is exactly the right word. In particular is it the right word in the context of what we are considering this evening. With a reassertion of Al-Islam, there is a corresponding reassertion of the Sharī'a – you cannot separate the one from the other. To me, reassertion conjures up a gentler picture in the first instance than fundamentalism. Fundamentalism is defined in the *Oxford English Dictionary* as 'strict adherence to traditional orthodox tenets (e.g. the literal inerrancy of Scripture) held to be fundamental to the Christian faith: opposed to liberalism and modernism'. When used in its proper sense that does not sound too extreme: but in the sense of current affairs today, this has come to mean, in common parlance, something much more violent, and in talking of a reassertion of the Sharī'a, I do not want to envisage any violent concept at the present time. If things go to an extreme, as alas they often do, then it may be another matter; but at the moment, sane, thinking, moderate men in the Arab world are seriously considering whether in adopting Western laws, they did not move too far too fast, and indeed make a basic mistake. Thus, we are not here talking of such extreme examples of so-called Islamic expression as the ghastly tragedy of the Iran-Iraqi war – the ideologically inconceivable picture not just of Muslim against Muslim, but Shi'a against Shi'a, with children going to their deaths in the promise and belief of glory in the 'aakhira' – the hereafter. No, we are not at the moment considering extremism over the whole scene, but, and I stress this, we may well be considering such extremism overall in a relatively short time if the moderate voices are not heeded and if something is not done to put the house in order. It is certainly true to say that throughout the Arab world 'fundamentalism' in accordance with the definition I have just given is on the dramatic increase.

We, in this country, consider the Christmas story repeatedly once a year. I think it is salutary here to consider very briefly the origins of Al-Islam. It is a very different story. Its relevance lies in the fact that its impact is the same today among Muslims as it was then over 13 centuries ago.

VIII Let us then recall that in the early 7th century of our era, the Prophet Muhammad, in the fortieth year of his life, fairly prosperous but otherwise an undistinguished member of the Quraish, began to dream dreams and see visions. One night in the month of Ramadhan, an angel appeared to him and said '*Iqra*' – read'. He answered, 'I am no reader – *ma ana bi qaari*'. Then, we are told, the angel seized him with a strong grasp, saying, 'Read', and as Muhammad still refused to obey, gripped him once more and spoke as follows: 'Read in the name of the Lord who created man of blood coagulated: read. Thy Lord is the most beneficent who taught by the pen, taught that which they knew not unto men'.* Well, the Prophet was obviously deeply troubled and at one time, we are told, thought that he was possessed

* In the lecture the original Arabic was quoted.

by a *jinn*. However, his wife, Khadija, comforted and reassured him, and eventually he became convinced that he had been called to prophesy and, indeed, after an interval of time, the angel appeared to him again and commanded him to prophesy. Thereafter began the series of revelations of the greatest beauty and power which are recorded in the *Qur'an*: 'By the morning, and by the night when it is still, thy Lord has not forsaken thee, nor is displeased: verily, the hereafter shall be better for thee than this.'*

I find it, of course, difficult to describe the force of the sound of the Qur'anic revelations – and sound is the essence, for these were messages not just to be read but to be proclaimed from the rooftops. Reactions to such forces are essentially personal, and as a confessed romantic, may I draw personal analogies. When I read of Sir Belvedere brandishing Excalibur and hurling it into the lake where it was grasped by an arm clad in white samite – mystic, wonderful – then I must confess that I am there, such is the power of authorship and imagination. However, to move up the scale a little, if I listen to a late quartet of Beethoven's, one of the mystic ones, then I become convinced that a higher power is reaching out through the genius of the man. How much more are these powers operative when one moves on to the plane of religion. Suffice it to say that for me and even my elementary knowledge of Arabic language, the revelations of the *Qur'an*, and in particular the early revelations, seem to be divinely inspired.

Well, the impact upon the Quraish tribe at that time must have been like a thunderclap. This new religious message of monotheism received in their own virile and rich language – the language which constituted virtually their only art form *per se*, and brought to what they no doubt had hitherto regarded as its highest form by their own poets – yet here was a merchant suddenly revealing messages from God of the highest power, in phrases such as they had never heard before (and indeed the *Qur'an* expressly challenged them to write something like it!). I try to impress upon my post-graduate students here the vital importance of realising the force of the Arabic language, and how it virtually adds another rule of construction to our interpretation of legal texts.

Well, of course, as we know, there was opposition, there were persecutions; but we all know what happened. Let the historian and orientalist Noeldeke speak for us:

* In the lecture the original Arabic was quoted.

> "On 14th September 629, the Emperor Heraclius again set up the true Cross in Jerusalem. He had vanquished the Persians after a desperate struggle, and compelled them to restore this most sacred of relics which they had carried off on their conquest of the Holy Land. It was a day of triumph for all Christendom which is still marked in its calendars as the 'Feast of the Elevation of the Cross'. At the very moment of this striking celebration of the victory of Christendom over unbelievers, we may suppose tidings to have been brought to the Emperor that his Arabian troops beyond Jordan had been attacked by a small band from the interior and had only with difficulty succeeded in repelling the violent onset. It is not likely that the news can have struck him as implying anything very serious. Nevertheless, this was the first assault of the Muslims; it was quickly followed by others, and in a few years Palestine and many other provinces had been forever torn away from the Roman Empire, to which they had for seven centuries belonged. The Empire of Persia had been destroyed, and in the native lands of Christianity and Zoroastrianism a new faith and a new people had attained an enduring ascendency. No overturn at once so great and so rapid is recorded in history."

Now as to the living message: this must be apparent to any who know the Arab world. I recall attending, in my early days in Bahrain, at a cinema where they were showing a film of the life of the Prophet Muhammad. At an early stage in the film, which was, of course, in Arabic, the Angel spoke to the Prophet as I have said, '*Iqra' bismi rabbik allathi khalaq* . . .' and it brought the house down. There was whistling and stamping of feet and one lost at least five minutes of the film. Let there be no mistake about the fervour which this arouses.

Well, we have seen this reassertion of the Sharī'a law in Iran and Pakistan – the obvious examples. As I have said, I want to deal this evening with the Arab world, and the picture is perhaps not so immediately clear to those who have not lived with it; but the message, in my view, is as strong, if not stronger. In particular, I want to deal with the States surrounding the Arabian Gulf – to take them in geographical progression from the north: Kuwait, Saudi Arabia, Bahrain, Qatar, U.A.E. (seven Emirates) and Oman – not merely because they constitute my own area of experience, but because they perfectly represent the forces and problems at issue: they present still, of course, an area of vital importance on the world scene, and it is they who were plucked from virtual obscurity to the fore-front of the economic stage, in some cases in as little as 25 or 30 years. It is, I think, essential to our purpose to point out how dramatic has been the transformation which has occurred in the Gulf States.

IX My first visit to Kuwait in 1948 revealed a small, golden, mudwalled town (the wall had been built earlier in the century to keep out the Saudis); Bahrain, a 1000-years-old entrepôt port, with a great history of civilization, but basically a simple island trading post; Abu Dhabi and the coast along to Fujairah with the exception of Dubai, an age-old smuggling port – nothing but a few barasti huts. As for Oman, at that time Muscat was a walled town under an entirely despotic Sultan, with a curfew at night, and where a lantern had to be carried in the streets. When I first visited Riyadh with Shaikh Hafith Wahba, it was still virtually the same mud-built town which Abd Al-Aziz took by storm. With the exception of Saudi Arabia, and latterly Muscat, all these States were protected States, where the British Crown exercised extra-territorial jurisdiction in virtually all cases concerning non-nationals. The British Courts applied codified Anglo-Indian law. In these circumstances, it is not surprising that little, if any, conflict arose with the Sharī'a. For historical reasons into which we need not go here, that jurisdiction terminated in 1961 in Kuwait, and in 1971 in the rest of the Gulf. The inevitability of this cession of jurisdiction was written large on the wall for years, and we could have left in the Gulf, as we did in India and elsewhere, a system of law which could have been taken over by the States and preserved the homogeneity which existed under the extra-territorial system. We neglected this. Politicians do not like law on the whole, or lawyers, who tend to be a nuisance.

When in 1961 Kuwait asked Al-Sanhouri, the architect of the Egyptian Civil Code of 1948 and subsequently of the Codes of Iraq, Syria and Libya, to write Codes for it, he did so in a remarkably short space of time, resulting in particular in the Kuwaiti Commercial Code of 1961. Now the thesis of that great jurist, Al-Sanhouri, in writing the Egyptian Code of 1948 and subsequently, was that the Sharī'a should and could be adapted and incorporated into modern Codes, but he did not pretend that this could be done immediately, and the Codes which he drafted inevitably contained more of the principles of Western secular law than of the Sharī'a. I well remember the heart searching of the Ruler of Kuwait in the late 50s, Shaikh Abdullah Salim Al Sabah, and his doubts as to whether he should promulgate modern Codes in, as it seemed to him, defiance of the Sharī'a.

1961 – only 27 years ago!

In the southern Gulf, jurisdiction was ceded in 1971, and there was alas no Al-Sanhouri to draft Codes for them, even if they could have agreed upon a unified effort. Only 17 years ago!

Now, we are dealing here with the Arabian heartlands, the area of the origins of Al-Islam, hardly touched by the outside world until the dramatic impact made by oil in this century, and it is hardly to be expected that the initial message has been lost in such a short time – and, indeed, it has not; it is as strong as ever. The Arabs have always had this feeling that, in adopting too quickly Western concepts of law, they were going the wrong way, or if the right way, much too fast. There have always been these doubts, fueled increasingly, latterly, by the fact that something has gone wrong economically – the golden dream of Utopia seemingly justified by the bonanza of the early oil years has gone sour. Moral and religious values swept under the rug of material prosperity are apt to surface in a welter of guilt.

To put the matter into its economic perspective – when I went to the Gulf in 1948, it was common form for oil concessions to provide for a fixed royalty on oil produced by the oil companies of 3 rupees 8 annas per ton! The rupee was then valued at 1s. 6d., and a ton of oil is seven barrels. In fact, virtually no oil was being produced because it did not suit the oil companies to fit it into the existing international marketing pattern, and the average 'rent' of a concession was Rs. 100,000 – £7,500! When I advised on the first 50/50 sharing agreement in Bahrain in 1952, the 50 per cent tax payable to the Ruler of Bahrain was calculated upon an inter-company price of $1.40 per barrel! These undoubted exploitations of the early years were gradually redressed by the increasing power of OPEC and the demands of that organisation, until, in the latter 1970s, the spot price per barrel of oil in the Gulf reached $41–$42, of which the OPEC countries were taking the major share. This led, of course, to astronomical increases in income. The current scene reveals an average price of $15 per barrel; it has been lower. In all the producing countries there have been drastic cut-backs, and recently Saudi Arabia even went to the length of restoring personal income taxation, not to control inflation or for any other like economic reason, but because the income was needed. This measure was almost immediately withdrawn, but it tells its own story.

X It is clearly impossible for me, within the ambit of this lecture, to deal other than superficially with the rôle which the Sharī'a plays in the various Arab jurisdictions, as opposed to the codes of secular law. What concerns us more, is to assess the trend of recent legislation. But to give brief examples in the overall situation:

> In Saudi Arabia, the Sharī'a continues to rule supreme within the old Constitution of the Hijaz, and such departures from Sharī'a principle as are perpetrated are *not* sanctioned by law. At the other end of the scale, we may refer to the Civil and Commercial Codes of Kuwait of 1981: while the Civil Code embodies many Sharī'a concepts, the Commercial Code as a 'special' Law takes precedence over it, and sanctions modern commercial principles without advertence to the Sharī'a, notably in regard to sanctioning interest on monies lent. In Egypt, Sanhouri's Civil Code of 1948 has survived virtually unamended, and again, Egyptian commercial law suffers little inconvenience by reference to the Sharī'a. In North Yemen, the Civil Code is, as one might expect, solidly Sharī'a based. In Bahrain, that trading centre par excellence, the new Commercial Code has moved away from the Sharī'a. In the United Arab Emirates, on the other hand, the new Civil Transactions Code is firmly Sharī'a-based. In Oman, the regime is Sharī'a; but it would be rare to find the Authority for Commercial Disputes, which takes the place of a Commercial Court, applying principles of Sharī'a in its judgments, but it *could* do so – therein lies the danger, as in most of these jurisdictions even under existing legislation. And so on. One can, and indeed must, when called upon to do so, analyze each jurisdiction on its merits.

Well, having made such brief analysis, if and to the extent that the Sharī'a applies, what is the effect of that? – and in particular, in what respect is the Sharī'a inconsistent or incompatible with modern Western commercial law? Clearly, I can in no way hope to answer such a question outside a many-volume comparative treatise, but at the risk of over-simplification, we may consider some of the main difficulties.

I have stressed that in talking of a reassertion of Islam, we are automatically envisaging a reassertion of the Sharī'a. Of the verses of the *Qur'an* opinion varies as to the number which can be interpreted as embodying legislation; but the number is not more than 500, and may be as low as 300: while of that number, in any event, the vast majority relate to 'ahwal shakhsiya' or what we might call personal relationships, and have little or no effect upon commercial legal relationships. In the dialogue between Western commerce and the Arab States, it is of course commercial relationships which highlight the conflict between the Sharī'a and secular law. Even having regard to the euphoria induced by the material circumstances over the last

30 years, to which I have referred, it is nonetheless surprising to recall how seldom in my 40 years experience that conflict has been allowed to arise. It is the fact that that position is, in my opinion, due for change, which highlights the importance of our subject this evening.

We must make an immediate distinction between those precepts of the Sharī'a which are immutable, and those which may be developed further by a new ijtihad. I come to that in a moment. Be that as it may, it must be accepted that some basic precepts of the Sharī'a stemming from the *Qur'an* and the *Sunna*, and thus universally regarded by Muslim jurists as immutable, militate directly against what Western society has made of commerce.

Writing in 1980, I said that:

> "The problem is that the Arabs have, to a greater or less degree, in wishing to adopt the existing international world of commerce, come face to face with the classic situation: an irresistible force against an immovable object. As is not uncommon in these circumstances (not by any means only in the Arab world), the question has been begged on all sides, and it will be, to say the least, interesting to see for how long and to what extent this apparent anomaly can continue."

To take an example from a modern international oil arbitration (*Ruler of Qatar* v *International Marine Oil Co. Ltd.*): Here the learned Arbitrator, while considering the law of Qatar to be the proper law of the Concession Agreement, declined to apply it. The Sharī'a law in the Shaikhdom of Qatar was (and indeed still is) Islamic law of the Hanbali school, which the Arbitrator held to be inappropriate to govern a modern oil concession. In his Award, he referred to the expert evidence of Professor (now of course Sir Norman) Anderson and Professor Milliot, and he said:

> "I have no reason to suppose that Islamic law is not administered in Qatar strictly, but I am satisfied that the law does not contain any principles which would be sufficient to interpret this particular contract . . . Both experts agreed that certain parts of the contract, if Islamic law were applicable, would be open to the grave criticism of being invalid. According to Professor Milliot, the principal Agreement was full of irregularities from end to end according to Islamic law applied in Qatar. This is a cogent reason for saying that such law does not contain a body of legal principles applicable to a modern commercial contract of this kind."

(One should point out that this is not the position now in Qatar, which has for some 20 years had a Civil and Commercial Code based upon the Kuwaiti 1961 Commercial Code.)

There are contemporary authors who pretend that even the basic '*nusuus*' of the *Qur'an* and *Sunna* may be diluted or shaped to contemporary needs, based upon the requirements of '*maslaha*' or benefit to the community. However, I believe that this theory would receive only very limited acceptance. Coming downstream, however, from these immutable principles, we may use the word '*ijtihad*' – logical reasoned deductions and developments emanating from the basic principles – as an umbrella phrase to denote all those processes of consensus between jurists, reasoning, analogy, etc., by which the fiqh, the science of Sharī'a jurisprudence, developed. Now, a further difficulty may be seen in the contentions of those purists who insist that even this process of ijtihad came to a stop in the Middle Ages, engendering in the Sharī'a a complete rigidity dating from that time. Fortunately, I do not believe that this view commands other than superficial acceptance at the present time. The question must be, therefore, whether, by a process of neo-ijtihad, the basic nusuus, the immutable precepts of the Sharī'a in the *Qur'an* and *Sunna*, could be brought into line with Western secular commercial law. (It will be noted that I say *could*, not *should* – and I turn to this again in a moment.) In my opinion, as indeed the learned Arbitrator was advised in the case to which I have referred, there are certain incompatibilities which it would be very difficult, if not impossible, to reconcile between the two systems. The greatest of these is *riba*.

XI We can clearly only touch upon these conflicting aspects here. However, it may be said that there are three things which are absolutely repugnant to the Sharī'a. One is '*gharar*', which is almost impossible to translate, but may be roughly rendered as risk or uncertainty; the second is '*riba*', which represents any unjustified, one-sided accretion and upsetting of the equivalence of the contract – the obvious topical example is the absolute ban on interest on monies lent; the other case is where you have a number of transactions within one contract: the precept is that each contract must be limited to one transaction. Al-Sanhouri, writing in 'Masaadir Al-Haqq' (*The Sources of Rights in Islamic Jurisprudence*) says:

> "You will observe that each of these three matters had a profound effect on detailed provisions to the extent that, in many such, the Islamic jurisprudence distanced itself from the

> requirements of the transaction. If it were possible to clarify our understanding of these three matters in accordance with the development of civilization, then much of the reasoning which stops the Islamic jurisprudence from going along with the requirements of such development would disappear."

We clearly cannot even deal with all these three; so let us single out *riba*, which has achieved fame because of the application of the principle to interest on monies lent.

It was related of 'Umar bin Al-Khattab that he said: 'I wish that the Prophet had not been taken from us until he had given us a satisfactory explanation of *riba* . . . We have forsworn things nine tenths of which were permissible, for fear of *riba*'.

There is no doubt that the prohibition on *riba* stems from the *Qur'an* itself, and is forbidden in the strongest terms in many verses.

In the simplest terms: the Sharī'a forbids interest on monies: the Western economies are structured upon it. With the onset of oil wealth, the Arab world has entered the Western system, and in the majority of cases, this conflict has simply not been allowed to arise. However, to the lawyer that is hardly satisfactory, when he has to advise his clients on the possible legal risks involved in, say, a syndicated loan transaction.

XII In some cases this nettle has been firmly grasped. As already pointed out, the Kuwaiti Commercial Code of 1981 expressly allows interest in a commercial loan. The new Bahraini Code of 1987 now, perhaps surprisingly in the present climate, does the same. The highest court in Egypt was, in 1985, faced with a case brought by no less than the Rector of Al-Azhar among others, for declaration that interest had become illegal. This plea was founded upon the amendment to the Egyptian Constitution made in 1980, the latter days of the Sadat régime, whereby the Sharī'a became not just *a* principal source of legislation, but *the* principal source. The Court however gave judgment that the effect of this was to enjoin the legislator in Egypt to bring Egyptian law into line with the Sharī'a, but did not affect existing principles of law.

To take a topical example on the other side of the fence – the Civil Transactions Code of the United Arab Emirates of 1985, while introducing for the first time conflict of laws provisions and respect for the principle of *autonomie de la volonté*, that is to say, the right of the parties to choose the proper law of the contract, detracts from much of this in Article 27 by expressly providing, 'It shall not be lawful to apply principles of law designated by the foregoing provisions if such principles are contrary to the Islamic Sharī'a or public policy or morals in the U.A.E.' Another part of the Code expressly forbids interest on monies lent. An extraordinary judgment issuing in Abu Dhabi after the promulgation of the Code, sought to recognize the legality of interest by deciding that the Code applied only to 'civil' transactions, not to commercial, and a half-hearted amendment to Article 1 of the Code has tried once more to fudge the issue in ambiguous terms.

XIII The position overall remains one of uncertainty, and it is this uncertainty which is the plague of the practising lawyer. Despite the Codes to which I have referred above, there is an undoubted trend overall to reassert the Sharī'a. In Kuwait, there have for some years now been committees studying the matter. In Egypt, for so long the source of codified law and doctrine which has formed the basis for so many of the Arab Codes, consequent upon the change in the Constitution to which I have already referred, Parliament constituted a special Commission with committees to study suggestions relating to adoption of the Islamic Sharī'a and its codification. As a result, five draft legislative Bills, among them a draft Commercial Law, all of them based upon the Islamic jurisprudence, have been prepared, and in 1982 Parliament agreed to refer the draft Bills to the Parliamentary Committee on Constitutional Affairs. At the first conference of the International Bar Association held in an Arab country (February 1987), the section on the Sharī'a, which I had the honour to chair, a paper submitted by no less than the Rector of Al-Azhar terminated:

> "It is unnecessary for us to note the urgent need to give constitutional effect to these legislative Bills, so that they may be implemented and that Egypt can thereby regain its Islamic standing, and that those dark clouds which have nearly obscured its true visage may be dispersed from before its face, with holy Al-Azhar being its people's model and precept. The codification of the provisions of Islam in the form of contemporary legislation paves the way for their study and for acting thereon in the hope of God's favour and mercy."

In the international sphere, the Learned Academy of Islamic Jurisprudence, whose establishment was decided upon at the Conference on Islamic Jurisprudence at Taif, has, if it adverts to principles of neo-ijtihad and endeavours to produce authoritative statements of Sharī'a commercial law adapted to modern conditions –

then it has the power to do something really momentous. In the existing climate, however, it has a formidable task: not the least formidable aspect being the necessity for new definitions of the immutable nusuus, among them the overriding concept of riba; but there is another side to this particular coin. Do the Arab States really wish, would they even be advised, to tamper with the existing concepts of riba at the present time? When they look at the world banking system, which is based essentially upon interest, and which may seem to them at times to be tottering on its base; when they see the most powerful nations in debt rather than in credit – may this not provide, apart from basic beliefs which exist anyway, a powerful argument that what the prophet uttered so long ago was entirely right, and that the principle of profit-sharing and partnership is better not only from the religious point of view, but in practice? There is also, now, of course, a huge vested interest in Islamic banking. Is Islamic banking not true merchant banking? Why then, they may say, erode the principles of riba as they exist, when it may be contended they provide the only solution to impending chaos? I am not saying that I subscribe to such an extreme view – I am not an economist – but it is a solemn thought. I hope that some of these issues will be discussed at our conference on Islamic finance which takes place here on April 15th.

XIV In conclusion, what, if anything, can be done by the Western lawyer, other than to sit back and wait for an inevitable crash application of the Sharī'a? First of all, realize the existence of the problem, and problem it is! Secondly, Western lawyers must show a great sympathy and understanding for this powerful religious and cultural background, and we have to devise where necessary (not as yet in all jurisdictions) our bridges – if indeed these can be built. There are many ifs. The Sharī'a is a sacred subject, and apart from understanding on the Western side, any dialogue must require the cooperation of the Muslim side in what in many quarters is regarded as a forbidden subject. Certainly, let us never under-estimate the importance of this subject at this time – a classical and rigid application of the Sharī'a to modern economic agreements would be catastrophic, and it is sobering to reflect that this could occur in most of the Arab jurisdictions with no need for prior legislation. Let it not be thought either that such application is relevant only within a Muslim jurisdiction – what of the situation in a Western court directed by its conflict rules to apply to a contract the Sharī'a law, proved by expert evidence, to be the law applicable as the proper law of the contract? Also, what of the enforcement of foreign judgments in the Muslim jurisdictions? These are grave matters.

Perhaps what is required in today's climate is not just a restructuring of the Sharī'a to fit Western economic concepts, but some restructuring of those concepts in order to meet the Sharī'a: a study of just how far Western and Sharī'a concepts are incompatible in the light of a new ijtihad. In so far as dialogue is possible, let us pursue it. The need for it is the reason that I insisted upon 'The Sharī'a in Transnational Transactions' as the leading subject of the first Conference of the International Bar Association to be held in an Arab country – Cairo, February 1987. The Arab Regional Committee of the IBA formed as a result of the outstanding success of that conference (of which I have the honour to be the first Chairman) will, I hope, provide an opportunity for such dialogue. Another hopeful initiative with which I am concerned is that of the Euro-Arab Chambers of Commerce in the field of arbitration. We must take the opportunity for discussion while wise and moderate men are available to participate in it. Really, this can only be done by lawyers, and, in the final analysis Muslim lawyers at that – such is the difficulty where the law is identified with the religion. The political implications are, of course, obvious; but for the issue to become an international political issue, or to be overtly treated as such, is, I hope, unthinkable – to say that that would be counter-productive is to understate the obvious. We are too apt to write learned memoranda based upon the material pros and cons of a situation. Our Arab friends can be supreme materialists; but also supreme romantic idealists, and, of course, religionists. We should in addition realize that *logic* as we understand it may play little part in their actions and reactions.

We can end as we began with two hopeful messages from the *Qur'an*: 'Do not dispute with the people of the Scripture' (i.e. the Christians and the Jews) 'unless it concerns something that is better, save with such of them as do wrong; and say (oh, Muhammad): We believe in that which has been revealed to us and revealed to you; our God and your God are one, and it is to Him that we surrender.'*

And to the people of the Scripture themselves: 'Oh, people of the Book, come to common terms as between us and you.'*

* In the lecture the original Arabic was quoted.

XII

The Bahrain Euro-Arab Arbitration Conference 1989: A Summing-Up

Bearing in mind the aims of this Euro-Arab initiative, I want to highlight if I may the difficulties and differences and the possible misunderstandings apparent to me from the proceedings of the past two days and try to put them into perspective. It would be foolish to pretend that they do not exist – that would indeed stifle progress.

I think that the correct simile to draw here is with the tributaries of a stream or river. This is an analogy which I make to my post-graduates in London when, in particular, drawing a distinction between the Shari'a and the Secular Laws. The streams run perhaps parallel towards a common goal, the sea. Sometimes, quite often, they touch and become one; sometimes bridges have to be built between one and the other. I hope (no more than that) I *hope* that in my 40 years' experience of the Arab world, I have been able at least to get my feet wet in both streams.

We do not talk here of fences, fences have to be demolished, and that is not our business.

Unfortunately, I did not attend the Port El Kantaoui Conference, but I did send a paper (printed in the proceedings at page 160) from which I quote:

> "If it were not recognised that there is a gulf still to be bridged between the Arab and European cultures in the field of dispute settlement, then there would probably be no need for this conference, and no need for the organisations which are sponsoring it. Of course there is such a need. There are still bridges to be built, and arbitration rather than litigation provides some of the answers."

So, I am not going to summarize for you what everyone has said; my colleague Samia Rashed has already done that to a large extent excellently and you have heard what the speakers said and you can read the papers afterwards.

It has been apparent to me that among all that we have heard two matters are outstanding: the absence of legislation in the Arab world to deal with international arbitration, and the Shari'a.

We heard many words of wisdom from Professor Fadhlallah, amongst them that there is no common Arab law – expressly there are no common arbitration rules in the Arab countries: there is a diversity. There are signs of evolution but that is all.

I am currently engaged upon lecturing in the Comparative Arab Commercial Law course at SOAS, and this is one of the initial messages which I put across to them – there is as yet no lex Arabica: in particular there is no lex mercatoria Arabica. Sometimes even my Arab friends argue about this but it is true. If we count from Morocco through to Oman, we have 18 jurisdictions and that includes counting the seven Emirates of the UAE as one, although they still have their peculiarities. Despite efforts within and without the Arab League, despite the initial path laid down by that great jurist Abdul Razzak Al-Sanhouri, we still have to view each jurisdiction separately.

But – a big but – those jurisdictions do have principles in common, points of concordance, which are extraordinary; they surmount the common principles which exist between European countries. The list which I now give is not necessarily exclusive:

1 Al Islam
2 The Shari'a
3 The Arabic language
4 Secular Laws on a common basis – civil based, due largely again to Al-Sanhouri
5 Much common doctrine and jurisprudence.
6 Sometimes, an inter-change of judges particularly in the Gulf States.

We may recall that the two books which are almost certain to be found at the right hand of every Judge in the Arab world are Al-Waseet the monumental commentary on the Civil Code by Al-Sanhouri, and the Majella.

And of course a great and enormous cultural affinity, greater often than the Western lawyer can appreciate.

Thus, although we cannot talk of a lex Arabica and although we still have to consider each jurisdiction separately, we can talk of general principles of *Arab* law, with a meaning more profound than attaches to this formula in, say, Article 38 of the Statute of the International Court of Justice as a source of public international law. There is here a homogeneity (tanasuq) which already gives hope and promises a possibility of legislation of the type which, as we have seen, is urgently needed in the field of international arbitration. Let us not forget also that at the Hague Conferences on International Law the Shari'a was recognized as one of the general principles of law.

So, I do not entirely agree with what Mr Carver said in derogation of the application of general principles of law in the *Arab* context – although I certainly agree with him in slating those arbitrators who seek to use those principles as avoiding the necessity to apply the proper substantive law.

Now I have nothing like the time to deal with all the above points of concordance but we have heard much at this conference about one of them; and, to my surprise, less about another. We have heard a lot about the Arabic language; very little until latterly under Jacques Hakim about the Shari'a. May I deal with these briefly:

The Shari'a – Here I am treading literally on 'holy ground'; please understand that there is no way in which I pretend to expertise on the Shari'a before *this* audience. We all know that all of our 18 States are Islamic States (with some reservations of course in the case of Lebanon): we should all know also that the Constitutions of all of them prescribe the Shari'a as *a* or *the* main source of legislation.

May I now for the benefit of my Western colleagues make a short excursus to quote yet again from myself at El-Kantaoui:

> "The Shari'a is of course the religious law of Islam, and those of us who are non-Muslim should appreciate that to say that Arabia (I use the term here to include the whole Arab-speaking world) is Muslim, is not at all the same as saying that Europe is Christian. Islam is a living religion, occupying the hearts and minds of its people, controlling their lives, and the Shari'a is its law. I have spoken of a 'reassertion' of Islam: I carefully do not speak of a 'revival' because it has never been dead or dying. There are great differences in basic thinking between Islam and other cultures."

The degree to which the Shari'a applies in each jurisdiction varies. In Saudi Arabia, Yemen and to a degree Oman, the Shari'a applies to a large extent; indeed in Saudi Arabia and the Yemen it virtually rules supreme. In Saudi Arabia, 'Regulations' are passed, not 'Laws' – to regulate matters within the Shari'a. In Yemen, the Civil Code is solidly

Shari'a-based; so is the new Code of the UAE. At the other end of the scale – Kuwait has a Commercial Code (1980) which expressly allows interest on monies lent; the new Commercial Code of Bahrain does the same.

Western lawyers must show a great sympathy and understanding for this powerful religious and cultural background and we have to devise where necessary (not, as I have said, in all jurisdictions) our bridges – we must if our Euro-Arab initiative is really to get underway appreciate these difficulties and minimize the conflicts, and this is not always easy. In the general reassertion of Islam and the Shari'a which is apparent in the Arab world, we have to examine the situation carefully first of all against the background of a possible application of the Shari'a in each jurisdiction. This is the first task of the practising lawyer: does the Shari'a apply at all and, if so, to what extent?

I think it was quite apparent that in order to engender the trust of the European part of this Euro-Arab initiative, in most of the Arab States liberalizing legislation is necessary really for two main reasons:

1 To create a jurisdiction within which international arbitration can be conducted without unknown quantities and with minimum court interference.
2 To maximize the possibility of enforcement of awards.

This requirement for legislation is by no means limited to the Arab States: Switzerland is in process of changing its Concordat – its federal arbitration statute – to the same end, largely due to the initiative of Pierre Lalive. In 1980 France 'liberalized' by limiting severely cases in which recourse may be had from international arbitration proceedings to the Courts (this did not prevent the Pyramids case from being upset). In England we had to pass a new Arbitration Act in 1975 to allow the famous Exclusion Clauses.

In countries like Kuwait and Bahrain, under their existing legal systems, there would be little difficulty; but what if the Shari'a applies?

Well let us examine the position in Saudi Arabia, the present Shari'a jurisdiction par excellence.

It must be said that the present Saudi Arbitration Regulation is not attractive to the European lawyer or party. Arbitrators must be Muslims, all the documentation and procedure must be in Arabic. But as we have indeed heard from Jacques Hakim, the Regulation does now expressly permit the submission of future disputes to arbitration, although this is contrary to accepted practice at the Shari'a. The point that arises is this: does that practice at the Shari'a stem from an express provision of the Quaran or Sunna? Or does it stem from the fiqh? I believe it may be the latter.

I have here to make a short excursus for the benefit of my Western colleagues and explain that the basic provisions of the Shari'a, deemed to originate in the Quran itself and the Sunna of the Prophet are by common accord all regarded as immutable, but subject to them the process of Ijtihad has allowed development of the law by deduction and analogy. The difference between the Shari'a and Western laws, as I understand it, is that society is supposed to develop in accordance with the Shari'a – the Shari'a cannot be expected to evolve in accordance with the material needs of society. However, this only goes to the immutable provisions, *unless* the door of Ijtihad is still reckoned to be closed – the majority opinion would appear to be that it is *not*, that it is open.

May I take an example; if the embargo upon the submission of a future dispute goes to a basic provision of the Shari'a, then why was it permitted in the new Saudi Regulation? Let us recall that the old Constitution of the Hijaz still provides the Shari'a as the only source of legislation and, indeed, this is the invariable practice in Saudi Arabia. So we must conclude that this dictate of the Shari'a was not regarded as presenting a difficulty to the enactment of modern international arbitration legislation, the position must be examined to see whether this is in fact the case. Are there basic provisions creating the difficulty? Or is it a question of flexibility inherent in Ijtihad?

(An obvious and topical example of a basic provision is Riba which is usually viewed in the context of banking interest but which is in fact a much wider concept.)

Let us recall that the principle of arbitration is favoured at the Shari'a. Let us also recall Dr Hoshan told us that the lack of arbitration legislation is not attributable to the Shari'a and that there is not much difference in procedures; and Shaikh Isa Bin Mohammed's Paper on the methods of proof.

We heard from Jacques Hakim again generally on the peculiarities of the Shari'a procedures, but how many of these are really immutable: that is the point. How inimical really is the Shari'a to the enactment of legislation for international arbitration?

The Arabic language – What a cohesive force this is over 18 jurisdictions! The language is revealed in its perfect form in the Quran. One can understand that there is some insistence upon it – anyone who is lucky enough to have Arabic as his mother tongue should be jealous of it!

However, we found great understanding and flexibility on the Arab side here. Professor Fadlallah said, as I understand it, that it would be the end of arbitration if *any* language not agreed by the parties were to be imposed. I agree with that: as a lawyer I would never agree to the compulsory imposition of any language. I would be equally diffident of course about a legal provision which required that all the arbitrators should be Christian: although, as I have said, there is a great difference between such a requirement and one that required him to be Muslim and I refer to the essential differences between the two cultures to which I made reference above. However, as far as language is concerned, we must realize that the Arabic language is not like other languages; may I quote again from myself at Tunis:

> The though processes to which the Arabic language gives vent make that language an essential element which almost adds another facet to the rules of construction.

I referred further in the Tunis Paper to the difficulties inherent in this question of language, difficulties of translation etc. (I refer to my Paper at page 162.)

I believe that I have dealt with those aspects of this conference which seemed to me the most important: the need for new legislation and the possibility in the Arab jurisdictions even against a strict Shari'a background of achieving it.

Now may I deal with a few more points.

The Parties and their Counsel

We heard (and I fully agree) of the importance of behaviour, essential to the success of arbitration. Mr Carver highlighted this and it was repeated more than once. Dr Redha cited the Aminoil Arbitration – I had the task of arguing Kuwaiti Law against the Kuwaiti Government in that Arbitration, the Government being represented in that respect by my friend Ahmed Kosheri. The whole proceedings were a pleasure. The result was a successful arbitration. The kind of understanding which we all shared in those proceedings would sweep away many of the difficulties referred to in this conference.

The Arbitrator as Advocate

The panel overwhelmingly endorsed the view that an arbitrator must never be in any way an advocate, he must always be objective. In my experience, this rigidity is difficult sometimes for some of my Arab friends to understand. I think the reason for that perhaps does lie in the Shari'a – again I commented on this at Tunis (proceedings at page 161):

> "The fallacy of the notion that an arbitrator is in some respects at least an advocate for his nominator is an attitude that dies hard, probably due in part to the fact that the traditional Shari'a does not essentially recognise or favour more than one arbitrator. Of course, if this attitude does exist, it puts the European party, believing in the opposite philosophy, at an obvious disadvantage where he has appointed his arbitrator entirely as an objective judge."

I believe that it would do much to put the European parties' minds at rest if the Euro-Arab Chambers could issue rules of ethics as quickly as possible – then parties would be able to see that the standards to which an arbitrator appointed under the rules must conform were in accordance with the accepted norms. I am not of course suggesting for one moment that any arbitrator appointed would obey any other norms in any event, but the rules of ethics would really be for the assurance of third parties, not the education of the arbitrators.

Bahrain as an Arbitration Centre

Bahrain is keen to become a Centre for arbitration; is it possible to imagine anywhere better? I think that having for many years had the honour to be regarded in some quarters as an Honorary Bahraini this enables me to speak with authority of these wonderful Islands and their people. Bahrain has early plans to subscribe to the New York Convention. New legislation, as we have seen, is necessary particularly to deal with international arbitrations but that should present no difficulty under Bahrain's existing legal system. After the great hospitality and efficiency which we have witnessed, who can doubt that this is the obvious place? My friend, Qasim Fakhro, recounted some of the legal history of Bahrain in his opening speech – when we met the Prime Minister, he did mention that 'our Father Ballantyne' knew very well all the old history and development and would remember personally the first Order in Council which was passed in 1913! Well I can claim to some experience, but not that much – I only go back to 1948! But that is long enough to have learnt something about this place and the quality of its people.

In conclusion, may I refer you to the very interesting handout 'Commercial Arbitration Principles and Procedures' provided to you all by the Bahrain Chamber of Commerce and Industry and the Bahrain Bar Society. (There is a very important omission on page 5 in the English text, the last paragraph on the page – the Arabic is correct.) May I stress that there is no right of appeal from an arbitration award if the parties expressly renounce appeal in the Arbitration Agreement. This is obviously of great importance.

I am quite sure that we shall build all the bridges we need and that this Euro-Arab initiative will forge ahead. It will take effort but we shall do it.

XIII

A Reassertion of the Shari'a: The Jurisprudence of the Gulf States

There can be no doubt whatever, in my view, that there is in the majority of the Arab jurisdictions the feeling that in adopting wholesale legislation based upon Western, mainly French, civil codes, they went too far too fast: the feeling that they should have adhered to the Sharī'ah as a base – possibly devising some kind of new *Majallah* (Ottoman codification of Sharī'ah civil law). Now, to anticipate and to try to put the crux of this issue immediately in the spotlight: the difficulty (perhaps impossibility) lies in the fact that the Gulf states, since the dramatic onset of oil wealth, have become economically tied to the West. The Western economic system of banking and interest is anathema to the Sharī'ah, and while that is perhaps the main difficulty, it is not by any means the only one. There are, as we all know, many incidents of complicated modern commercial contracts which would simply be illegal at the Sharī'ah. Those who talk of a new *ijtihād* (interpretation) tend to overlook the fact that, even admitting that the door of *ijtihād* may be reopened (now, I think, admitted by the majority), there are few indeed who would venture to contend that express provisions (*nuṣūṣ*) of the Quar'ān and Sunnah can be tampered with. Of such is *ribā* (interest). It may be that the way forward is by a new and restrictive definition of *ribā*, *gharar* (hazard or risk), and other such aspects of the Sharī'ah, but that will take great unity and political courage at the present time. In my opinion, anything short of a new *Majallah* redefining Sharī'ah concepts in the light of contemporary conditions – a new *Majallah* passed by the Arab states as a uniform law – must continue to beg the question and leave in the Arab jurisdictions that uncertainty which will increasingly bedevil the Western lawyer. What a dream – a true *lex arabica*! There are at the moment few signs that it can be achieved or that such a code could be devised without resorting to what many Muslims would regard as heresy.

In order to assess current trends, we must consider briefly the position occupied by the Sharīʿah as a source of legislation in Kuwait, Bahrain, Qatar, the United Arab Emirates, Oman and Saudi Arabia. They are all Islamic states, and it is almost trite to point out to this audience that where there are written constitutions – in all save Saudi Arabia and Oman – the Sharīʿah is prescribed as a, or the, main source of legislation. Saudi Arabia has no written constitution in the current sense, but the ancient Organic Instructions of the Hijazi Kingdom of 1926, amended or supplemented by the Statute of the Council of Deputies of 1932 and the Constitution of the Council of Ministers of 1953, make it clear that the law of the Kingdom is the Sharīʿah, and it may be confidently submitted that no regulation of the Kingdom which could be shown to be contrary to the Shariʿah would be applied by the courts. In Oman, the position is perhaps least defined of all the states; there is no written constitution, and it must be stressed, therefore, that despite the apparently liberal trends to which I shall refer, the Sharīʿah could be applied to any matter in Oman at any time.

Apart from Saudi Arabia and Oman, we find varying shades. In my long practice, I have found that, in other than matters of personal affairs (*aḥwāl shakhṣīyah*), the Sharīʿah has had minimal relevance, particularly in commercial matters. However, whatever may have been the position in practice over recent years, the trend towards a reassertion is quite apparent, and it is thus illuminating to consider the extent to which the Sharīʿah *could* be applied under the existing constitutions and the variety of legislation promulgated under them.

Now, one hears too often from one's Arab colleagues the dictum, 'No, we have civil courts in our country; the Sharīʿah is not relevant.' That is, of course, a dangerous non sequitur; the crucial matter is not the label put upon the courts, but the law which those courts are directed to apply. While it may be true to say that a Sharīʿah *qāḍī* will apply the Sharīʿah exclusively, it is certainly not true, indeed it is entirely misleading, to say that a civil or commercial court will *not* apply the Sharīʿah. In considering the Gulf states, we may indeed indicate two extremes – in Saudi Arabia, it may be submitted that no court or judicial committee may do other than apply the Sharīʿah; whereas in Kuwait, at the other end of the scale, it would be rare indeed to find the Sharīʿah mentioned in a commercial court; the same may be said of Bahrain or, to a lesser extent, Qatar. We find, however, as we have said, varying shades.

Given, then, that the Sharīʿah may be taken in these states to be at least a principal source of legislation according to the constitution, what is the extent to which it is applied by law and in practice, with especial reference to commercial matters? To a large extent, this issue, embarrassing to regimes which have perforce adopted in the last two decades Western codes and, even more importantly, become absorbed into the Western economic system, has been swept under the rug. I do not believe that it will continue to be so.

As we have seen, in Saudi Arabia the Sharīʿah reigns paramount, and such regulations as have been promulgated must in my opinion be subjected to the test of validity at the Sharīʿah. Let us take the other states from Kuwait round the Gulf to Oman.

Kuwait

Article 1 of the Kuwaiti Civil Code of 1980[1] provides for an apparent hierarchy of sources to which a judge shall make reference: (1) express legislative provisions, which apply to matters to which they relate both expressly and by implication, (2) custom, and (3) the *fiqh*. Although contract is not expressly referred to in this context, Article 196 of the code covers this by the hallowed precept that 'the contract is the law of the parties' (*alʿaqd sharīʿat al-mutaʿāqidayn*).

While the Kuwaiti Civil Code shows a great deal of Sharīʿah influence in its make-up, by Article 3 of the law issuing that code special laws are expressed to take precedence over general laws such as the Civil Code. One such special law, the Kuwaiti Commercial Code, was published contemporaneously with the Civil Code, and legislates specifically in the modern commercial context.[2] In particular, while loans according to the Civil code must be without interest, the Commercial Code, as a special law, allows interest on commercial loans, and indeed contains detailed provisions as to its regulation. Thus, in general, it would be rare indeed to find the Sharīʿah adduced as an authority in a purely commercial transaction in Kuwait, where express legislative provisions exist. However, where there is no such provision, and where the judge is directed to custom, the position is different. The learned commentary to the code points out that customs must not offend public policy or morals (*al-niẓām al-ʿāmm wa-ḥusn al-ʿādāt*), and it goes on to state: 'Customs (*ʿādāt*) which contradict the social, political, economic or moral principles upon which the community rests can never be elevated to the rank of custom (*ʿurf*) even if of long duration; in a country such as Kuwait, whose religion is, by the constitution, Islam, it is not possible that anything which contravenes one of the bases or established precepts of Islam should constitute custom.'

Bahrain

In Bahrain, the matter of sources was, until the promulgation of the new Commercial Code in March 1987[3] regulated by the Judicature Law of 1971.[4] The structure prescribed by that law, which must, from its wording, be taken to be hierarchical, is: (1) provisions of law, (2) the principles of the Sharī'ah, (3) custom, and (4) natural law or the principles of equity and good conscience.

This formula is interesting as clearly envisaging that secular legislation is to be preferred to the Sharī'ah, even, presumably, if it does not accord with the Sharī'ah. It also envisages that the Sharī'ah may be deficient in supplying a solution to a problem, in which case custom applies. Would such custom be applicable if itself contrary to the Sharī'ah? Finally, would the tenets of natural justice or the principles of equity and good conscience be applicable in defiance of the Sharī'ah?

As far as commercial matters are concerned – and it must be remembered that Bahrain is par excellence, and has been for thousands of years, an entrepôt state with great commercial interests, and latterly a developed banking community – the new Commercial Code of 1987 takes the matter a step further. As far as I am aware, this code has not been generally published in English. I have translated the relevant Article 2:

"1 There shall apply to commercial matters that which the two contracting parties have agreed to unless such agreement conflicts with mandatory legislative provisions (*nuṣūṣ tashrī'īyah āmirah*).
2 In the absence of express agreement, the principles of commercial custom shall apply unless there be in that respect provision in this law or in any other law relating to commercial matters. Special or local custom shall be preferred over general custom.
3 If there be no commercial custom, the laws relating to civil matters shall apply, failing which the judge shall deduce the bases of his judgment from the principles of the law of nature and the principles of justice."

It may now be said in the light of these provisions that, as with Kuwait, in Bahrain in a commercial matter where there is express legislative provision, such provision would be applied even if contrary to the Sharī'ah.

Taking *ribā* once again as the yardstick in our current context, we find that the new Bahraini code has, like Kuwait's in 1980, finally grasped this nettle and legislated sanctioning banking interest. Article 76 defines a commercial loan, and goes to the length of providing for a presumption that interest be charged in the absence of a contrary intention expressed by the contracting parties. The article further provides for an upper limit of interest to be set by the Central Bank. Article 275 of the code, which deals with bank deposit, again expressly allows the stipulation of interest thereon, and refers back in this respect to the general provisions of Article 76.

One may recall in passing that Bahrain still has a contract law and a law of torts based on the common law.[5] It is to be presumed that the state will eventually issue a comprehensive civil code in replacement of these two survivals, but in the meantime it will be interesting to study the conflicts which must inevitably develop between the old code and the new commercial code, based as it is upon European commercial concepts.

Qatar

The Civil and Commercial Code of Qatar of 1971[6] provides for the sources of law to be in essence as follows: (1) the contract between the parties provided it accords with the law, (2) express legislative provision, (3) custom, and (4) the Sharī'ah.

We may recall that, unlike the constitutions of Kuwait, Bahrain, and the U.A.E., which provide for the Sharī'ah as *a* principal source of legislation, the Qatari constitution provides that it shall be *the* principal source thereof. The question therefore arises as to whether the hierarchy of sources prescribed under the civil and commercial code must be read subject to the proviso that they are not contrary to the Sharī'ah. My own view is that, despite the more stringent wording of the constitution, this should not be the test, but the matter is clearly controversial and confirms doubts about the ever-looming presence of the Sharī'ah which exists in greater or less degree in the other jurisdictions. We shall note in a moment recent important and illuminating judgments delivered by the Supreme Constitutional Court of Egypt construing the effect upon past existing legislation of the changes in the constitution made in 1980, whereby the Sharī'ah was promoted from being *a* principal source of legislation to *the* principal source.

The United Arab Emirates

The sources of law to be applied by the courts in the U.A.E. are to be found basically in Union Law No. 10 of 1973 setting up the Union Supreme Court[7] where it is provided (Article 75):

> "The Supreme Court shall apply the provisions of the Islamic Sharī'ah, Union laws and other laws in force in the member Emirates of the Union conforming to the Islamic Sharī'ah. Likewise it shall apply those rules of custom and those principles of natural and comparative law which do not conflict with the principles of the Sharī'ah."

Here the paramountcy of the Sharī'ah is evident. Again, Union Law No. 6 of 1978[8] setting up the Union Courts of First Instance and Appeal prescribes the following sources (Article 8):

> "The Union courts shall apply the provisions of the Islamic Sharī'ah, Union laws, and other laws in force, just as they shall apply those rules of custom and general legal principles which do not conflict with the provisions of the Sharī'ah."

The matter is taken further by the new Code of Civil Transactions for the United Arab Emirates,[9] which came into force in March 1986, and which provides (Article 1) that legislative provisions shall apply to all matters contained therein either expressly or by implication; that there shall be no place for construction or interpretation where a provision is clear; and that if the judge does not find any provision in the law, then he must adjudicate in accordance with the Islamic Sharī'ah. In so doing, the judge is directed to the Mālikī and Ḥanbalī schools; if he finds no answer there, then he adverts to the Shāfi'ī or Ḥanafī schools as the matter may require. If the judge still does not find the guidance he requires, then he gives judgment in accordance with custom, which custom, however, must not be contrary to public policy or morals, and if it is a custom peculiar to a particular emirate, then his judgment applies to such emirate. Article 2 of the code provides definitely that in the comprehension and interpretation of a provision, reference shall be made to the principles of the Islamic *fiqh*; while Article 3, in defining public policy, lays it down that nothing shall be contrary to the mandatory provisions and the basic principles of the Sharī'ah. The new code contains for the first time conflict of law provisions but, although Article 19 respects the principle of *autonomie de la volonté*, Article 27 provides that 'it shall not be lawful to apply principles of law designated by the foregoing provisions if such principles are contrary to the Islamic Sharīʻah or public policy or morals of the U.A.E.'

It may be deduced, therefore, that in the U.A.E. principles of law contrary to the Sharīʻah should not, whether in a civil or commercial transaction, be adverted to by the courts. Be that as it may, in a recent case in Abu Dhabi, the judge, in finding interest on a loan to be legal despite arguments produced before him based upon the new code, made a differentiation between a civil loan and a commercial loan. This was a commercial loan, he said, and thus the provisions of the civil code did not apply to it! I would submit that, in view of the weight of legislation existing in the U.A.E. to which I have referred, it is difficult to conceive how the judge could possibly have come to that conclusion. There is, as yet, no commercial code in the U.A.E.

Oman

Article 44 of the Law of Procedure for Hearing Cases and Applications for Arbitration before the Authority for Settlement of Commercial Disputes[10] prescribes:

> Decress and laws in effect in the Sultanate; contracts between the litigants provided that such do not conflict with the laws, public order or morals; established and observed customs in the field of commercial activity; and that which will achieve justice between the adversaries and lead to stability in commercial transactions.

It may be noted also that certain provisions of the Omani Banking Law would appear to confer on contracting parties the right to choose both jurisdiction and law in their contract, although it seems doubtful whether those provisions go beyond matters of banking as therein defined. However, we may recall the basic constitutional position in Oman to which I have already referred and note that there is nothing to preclude the application of the Sharīʻah by the Authority; indeed, as a matter of jurisprudence, it may be anticipated that if points of Sharīʻah were made before the Authority, it would be obliged to take them.

In 1980, in the latter days of the Sadat regime, Article 2 of the Constitution of Egypt was amended to provide that the Sharīʻah should be *the* principal source of law. On 4th May 1985, the

Constitutional Court of Egypt issued a judgment in this respect which was of great importance, not only for Egypt but for the other Arab jurisdictions whose codes owe so much to Egypt and where deference is paid to Egyptian jurisprudence. The case was brought before the Constitutional Court by no less a person than the Rector of al-Azhar, against the President, the Prime Minister, the President of the Legislative Committee of Parliament, and finally against the heirs of one Fuad Goudah, the latter being the person concerned with the substance.[11] In essence, the court held that the change in Article 2 of the Constitution did not affect existing legislation – notably Article 226 of the Civil Code of 1948, which the Rector claimed to be against the Constitution in its amended form in that it provides for interest in case of delayed payment. In another more recent judgment announced by the same Constitutional Court on 4th April 1987 the court ruled on a case brought by the public prosecutor, who was not satisfied with the sentence of fine or imprisonment prescribed for drinking wine and being intoxicated in a public place place.[12] The prosecutor endeavored to invoke Sharīʿah punishment, but the court ruled, as before, that the new Article 2 of the Constitution applied only to subsequent legislation.

At the first conference of the International Bar Association to be held in an Arab country, that held in Cairo in February 1987, I had the honour to co-chair the section on 'The Sharīʿah and its Relevance to Modern Transnational Transactions.' The burning interest in this subject at the present time and the appreciation of the current reassertion of the Sharīʿah generally were apparent. In particular, the first of the constitutional cases to which I have just referred came in for much criticism from Egyptian lawyers. The Sharīʿah as a main source of legislation was recognized, as was the problem of whether the Sharīʿah can be made compatible with modern transnational commercial transactions. Inevitably, these themes were developed by consideration of new *ijtihād*, and the papers read reflected the differences of opinion in this respect. A fascinating paper was read on behalf of the Rector of Al Azhar, in which he referred in particular to the Hague conferences and the resolutions that: (1) the Sharīʿah be considered as one of the sources of the general principles of law, (2) the Sharīʿah is living and capable of development, and (3) the Sharīʿah is unique and not taken from any other source. The paper outlined in particular how apposite was the Sharīʿah to commercial transactions, and dealt with this in detail. However, at the end of the paper came the punch line: the Rector's analysis was to illustrate the competence of the Sharīʻah to deal with commercial transactions, but it was now essential to return to the principle of Islam in the laws of Egypt, and much drafting had already been completed to that end. The Rector referred expressly to the amendment of the Constitution of Egypt to which I have referred.

The other papers, while stressing the need for a new *ijtihād*, did not explain – indeed, how could they? – how such a process could overcome immutable provisions which seem to conflict directly with occidental legal theories.

To sum up. At the present time it can only be said that uncertainty remains, not only in the Gulf states, but overall. I have ventured to express the view that only uniform legislation can solve the issues involved so as to remove all doubts; I have also referred to the unfortunate unlikelihood of this happening. We all know of the drafting committees operating within the Islamic conferences, but so far little has emerged. I must repeat that I for one fail to see how, even if it be desirable, such uniform legislation could, while remaining true to the basic precepts (*nuṣūṣ*) of the Sharīʻah, be consonant with Western legal systems or compatible with Western commerce and commercial law.

Invidious as it may be to quote too much from oneself, may I nonetheless do so from a book which I wrote in 1980.

> "It is often said that the Qur'an (and hence the Shari'a) provides all the principles necessary for the regulation of relationships even in the world of commerce. As with Christianity or other major religions, that would be true in the context of the ideal society, wherein every member accepted and obeyed its dictates under spiritual sanction; in the modern commercial world, this would envisage also such obedience in general internationally by members of other cultures, including States. This is unfortunately at the moment unthinkable, and in the context of society as it exists, the lesser merits of man-made law must obtain. It is in the latter context that the Shari'ah must be viewed and, in its very nature, necessarily found inappropriate. It may be said that it is the material world that is at fault in this, and that either Islam or Christianity, restored to their essential validity amongst us, would do a better and more adequate job. Be that as it may, the inherent immutability of the Shari'a militates against its suitability in the system of international commerce which man has created. Acceptance of this truth is reflected in the

> publication by most of the States of the Muslim world of Commercial and other Codes in replacement of the Shari'a, which is now in many cases limited to matters of personal status."[13]

If I am correct in this overall view, then the Arabs are inevitably ever faced with the alternatives of adhering to Western-type codes (*vide* Kuwait, Bahrain) or adhering or reverting to Sharīʻah principles, perhaps with new *Majallahs* which merely codify the appropriate Sharīʻah principles (as an example we may recall the new *Majallah* issued in Saudi Arabia based on Ḥanbalī principles). No doubt the whole question will continue to be begged for as long as possible; but the pressures are there and are increasing; the swing back to the Sharīʻah is apparent in current legislation. It is the duty of the practising lawyer always to point out the possibility of its application.

Notes

1 Promulgated by Law 67 of 1980; published in *Al-Kuwait al-yaum* No. 1335 (1981).
2 Promulgated by Law 68 of 1980; published in *Al-Kuwait al-yaum* No. 1338 (1981). Article 96 of the Commercial Code confirms the precedence of that code's provisions in the matter of commercial obligations and commercial contracts, where there is any variance with those of the Civil Code.
3 Promulgated by Decree Law 7 of 1987; published in the *Supplement to Official Gazette* No. 1739.
4 Law 13 of 1971, *Official Gazette* No. 929.
5 The Bahrain Contract Law first appeared as Queen's Regulation No. 1 of 1961 in Supplement No. 32 to the *Persian Gulf Gazette*. It was reissued by the Ruler of Bahrain in 1969 (see *Official Gazette* No. 852). The Law of Civil Wrongs first appeared in 1970 (see *Official Gazette* No. 870).
6 Law 16 of 1971, *Official Gazette* No. 7 (1971).
7 *Official Gazette* No. 12/1973.
8 *Official Gazette* No. 58/1978.
9 Promulgated by Law 5 of 1985; published in *Official Gazette* No. 158.
10 Promulgated by Sultani Decree 32/84; published in *Official Gazette* No. 286.
11 Case No. 20, judicial year 1.
12 Case No. 141, judicial year 4.
13 Ballantyne, *Legal Development in Arabia* (London: Graham & Trotman, 1980), pp. 109–110.

XIV

The AMF Case and Arab International Corporations[1]

Introduction

The purpose of this paper is to set a basis for discussion of the recent House of Lords decision in the case of *Arab Monetary Fund* v. *Hashim and others (No. 3)*,[2] and to examine how it affects the position of Arab International Corporations, particularly with regard to their ability to sue and be sued in English courts.

As there is as yet comparatively little judicial discussion in general upon the nature of International Corporations, which are also referred to as International Companies and International Legal Persons, brief reference will be made to the attempts of academics to define such entitles (which I shall refer to as ILPs for short). Some of the problems created by ILPs *vis-à-vis* the liability of their members for debts in municipal jurisdictions, as witnessed in the mamoth *Tin* litigation and the *AMF* case will be examined, as will the International Arbitration which involved Westland Helicopters and the Arab Organisation For Industrialisation, with which I have been concerned for many years.

The scope for discussion is enormous and could involve questions such as the immunities or responsibilities of ILPs, the application of the *ultra vires* rule to their acts, and the problems which might occur upon their dissolution. I hope these problems will be the subject of wider discussion.

Definition of an ILP[3]

Firstly, I will deal with the nature of an ILP. Clive Parry has stated in graphic terms that an ILP, 'is everywhere abroad nowhere at home'.[4]

Attempts have been made by various academics to provide a definition of an ILP with a certain amount of confusion. One can advantageously refer to the definition provided by F.A. Mann,[5] who suggested that the term 'International Company' bore at least three meanings. In the present context, it is only necessary to note that we are not referring to national companies which have an international business. Nor are we referring to companies created under national law but described as international because they are conceived in a treaty concluded by States. The truly International Company, according to Mann, is one that is not only contemplated but is also created by the treaty between states. It must also be organised and live under Public International Law alone, and not derive its status from national law. Brownlie[6] would add to the definition the need for a distinction in terms of legal power and purposes, between the organisation and its member states. Seidl Hohenveldern[7] further provides that an ILP is established by its member states where they use means which if pursued by a single state, could be qualified as *acta jure imperii*.

While Friedmann[8] would argue that some national corporations ought to be elevated to the International plane because they have resources available to them which equal or exceed those of some states, his view does not appear to have any significant support.

It is worth remembering that it is not only a treaty which can create an ILP. Whilst this is the norm, according to Brownlie[9] it could equally be possible for the necessary contractual consensus to be provided by a resolution of a conference of states,[10] and he cites The World Tourism Organisation as being a case in point.

The existence of ILPs is by no means a new-found phenomenon. One could cite the Central Commission for the Navigation of the Rhine set up in 1815 by the Congress of Vienna as an early example.[11]

It is true to say that ILPs have proliferated since the Second World War, the reason being the recognition by states of the need for greater co-operation between them and the inherent advantages in creating a separate legal entity to facilitate such co-operation, particularly in the commercial field with which we are presently concerned.[12]

Arab International Corporations

Having briefly dealt with the nature of an ILP, I turn now to consider how Arab ILPs differ from other such entities. At first sight, there is no reason to distinguish an 'Arab' International Organisation from any other, governed as they all are by Public International Law.

However, upon consideration of the sources of Public International Law, one recalls that for the purposes of Article 38 of the Statute of the International Court of Justice, they include the general principles of law as recognised by civilised states.

It is at this point that one realises that the one essential feature distinguishing the Arab States is al Islam and the *Shari'a*, the law of Islam. The *Shari'a* has been recognised by at least two International Conferences at the Hague as one of the sources of general principles of law. Also, of course, the *Shari'a* is prescribed as a principal source of legislation in the Constitutions of the vast majority of Arab States. Hence, we have a feature which may be relevant in construing a treaty between Muslim States which might not be relevant otherwise in applying principles of Public International Law. This question has never arisen to my knowledge in the context of treaty interpretation, but must be borne in mind. In this present context, it may be noted that the *Shari'a* does not recognise the concept of juridical personality – quaere, even, limited liability.

There are numerous ILPs made up in whole or in part by Arab States. I name but a few:

1 The Organisation of Petroleum Exporting Countries (OPEC);
2 The Arab Monetary Fund (AMF);
3 The Arab Shipping Company (founded in 1972);
4 The Arab Petroleum Company;
5 The Inter-Arab Investment Guarantee Corporation established in 1971;
6 The Arab Organisation for Agricultural Investment and Growth;
7 The Gulf Industrial Consultancies Organisation;
8 The Arab Organisation for Industrialisation.

Litigation Involving ILPs

There are well over 400 ILPs in existence operating in profit and non-profit making endeavours and there has been astonishingly little litigation involving them.

There is, of course, the *Reparations* case[13] which involved the United Nations, but the decision has been subjected to much academic scrutiny,[14] and is now regarded as being unique in its application to the United Nations.

In the jurisdictions of New York and Switzerland, there appear to be no qualms about allowing ILPs to engage in litigation in the municipal courts. Academic opinion also suggests that the municipal courts of the Federal Republic of Germany and Luxembourg would recognise ILPs for such purposes.[15]

In the UK, the position is rather different – the reason being the apparent reluctance of the municipal courts to deal with treaty law, or indeed, Public International Law as such. This is attributable to English Constitutional Law, which prevents a treaty entered into by the Crown from being capable of affecting the rights of subjects unless and until it is incorporated into English law by legislation.[16]

The Tin Case[17]

As ILPs (with a few exceptions), find their existence in treaty provisions, the English courts, as demonstrated by the House of Lords in the case of *J.H. Rayner* v. *D.T.I.* (*The Tin Council case*),[18] have held that ILPs do not *per se* possess legal personality under English law in the absence of municipal legislative provision which has the effect of conferring such personality upon them.

In brief the Tin Council was an ILP operating under the Sixth International Tin Agreement 1982 (ITA 6), the treaty to which the EEC and twenty-three States were parties, including the UK, where the ITC was based.

Article 16 of ITA 6 provided that the ITC was to have legal personality including, 'the capacity to contract, to acquire and dispose of moveable and immoveable property and to institute legal proceedings'.

This provision was repeated in the headquarters agreement concluded between the ITC and the UK.

Article 5 of the ITC (Immunities & Privileges) Order 1972, a statutory instrument made under the International Organisations Act 1968 provided that the ITC should have 'the legal capacities of a body corporate'.

The House of Lords held that the 1972 Order did not merely recognise and give effect to a personality which the ITC already possessed but rather created the personality of the ITC for the purposes of English law.[19] One of the consequences of this approach is that without an Order in Council, the courts would not have recognised the Tin Council as having a juridical existence for the purposes of English law.

Whilst the House of Lords accepted that the ITC already existed, and indeed was implicitly accepted as having already existed by the

1972 Order, they considered that this existence was strictly confined to the plane of relations between States. Lord Oliver's attempt[20] to make a distinction between the legal personality of the ITC on the plane of International Law and its personality in English law, with respect, appears to have relied upon a misconceived analogy with a foreign municipal company which chose to do business in England through the medium of a locally-incorporated subsidiary.

Whilst the Court of Appeal's judgment deals with some of the questions of International Law,[21] their Lordships' House adopted an approach that, with respect, was unfortunate (and perhaps inevitable), in that they completely ignored the International Personality of the Tin Council as such, focusing upon the provisions of the International Organisations Act 1968 and the Order in Council.

The AMF Case[22]

The approach adopted by the House of Lords in the *Tin* case necessitated a resort to other principles by Hoffman J, the judge at first instance in the case of *Arab Monetary Fund* v. *Hasim and others (No. 3)*.[23]

The brief facts of the case are that the Arab Monetary Fund (AMF) had been created by Treaty agreement in 1976 between twenty Arab States and 'Palestine', the UK not being a party to it.

By the terms of the agreement Article 2 provided:

> The fund shall have an independent juridical personality, and shall have, in particular, the right to own, contract and litigate.

There was no Order in Council in existence under the International Organisations Act 1968 in respect of the AMF, but it had its headquarters in Abu Dhabi and was the subject of a UAE decree in 1977, which according to expert evidence had provided the AMF with independent legal personality and the right to sue according to UAE law.

The AMF brought proceedings in England for damages and tracing orders and other relief against Dr Hasim, who formerly was its Director–General, members of his family, and financial institutions, in respect of the alleged misappropriation of around US $50 million by Hashim. The defendants sought to strike out the action on the grounds that the AMF did not exist as a legal person in English law.

As to the UAE decree (Union Decre 35/1977), its wording provided that:

> Consent is accorded to the Agreement of the Arab Monetary Fund signed in the city of Rabat Morocco, Tuesday the Twenty Seventh of Rabi'al Akhir 1396 equivalent to the twenty seventh day of April 1976, the text of which is annexed to this Decree.

The effect had been to give effect to the Articles of Agreement of the AMF within the UAE. The defendants submitted that the Treaty agreement, which formed the constitutional basis of the AMF, was non-justiciable and did not confer capacity on the AMF to bring legal proceedings in England.

Hoffman J cut through the complication by holding[24] that since the Treaty establishing the AMF had been incorporated into the law of the UAE and Abu Dhabi, he could use the English conflicts rules to recognise the AMF as an entity existing under UAE law, with the result that it had the capacity to sue in the English courts.

The Court of Appeal, by a majority, allowed the defendants appeal on the ground that the AMF remained the creation of a non-justiciable Treaty, and that the UAE legislation had given effect to the Treaty solely within the UAE territory without creating a UAE entity capable of being recognised under the English conflicts rules.

The Master of the Rolls, Lord Donaldson, stated in graphic, even romantic terms, what he perceived to be the effect of the Tin Council decision. As he saw it at page 156 of the report:

> Absent an Order in Council, an international organisation is something which in the eyes of English law, is as much a fact as a tree, a road or a hill. But it is not a person and the law can only deal in the rights and liabilities of persons. Once it is touched by the magic wand of the Order in Council, it becomes a person but one which is quite unlike other persons. Self-evidently it is not a natural person. But equally it is not a United Kingdom juridical person. Nor is it a foreign juridical person. It is a person sui generis, which has all the capacities of a United Kingdom juridical person, but is not subject to the controls to which such a person is subject under United Kingdom law. It is not a native, but nor is it a visitor from abroad. It comes from the invisible depths of outer space.

Bingham LJ dissenting[25] saw no inconsistency in holding that in the *Tin* case and the *AMF* case, the Order in Council and the Decree respectively did not *create* (my emphasis) a domestic corporation, but each was effective to *confer* legal personality in its respective municipal law on a body which would otherwise have lacked it.

He was of the view that comity required the UK to recognise the AMF by virtue of the Decree, just as the UAE would (one hopes) recognise the ITC by virtue of the Order in Council.[26]

In the House of Lords,[27] the AMF appeal was allowed, the majority concurring with Lord Templeman who held that the UAE Decree had *created* a corporate body and that under the domestic English conflicts rule the courts would grant standing to sue to corporate bodies created by foreign States recognised by the Crown, as in the case of the UAE.[28]

On this basis their Lordships were of the view that the *Tin* case did not prevent them reaching such a conclusion. I am in respectful agreement with this conclusion, which provides a commonsense conflicts solution. It would however perhaps have been better to base the conclusion on the principle that if an entity is recognised as having juridical personality by the laws of a State itself recognised by the UK,[29] then such personality should be likewise recognised by the English Courts. The whole approach appeals directly to English conflict rules, wherein lies the commonsense. However, the difficulties inherent in this approach are manifest.

The critics of the decision would argue that to enable the AMF to sue in the English courts, its obvious international character was disregarded and it was treated as a creature of UAE law which it obviously was not.

Indeed, the effect of such a process is to locate an ILP within a national legal system, which runs counter to the manifest intention of its members to elevate the ILP above the municipal plane, on to the International level.

A further effect of the House of Lords judgment in the AMF case is that an ILP which has its legal personality embodied in the laws of more than one Member State as is often the case, will have a separate personality in each such State. The courts might consequently face problems of deciding between these personalities for the purposes of recognition, and such difficulties could be exacerbated by the English conflicts of law rules.[30] They could be further exacerbated in the case of Arab ILPs where the *Shari'a* formed an operative element in the applicable law, either as one of the general principles of law contributing to Public International Law, or as one element in the municipal law of the Member State.

The Status Quo

The legal position of ILPs seeking to sue in the English courts after the *Tin* case and the *AMF* case appears to be as follows: in the absence of express UK legislation conferring legal personality upon an ILP which has not been the subject of foreign municipal legislation embodying its constituent treaty, the ILP will not be entitled to sue in the English courts.

Whilst such a conclusion also means that the ILP cannot be sued in the English courts, it is unlikely to be of much comfort to ILPs which possess assets and engage in business in the UK. Although I have not yet had the opportunity to research this matter fully, I believe that in the majority, if not all of Arab ILPs, the treaty setting up the ILP has been passed into law by each of the contracting States. In the case of the Arab Organisation for Industrialisation (AOI), for example, each of Egypt, Saudi Arabia, Qatar and the UAE passed laws to that effect.

It is submitted that the solution sought[31] calls for the International Organisations Act 1968 to be extended in scope, and for Orders in Council to be promulgated to enable otherwise incapacitated ILPs to sue in English courts is unnecessary.

With the very greatest of respect to their Lordships in the *Tin* case and the *AMF* case, they reached their conclusion by adopting tautologous reasoning when a simpler and more consistent approach may have been available to them.

The frantic searching for municipal legislative underpinning of an ILP is thought to be necessary because, as Lord Oliver[32] put it in the *Tin* case:

> It is axiomatic that municipal courts have not and cannot have the competence to adjudicate upon or to enforce the rights arising out of transactions entered into by independent sovereign states on the plane of international law.

This view leads the court inevitably it would seem, to the conclusion that the International Organisations Act 1968 and Orders in Council thereunder are the exclusive source for the conferment of legal personality upon ILPs under English law. The alternative view, that this Act and its predecessor, the Diplomatic Privileges (Extension) Act 1944, do not affect the position under Customary International Law and at common law, namely that ILPs are entitled to recognition by virtue of their existence was canvassed as long ago as 1945 by Jenks,[33] and has been voiced by the dissenting opinion of Bingham LJ[34] in the *AMF* case and numerous academic commentators.[35]

The main argument against this view, and one which I support, stems from such recognition arising out of the principle of recognition of States, and hence removing recognition of ILPs from the courts and placing it in the hands of the executive.

The view put forward by Jenks has undoubtedly received a warm reception in other jurisdictions, the ITC having being recognised for litigation purposes in the State of New York even though the US was not a party to the Tin Agreement. Although the recognition theory found little favour with their Lordships, a further opportunity may arise for it to be incorporated into English law. Whether it is acceptable for such an issue to be placed in the hands of the executive is undoubtedly a question which ought to be discussed further.

Concurrent and/or Secondary Liability of Members of ILPs

Assuming that the ILP in question is able to sue and be sued, the possibility of its members being concurrently and/or secondarily liable for its debts must be examined.

There are no judicial decisions providing for such liability and there appear to be only two examples of State practice, the first involving payment by the members of Eurochemic to the State of Belgium, apparently as an incentive for Belgium to take over the functions of Eurochemic[36] and secondly, the settlement payment of £182.5 million agreed by the members of the ITC in December 1989 satisfying approximately 40 per cent of the claims of its creditors.[37] In neither case did the members accept liability.

The argument for concurrent and/or secondary liability is propounded by amongst others Mann,[38] Adam[39] and Seidl[40] who view the absence of any rule of Public International Law protecting members from liability as leading to a necessary inference that such members are liable. Shihata[41] and Amersinghe[42] reject this approach and are of the view that the absence of conclusive State practice, taken together with the nature of legal personality in Municipal Law, lead to the conclusion that the liability of an ILP for its debts is limited and does not extend to its members. Support for their view can be found in The Vienna Convention on the Law of Treaties between States and International Organisations or between International Organisations (21 March 1986),[43] which by Articles 34 and 35 provides that where there is a treaty to which an International Organisation is a party, liabilities arising from the treaty shall not attach to third States without their consent. As a result, members of an ILP could not be held concurrently and/or secondarily liable without their consent for its failure to fulfil a treaty obligation.

Further support for the limited liability view can be found under English law in the *Tin Council* case, where limited liability was held to be a concomitant of separate legal personality. This was in accordance with the common law rule established by the House of Lords in 1897 in the case of *Salomon* v. *A. Salomon & Co. Ltd.*,[44] although Nourse LJ dissenting[45] in the Court of Appeal held that the only inference that could be drawn from an examination of the Tin Agreement was that the members would be liable in the event of the Tin Council being unable to meet its debts. This view appears to have been based less upon the common law concept of limited liability and more upon the civil law concept, which in contrast provides for liability of the members of the juridical entity known as the *Société en Nom Collectif*.

In the case of an Arab ILP, important *Shari'a* principles could be involved. The *Shari'a* does not in principle recognise corporate personality or limitation of liability (*supra*).

The Westland Arbitration

The concept of the *Société en nom Collectif* was also significant in the International Arbitration brought by Westland Helicopters Limited, in respect of the debts of the Arab Organisation for Industrialisation (AOI).[46] Briefly, the facts are that the AOI was formed by Treaty in 1975 between the UAE, Saudi Arabia, Egypt and Qatar, with the aim of developing the arms industry of its members. As far as its juridical personality was concerned, by Article 1 of the Treaty, the AOI had total administrative and financial independence from its members, and Articles 1(2) and 8 provided that it was not to be subject to their internal laws and regulations. There was no attempt to limit the liability of its members and its operation was swathed in a complicated connexity of contracts.

The AOI entered into a contract with Westland Helicopters Limited which contained an arbitration clause, by which the ICC was to designate the arbitrators for arbitration to take place in Geneva and to be governed by Swiss law.

In 1979, as a result of the Camp David accord between Egypt and Israel, the other three members of the AOI declared it at an end, with the initial concurrence of Egypt.

The International Tribunal had recourse to the Treaty entered into by the Member States in 1975 which created the AOI, in finding that it was competent to hear the dispute. In its interim award of 5 March 1984 it held that in the absence of an express provision in the constituent documents limiting liability, the members of the AOI could conceivably be concurrently liable for its debts. This conclusion was reached by treating the AOI as a mixed entity akin to the *Société en Nom Collectif*. The decision has been the subject of appeals within the Swiss courts, and in 1988 the Swiss Federal Tribunal held that there could be no competence *vis-à-vis* Egypt. This result followed from the fact that Swiss law required express signature to an arbitration clause. However, as Egypt was the only party appearing before the Tribunal, the other three members were still subject to the competence of the International Tribunal. Publication of a Final Award on liability is awaited.

State Practice

Whilst there does not appear to be a general consensus either in State practice, judicial precedent or academic opinion as to the existence of a firm rule providing for members of an ILP to be concurrently and/or secondarily liable for its debts,[47] in the event of liability becoming an issue it will of course always be necessary to examine the constituent documents of the ILP concerned to determine whether they make an express provision. In particular, this is essential in the case of an Arab ILP, where the original Arabic must always be carefully examined.

Amersinghe[48] analysed the constituent documents of ILPs and concluded that, whilst in less than one third of existing constituent instruments examined by him express provision is made for the limitation of liability of the ILP, most of the constituent instruments of banking, commercial and financial ILPs contained express provision which purported to limit the liabilities of their members.

One such example is the World Bank, which by Article 11(6) of its constituent instrument seeks to limit the liability of members to the unpaid portion of the issue price of shares.

In others, the formulation of the limitation of the members liability is wider and more general to the effect that: 'no member shall be liable by reason of its membership, for acts or obligations of the fund'.[49] Provisions to this effect are contained in the constituent instruments of several Arab ILPs including:

1 The Arab Fund for Economic and Social Development – Article 8(1);
2 The Arab Monetary Fund – Article 48(a);
3 The Islamic Development Bank – Article 7(3);
4 The Inter-Arab Investment Guarantee Corporation – Article 7(4).

Currently, there appears to be only one example of members of an ILP expressly agreeing to be liable concurrently and/or secondarily liable for its debts, and that is provided in the Euratom Agreement.

Examples of ILPs (admittedly of a non-commercial nature), where the constituent instruments do not refer either to concurrent or secondary liability of members or the exclusion of such liability include:

1 The United Nations;
2 The Arab League;
3 IMF;
4 OPEC;
5 OAPEC.

The unsettled state of the law leads one to conclude that in any case where liability of members is in issue, the constituent documents of the ILP will have to be examined thoroughly, the common law tradition supporting the view that even in the absence of any express provision on the point in the constitution, the members will not incur liability for its debts. Civil analogies however may suggest otherwise. As pointed out (*supra*), Public International Law should refer to the general principles of law, by analogy a concordance of municipal systems. It is also worth remembering that even if separate legal personality has *per se* created a veil behind which the members can hide from liability, the possibility of piercing the veil exists on the international plane, as stated in the *Barcelona Traction* case[50] albeit that exceptional circumstances may have to be shown to enable this to take place.

Forum Conveniens? – Common Law or Civil Law

Perhaps nothing illustrates more clearly the fundamental importance of the jurisdictional aspect than a comparison between the approach of the House of Lords in the *Tin* case and that of the Tribunal in the Westland Arbitration. It would appear from such a comparison that the answer to the problem of concurrent and/or secondary liability of the members of an ILP will to a large extent depend upon whether the tribunal trying the issue is a common law court, a civil law court, or an International Tribunal. Ultimately, the composition of the tribunal utilised will most probably determine whether the members of an ILP can hide behind a veil (most likely on the common law view), or whether they will be held jointly and/or severally liable for its debts (most likely in a civil law jurisdiction, as in Scotland and on the Continent).

The view of the writer is that given the possibility of States being able to limit their liability for the debts of ILPs which they have created, this should be done by express provision in the constituent documents of the organisation, to enable third parties to be put on notice. Otherwise third parties should be able to assume that the Member States stand behind the organisation and accept liability for the debts which it incurs. In the case of Arab ILPs formed between Muslim States, it would be difficult to exclude from the general principles of law applicable to the Treaty, the *Shari'a* law of Islam.

Conclusion

ILPs will undoubtedly generate problems upon their dissolution and in respect of their immunities and responsibilities, but the scope of such topics is too great to encompass in such a short space of time. Indeed, there may even arise problems in ascertaining the point at which an ILP ceases to be International, in view of the potential for the members of some ILPs, including Gulf Air, to alienate a proportion of their shares to their nationals. One thing is certain, English law is at an early stage of development in respect of ILPs and it may not be too long before it comes to recognise ILPs as existing in their own right, thereby banishing the seemingly impenetrable haze in which they have recently been immersed by the English courts.[51]

Notes

1 This was a paper read to the Legal Practitioners Group, CIMEL, at the University of London. The paper was as its name implies an attempt to set the stage for discussion, and in no way purports to be a complete analysis. The detailed material in this paper was compiled by Mr Khawar Qureshi, a member of my chambers at 1, Hare Court, Temple, to whom I am thus greatly indebted.

In the event, the paper succeeded in its object, and the ensuing debate was lively and informative. It is regretted that no transcript was kept, a deficiency which will, it is hoped, be remedied in future meetings of the group.

2 [1991] 2 WLR 729.

3 See Jenks 22 (1945) BYBIL 267–75; Rama-Montaldo 44 (1970) BYBIL, p. 111 at p. 154; Brownlie, *Principles of Public International Law*, 4th ed. (1990), p.681; see also *Institut de Droit International Annuaire*, vol. 61 (1985), Part II, at p. 185 for the Institute's Resolution concerning ILPs.

4 In Friedmann (ed.), *The Public Corporation* (1954), p. 514.

5 'International Corporations and National Law' (1967) BYBIL 145.

6 *Supra* note 2 at p. 681.

7 *Corporation in and under International Law* (1987), at p. 72.

8 *The Changing Structure of International Law (1964), pp. 221–331.*

9 *Supra* note 2 at p. 682.

10 For example, the United Nations Conference on Trade and Development (UNCTAD) and the United Nations Industrial Development Organisation (UNIDO) were both founded by resolutions of the UN General Assembly.

11 See P. Wood, *The Law and Practice of International Finance* (1980), at p. 37.

12 See Seidl Hohenveldern, *supra* note 6 at p. 67.

13 [1949] ICJ Reports p. 174.

14 Rama-Montaldo, *supra* note 2 at p. 124 *et seq*.

15 See Wood, *supra* note 10 at p. 39.

16 For a recent application of this principle see the House of Lords decision in the case of *R* v. *Secretary of State for the Home Department, exp. Brind* [1991] 2 WLR 588. The Treaty in question was the European Convention on Human Rights.

17 For academic analysis of the House of Lord's judgment see Greenwood (1990) CLJ 8; for analysis of the judgments of the lower courts see J. Kodwo Bentil (1989) 8 *Litigation* 91.

18 [1990] AC 418.

19 See the speeches of Lord Templeman at p. 4789–4798 and Lord Oliver at 506 C–E.

20 At 508H–510F of his speech.

21 See, in particular, the judgments of Kerr LJ and Nourse LJ at p. 169 C p. 173 and p. 206 D-220 G (1989) Ch. 72, respectively.

22 For academic comment on the decision of the House of Lords see G. Marston [1991] CLJ 218.

23 [1990] 3 WLR 139; the judgment of the Court of Appeal begins at p. 151 of the same volume.

24 Pp. 147 E-148 B.

25 Pp. 163–6.

26 This is by no means certain. Although the UAE Code of Civil Transactions 1985 contains, for the first time in that jurisdiction, basic principles of conflict of laws, such principles are expressed to be subject to the *Shari'a*. For an analysis, see Ballantyne in the *Arab Law Quarterly*.

27 *Supra* note 1.

28 For the relevant English conflicts rule see Dicey & Morris, *The Conflict of Laws*, 11th ed. (1987), Vol. 2 at p. 1128.
29 See now the Foreign Corporations Bill 205, which seeks to alter the position of corporations created in unrecognised States vis-à-vis their capacity to sue and be sued in the UK.
30 See P.J. Smart, 'Corporate Domicile and Multiple Incorporation in English Private International Law' [1990] JBL 126 at p. 130.
31 See the judgment of Nourse LJ in the *AMF* case at p. 161 A–C.
32 At p. 499F.
33 'The Legal Personality of International Organisations' (1945) BYBIL 267 at p. 273.
34 See pp. 162 H-166 of his judgment.
35 For an analysis of the International Organisations Act 1968 and its precursor, the Diplomatic Privileges (Extension) Act 1944, see G. Marston, 'The Origin of the Personality of International Organisations in United Kingdom Law' [1991] 40 ICLQ p. 403. The writer concludes that the personality of an International Organisation ought to be analogous to that of a foreign state for the purposes of recognition; see also 49 (1978) BYBIL 347–84 for the reply to a question put by the Bank of England to the Foreign and Commonwealth Office, which supports this recognition theory with regard to financial ILPs such as banks.
36 See Seidl-Hohenveldern, *supra* note 6 at pp. 51–2.
37 See *The Financial Times*, 23 December 1989, p. 22, col. 4.
38 F.A. Mann, 'International Corporations and National Law' 42 (1967) BYBIL 145 at pp. 160–61.
39 H.-T. Adam, *Les Organismes Internationaux Specialisés* 130 (1965).
40 Seidl-Hohenveldern, *supra* note 6 at pp. 88–9 and 119–21; see also Schermers, *International Institutional Law* (1980), at p. 780.
41 *Revue Egyptienne De Droit International* 25 (1969), 119 at p. 125.
42 'Liability to Third Parties of Member States of International Organisations: Practice, Principle and Judicial Precedent,' 85 (1991) AJIL 259 at p. 280.
43 25 (1986) ILM 543.
44 [1897] AC 22 (HL).
45 At [1989] 1 Ch. 72 pp. 221H–222A, 223D–E.
46 Westland Helicopters Ltd and Arab Organisation For Industrialisation, United Arab Emirates, Kingdom of Saudi Arabia, State of Qatar, Arab Republic of Egypt and Arab British Helicopter Company 80 ILR 596.
47 See the judgment of Ralph Gibson LJ in the *Tin* case at pp. 242E–246B and the speech of Lord Oliver in the House of Lords at p. 512H–513F where they both conclude that there is no settled rule of concurrent and or secondary liability falling upon the members of an ILP for its debts.
48 See *supra* note 41 at pp. 269–73.
49 See The Agreement Establishing the International Fund for Agricultural Development (IFAD), Art. 3(4), 15 ILM 922 (1976).
50 *Barcelona Traction, Light and Power Company Ltd.* (1970) ICJ Reports at p. 39, paras. 56–8.
51 Postscript: for a recent attempt by the legislature within the UK to tackle the problems of recognition, see again the Foreign Corporations Bill [Bill

205 – brought before the Lords on 3 July 1991; see also *Hansard* 17th July 1991, pp. 417–423]. Unfortunately, it would appear that the ambit of the Bill is restricted exclusively 'to enabling foreign corporations incorporated under the laws of territories which the United Kingdom does not recognise as States to be treated for the purposes of the law in the United Kingdom as having legal personality'.

XV

Secular Law and the Shari'a: *Pacta Sunt Servanda* and the Theory of *Imprévision*

Against the background of the general principle that there may be exceptions to the rule that *pacta sunt servanda*, if contractual justice so requires, the theory of imprévision must be considered.

Any legal system other than the most unsophisticated will develop some means of offering at least a measure of relief from the rigours of the rule that *pacta sunt servanda* in cases in which events have occurred after a contract has been entered into which have rendered its performance impossible or (in some cases) significantly more onerous than that which was originally undertaken. The civil law systems have developed various such doctrines, including the French doctrines of *force majeure* (civil law; also known as *cas fortuits*) and *imprévision* (administrative law). The modern Arab Codes have adopted the theory of *imprévision*, to a greater or lesser degree; the operation of the theory within these Codes is then in varying degrees, subject to the Shari'a, which, it will be seen, has shown more flexibility in this respect than the Western systems of law.

Features of *imprévision*: the Arab Codes

Article 198 of the Kuwaiti Civil Code, which we may take as a model, provides as follows:

> 'If there occur, after the contract and before completion of its execution, general exceptional circumstances which could not have been expected when it was concluded, and there result from such occurrence that the execution of the obligation arising from the contract, if not becoming impossible, yet becomes oppressive

to the obligor such as to threaten him with grievous loss, then the Judge may, after weighing up the benefits of the two parties, restore the oppressive obligation to a reasonable extent, so as to narrow the scope thereof or increase the consideration therefor, and any agreement to the contrary falls void.'

A provision similar to this is common to virtually all the Arab Codes.[1] From this provision the basic features of the doctrine of *imprévision* appear: where general and exceptional events occur after the conclusion of a contract, which render performance oppressive or impossible, the Judge may, at the request of one of the parties, intervene to restore the balance of the contract. Thus, there are two stages: the first a question of fact, and the second a matter for the exercise of judicial discretion.

Even although the applicability of the doctrine rests on the facts of each individual case, there are clearly certain situations in which the doctrine is likely to be applied. The Codes themselves do not provide any examples, but Sanhouri gives several, including: earthquake; war; sudden strike; official price fixing or cancellation thereof; marked increase or reduction in prices; requisition; epidemic; locust swarms out of the ordinary. It is clear from these examples that the relevant circumstances are exceptional and rarely occur, that they could not have been expected, or foreseen, and that the test is a general objective one, not referable to the person or circumstances of the obligor, but embracing a whole class of people. Thus, the flooding of the Nile would not qualify, because it is something which one knows is likely to happen from time to time, and which might therefore fairly be described as expected, or foreseeable. Exceptionally severe flooding, however, might qualify. Similarly, damage to a crop of cotton due to cotton worn is expected, or foreseeable, and so would not qualify.

For the doctrine to be invoked, there must be an application to the Court. Any relief is in the discretion of the Judge, which is very jealously and sparingly applied. The theory of *imprévision* goes to *ordre public* (*nitham al-'am*), and therefore cannot be excluded, modified or brought into operation by contract: the discretion of the Judge cannot be fettered (this is reflected in the concluding phrase of Article 198 of the Kuwaiti Civil Code, translated *supra*).[2] If the Judge elects to exercise his discretion, he reapportions the burden of the obligation: the contract remains on foot, with the balance or equilibrium of the contract adjusted to take account of the exceptional events which have occurred.[3] Such judicial intervention would be unthinkable in England, but is commonplace in the civil jurisdictions.[4]

Imprévision and the French Courts

The theory of *imprévision* was developed by the Courts and legal writers in France. Interestingly, while the Administrative Courts, and in particular the *Conseil d'Etat*, have been particularly active in this respect, the Cour de Cassation has consistently refused to apply the doctrine, or anything which resembles it. This may be partly due to the fact that the rationale of the theory of *imprévision* seems to be the public interest in ensuring the discharge of contracts which are essential to the orderly conduct of public affairs; such a rationale of course has no application in relation to private transactions. The result is that the doctrine is confined to public law in France. In the Arab jurisdictions the doctrine is of general application.[5]

A famous application of the theory of *imprévision* took place during the First World War,[6] and involved a contract for the provision of gas and electricity, at a fixed price per cubic metre, which had been entered into in 1904 between a private company and the City of Bordeaux. With war came a dramatic increase in the price of coal, and thus in the price of gas. Contrary to the decision of the lower court, the Conseil d'Etat allowed an application by the company that the price of gas under the contract should be increased.

Interestingly, the Cour de Cassation has refused to grant relief in similar circumstances. The famous case of the *Canal de Craponne*[7] involved an agreement entered into in the sixteenth century, under which one party had agreed to irrigate an orchard, for a fixed sum, by means of a canal which was to be built. The contract remained valid in the late nineteenth century, by which time the fixed sum payable bore no relation to the cost of performing the irrigation and maintaining the canal. The lower courts granted an application to increase the fixed sum payable for the irrigation service; however, when the case reached the Cour de Cassation the result was reversed, and the terms of the contract as written reasserted.

As one might expect, the drafters of commercial contracts have provided their own solution to the problem, and commonly include provisions designed to cover situations such as severe currency fluctuation or war.

Frustration, *force majeure*, 'basis of transaction'

The common law doctrine of frustration terminates the obligation entirely, and is operable only in cases of impossibility, or virtual impossibility. The essence of the doctrine of frustration was described thus by Lord Radcliffe in the course of delivering his judgment in the House of Lords in *Davis* v. Fareham U.D.C.:[8]

> . . . frustration occurs whenever the law recognizes that without default of either party a contractual obligation has become incapable of being performed because the circumstances in which performance is called for would render it a thing radically different from that which was undertaken by the contract. Non haec in foedera veni. It was not this that I promised to do.

As we have seen, the theory of imprévision goes to *ordre public* (*nitham al-'am*), and therefore cannot be excluded, modified or brought into operation by contract. It is quite otherwise with the doctrine of frustration: the parties may, and commonly do, insert clauses into contracts the purpose of which is to provide for the happening of 'unexpected' events such as war, strike, natural disasters. These clauses are commonly referred to as 'force majeure' clauses, after the French doctrine of that name.[9]

The French doctrine of *force majeure* (which is a civil, rather than administrative, law doctrine) terminates the obligation entirely, but is operable only where the performance of the obligation has become impossible, rather than simply oppressive.

In Germany, where there is no statutory mechanism regulating the effect of change of circumstances, the doctrine of *Geschäftsgrundlage*, or basis of transaction, has been developed by the academic writers and by the Courts. Where the Court finds that basic unexpressed assumptions common to both contracting parties have been destroyed by the subsequent events, it may adapt the contract or, in extreme situations, discharge the parties from their obligations under the contract.

The Shari'a

The approach of the Shari'a is fundamentally different from that of English law. The operation of the theory of *imprévision* above referred to in the civil law systems means that the contrast there is not so marked. As a result, it has proved easy to adopt into the modern Arab

Codes the *imprévision* theory without offending against the principles of the Shari'a. In fact, in this instance the Shari'a is more flexible than the Western law. The approach adopted by the Shari'a, and the reasons for it, are aptly described by Professor Coulson:[10]

> "In English law the sanctity of contract means that the promise endures despite the normal vicissitudes of fortune. It is right that the promise should be kept 'for better or worse' 'through thick and thin', because this is in line with the popular belief that tenacity of purpose to some degree controls events and that the human will determines the future. The promise must dominate the circumstances.
>
> For Islam precisely the converse is true. Circumstances dominate the promise. Future circumstances are neither predictable nor controllable but lie entirely in the hands of the Almighty. In the face of the predetermined march of events human activity assumes a relative insignificance and the contractual promise becomes a relatively ephemeral thing. If the tide of affairs turns then the promise naturally floats out with it. The ubiquitous phrase of the vernacular: *in sha Allah* (if Allah so wills) is no empty expression. It could, in fact, be read as a vital proviso into any contract for future performance."

Generality of application of the theory of *imprévision*

Thus, the theory of *imprévision* is applied in the majority of the Arab jurisdictions, and in French administrative law, and doctrines allowing for judicial intervention to restore the balance of a contract are found in many other jurisdictions. The theory may therefore be said to be a general principle of law recognised by civilised States, which, by virtue of Article 38 of the Statute of the International Court of Justice,[11] is to be applied by the International Court of Justice in the resolution of disputes brought before it.

International law may also reach the same result as would an application of the doctrine of *imprévision* in municipal law, by a different route:[12]

> "While the principle of good faith prohibits the evasion of an obligation as established by the common intention of the parties, it also prohibits a party from exacting from the other party advantages which go beyond their common and reasonable

intention at the time of the conclusion of the treaty, as, for example, by invoking the treaty to cover cases which could not reasonably have been in the contemplation of the parties at the time of its conclusion. In this limited sense, the doctrine of *clausula rebus sic stantibus* is founded on the principle of good faith and is recognised by international law."

Notes

1 Inlcuding the Civil Codes of Jordan (Article 205), the U.A.E. (Article 249), Iraq (Article 146(2)), Egypt (Article 147(2)), Syria (Article 148(2)), Libya (Article 147(2)), Sudan (Article 117(1)), Algeria (Article 107(1)), Qatar (Article 48) and Yemen (Article 214).

2 This sits rather oddly with the Courts' willingness to recognise *force majeure* clauses, as to which, *vide infra*.

3 The Civil Codes of the U.A.E., Jordan and Iraq require the Judge to take into account considerations of equity in deciding whether to reapportion the burden of the contract and, if so, how much (see Articles referred to *supra*).

4 The English courts have consistently refused to rewrite contracts. See, for example, chitty on Contracts, 27th Edition (London, 1994), paragraph 16–166*ff*.

5 Although the application of the doctrine in practice may differ, since in exercising his discretion in a case involving a contract to which a public body is a party, the Judge will have regard to the public interest in the continued performance of the contract, which would not fall to be considered in a normal case.

6 CE 30.3.1916, S. 1916.3.17, D. 1916.3.25.

7 Civ. 6.3.1876, D.P. 1876.1.197.

8 [1956] A.C. 696, at 729.

9 See, further, Chitty on Contracts, *op. cit.*, paragraph 23–045*ff*.

10 Coulson, 'Commercial Law in the Gulf States – The Islamic Legal Tradition', London, 1984, at pp 81, 82.

11 Article 38 provides that the Court 'shall apply . . . the general principles of law recognized by civilised nations'.

12 Bin Cheng, 'General Principles of Law as Applied by International Courts and Tribunals,' London, 1953, at pp. 118 to 119.

XVI

Commercial Law in the Middle East: Law and Legal Change: Syndicated Loans

Introduction

This title is self explanatory. My task is to try to give an overview of what is likely to happen to syndicated loan agreements over the next decade. A syndicated loan is not, in this respect, different from any other kind of loan – so we ask ourselves, what is likely to happen to loans over the next decade?

This is virtually equivalent to asking: What will be the role of the Shari'a in the next decade, and: what will be the role of Islamic banking as against conventional banking?

I am fortunate to have with me on this panel two experts who, I have no doubt, are much more versed in this subject than I am.

The object of this paper is to set the scene for discussion.

We are dealing here with law, not politics or economics, although the three are of course so interrelated as to be virtually inseparable.

As we are here dealing with the future, I will try to limit myself as far as possible as regards the past and the present; but it is I think essential for an understanding of our subject to say something of the syndicated loan and its immediate history, in order to try to forecast the direction which these and indeed loans generally, are likely to take. What difficulties or potential difficulties exist at the present time, and how are these likely to be alleviated or exacerbated in the future? It will also be necessary to refer briefly to the existing legal situation in some of the Arab jurisdictions on a comparative basis.

In a foreword to an excellent new book on syndicated lending, Mr Eddie George, now governor of the Bank of England, writes:

> "Readers of Tony Rhodes' book will reach their own conclusions as to whether the re-trenchment of syndicated lending activity in the past year or two represents the beginning of a longer term contraction, or as in the past simply a pause in an expansionary trend. I myself have little doubt that syndicated loans will remain a very important technique for meeting the credit needs of large borrowers. But the confidence of those lenders and borrowers has been damaged by recent experience and the scale of the syndicated loan market's future activity will, in my view, depend to a substantial extent on how successfully its participants absorb the lessons of the past."[1]

I hope that in our discussions here today we may be able to make some contribution in respect not only of learning the lessons of the past but, against the constitutional and legal backdrop in the Middle East, trying to assess the trends for the future.

The Syndicated Loan

Definition

My role has for many years been that of the lawyer giving the necessary clearing opinions in these Loan Agreements in various Arab countries. It is with that background that I try to look at the future.

These loans have been defined as:

> A loan made available by a group of banks in predefined proportions under the same credit facility.

The loan is priced i.e. interest rates are determined by reference to a basic rate in the medium to long term floating rate bank market. Usually, with reference to those Arab countries with which I am concerned, there will be guarantee cover by ECGD or one of the equivalent national organisations.

The loan is usually with a sovereign state or state agency; this factor itself is very germane to our subject.

Brief History

Very briefly: the syndicated loan market had its origins in the sixties with the creation of 'eurodollars' and the introduction of variable interest rates during the period of the loan. Initially, the US$ was almost universally the currency, but what started as simple transactions have now become extremely complex – provisions relating to multi tranches, different currencies, various objects, options and a multiplicity of borrowers. Even were I qualified to do so (I am not a banker nor yet a city solicitor) there is no need to deal with all these complications in our present forecast. The loans with which I have dealt in the Arab countries have been largely US$ and/or sterling loans and for present purposes we must simplify, analysing the main features in order to assess which of them is liable to be affected by legal developments over the next decade. Before we do that however, a very short piece of further history.

We recall the almost frenetic activity in this market in the late 1970's and early 1980's accelerated in particular by the dramatic rises in the price of oil in 1973, when that price quadrupled over a short period. Let us recall that at that time the basic philosophy was that sovereign borrowers were gilt edged and did not fail. That shibboleth was soon turned on its head in the 1980's when we had a plethora of suspended payments and re-scheduling. We do not have the time to go in to all that now, even if it was relevant to do other than note it. The immediate point that I make here is that it is one thing perhaps for a sovereign state to be obliged to renegotiate cap in hand; it could be another in a final or desperate analysis where such state has a constitutional or other legal excuse for so doing or for avoiding the loan. This is really one of the essences of what we have to consider. Of course, in the ultimate analysis it is a question of international credibility or creditability; the sanctions are economic, lack of credit. Here, however, we are dealing with the legal aspects.

There can be no doubt that the lessons of the 1980's led to a good deal of re-thinking in this market and significant changes occurred in the early nineties. To quote from the excellent book to which I have already referred:

> "One is the increased emphasis placed by banks involved at all levels in the market on the credit quality of the borrower and the credit structure of each transaction. This is manifested by the move away from the 'name lending' which was common place in the 1980's to detailed and rigorous analysis."

In other words, not surprisingly, there does not seem to be the rush to lend which was the tendency at the time of that frantic boom; there is more caution, more investigation of the credit rating of the borrower and so on. There are those who say that on the basis of Shari'a principles of equity sharing and had syndicated financing adverted more to that principle and less to loan financing, there would have been more investigation into credibility; more importantly, the viability of the project.

The essential contents of the syndicated loan agreement

Once again, we have to generalise, to take an overview; to do otherwise would of course require a book of its own.

In the simple case which suffices for our purposes, there will be a syndicate of banks each bank being severally liable under the agreement; a managing or agent bank; and a guarantor, probably ECGD or some like organisation. There is usually a long definition section followed by a spelling out of the facilities to be granted. These may be of varying degrees of complication and variation. There may be various rates of interest linked to LIBOR or some other base rate.

There are of course detailed provisions for payment, re-payment, pre-payment and cancellation.

There are provisions for changes in circumstances – taxes increased costs relating in particular from changes in law or regulations which result in increased costs to the lenders – supervening illegality – market disruption etc.

The agreement will contain representations, covenants and provisions for events of default.

There will be a section providing for the guarantee.

There will be provisions for default interest and indemnity – default interest usually being charged above the normal rate charged on the loan. I need hardly state the danger here, that in almost any jurisdiction such a clause may be regarded as a penalty unless carefully worded. It is doubly relevant when viewed in the light of the Shari'a.

There is then a section dealing with payments; a section for fees; costs and expenses; agents; assignments and transfers with rights of assignment in the lending bank subject to safeguards.

Finally, of course, that essential section covering law and jurisdiction. I hardly need to tell this audience that it is essential for a system of law to be chosen to govern the contract. Normally in a sterling or dollar loan, the law chosen will be English law or US law – some such phrase as 'This agreement shall be governed by and construcd in accordancc with English law'.

As to jurisdiction, this would be vested in the English courts and in designated state courts and the federal courts of the United States. Other courts may also be specifically chosen: the position is further kept open by a clause to the effect that other appropriate courts shall also have jurisdiction – some such clause as the following:

> "The submission to the jurisdiction of the courts referred to in clauses – and – shall not (and shall not be construed so as to) limit the rights of the other parties hereto or any of them to take proceedings against any of the obligors in any other court of competent jurisdiction, nor shall the taking of proceedings in any one or more jurisdictions preclude the taking of proceedings in any other jurisdiction (whether concurrently or not) if and to the extent permitted by applicable law."

In a sovereign loan, where a state or state agency is involved, there will be, in addition to the submission to jurisdiction, an express waiver of sovereign immunity and an acknowledgment that the state acts *jure gestionis* in a commercial transaction.

I used to find very surprising, in particular during my early days of practice in the Gulf, the number of lawyers who should have known better who thought that by the insertion of comprehensive law and jurisdiction clauses, that was the end of the matter and that their clients were safeguarded accordingly. Well of course I do not have to mention to this audience the folly of such an attitude, but that does bring us back to a clause which normally occurs about clause 4 in the syndicated loan agreement, and that is the clause which sets out the conditions precedent to any draw down under the Agreement. The condition which concerns us here is that requiring a clearing opinion from a lawyer qualified to advise on the jurisdiction of the borrower to the effect that the loan agreement is valid and binding according to the law of that jurisdiction. Once again, I do not need to stress to this audience the importance of such an opinion; we all know that there may be for example public policy provisions in the forum of the borrower which may militate against the legality of the loan agreement; in the case of the Muslim Arab State, there may even be provisions, very basic provisions in the loan agreement as we shall see, which go against the constitution where the Shari'a is prescribed.

The Clearing Opinion

A clearing opinion is of course necessary to point out these possible shortcomings: their importance in the courts of the jurisdiction of the borrower is obvious; but there may also be an effect in the courts of the jurisdictions chosen in the agreement where, for example, the conflict laws of such courts give weight or credence to basic illegalities according to the law of the jurisdiction of the borrower. All these matters have to be very carefully considered. In a sovereign loan, as I have pointed out, it is one thing where a sovereign state applies ad misericordiam to recycle or reschedule its commitments – it is quite another where it has a legal peg upon which to hang it! The duty of the lawyer giving the clearing opinion is to point out any legal risks which exist at the time of signing the agreement. At this conference we go further and try to take a look at possible developments in this respect over the next decade, in the Arab countries of the Middle East.

Thus, in giving his clearing opinion, the counsel concerned must warn against any provisions in the law of that country going to mandatory requirements of public order (An nitham a'am) and in so doing it is probably necessary for him to advert, not only to the secular law of the state concerned, but also to the Shari'a law of Islam. In all cases in giving such opinions, I advert firstly to the question: Does, or could, the Shari'a have any relevance to this agreement? If it does or could, then a proviso has to be inserted in the clearing opinion to that effect, for a syndicated loan agreement contains in its very essence, provisions which would be avoided by the Shari'a. If the Shari'a has no relevance in the particular jurisdiction, then reference is made to the secular laws to see whether there are any similar mandatory provisions which require provisos to be made in the clearing opinion; but without doubt, the main difficulty arises if the Shari'a applies.

Thus, as I have pointed out at the beginning of this paper, the essence of the problem in considering the next decade of legal change in relation to these agreements, lies in assessing the extent to which there is likely to be a re-assertion of the Shari'a in the states of the Middle East. If there is to be such re-assertion, then its logical concomitant is the development of business along Islamic banking or profit sharing lines, moving away from the present structure based upon conventional banking and credit arrangements bearing interest and indeed interest upon interest.

A further express question which counsel giving the clearing opinion must ask himself, goes to private international law or conflict – is there an adequate system of conflict in the jurisdiction whereby the principle of autonomy of the parties would be recognised, that is to say the right of the parties to choose the law which they wish to govern a commercial contract? Will the courts of the country respect such choice of law? To take two extremes – in Saudi Arabia, for example, there is no conflict code, the Shari'a is paramount as the source of legislation in the state and technically the Shari'a would govern the loan agreement; in Kuwait, by contrast, there is an excellent conflict of laws code wherein the principle of autonomy of the parties in a commercial contract is expressly recognised. In Bahrain, although there is as yet no conflict code, the same principle would in my opinion be recognised. The same would obtain in, for example, Egypt.

Another aspect which must be carefully considered, is whether there are any special requirements in the jurisdiction concerned which go to execution of the agreement – there are for example special signing arrangements and safeguards for government contracts in Oman. In Bahrain and other states, it is always essential to assure oneself that the loan falls within the budgetary sanctions for the year in question.

A comparative overview of the existing law

Once again we have to paint with a very broad brush.

I spend a lot of my time impressing upon my students that there is no such thing as 'Arab Law'. We should talk of Arab laws of which there are a great number of great diversity. There are, however, common features between the Arab jurisdictions which I would list as follows:

1 Al Islam – hence the Shari'a – in varying degrees.
2 Similar features in the constitutions.
3 Civil and Commercial Codes stemming often from common origins – Egypt – France and the other great continental codes.
4 An interchange of judges and jurists.
5 By no means least, the great influence of Egyptian jurists.
6 The Arabic language.

It is of course impossible to overestimate the influence of Egypt and par excellence of Al Sanhouri who wrote the current Egyptian civil code in 1948. We may recall also that when Sanhouri wrote the code, he stated that he had made it as consistent with Shari'a principle as was appropriate at the time, but that the object of legislation in Egypt must be to accord more and more closely in the future with the Shari'a. We may also recall that in 1980, in the latter days of the Sadat regime, the constitution of Egypt was changed to provide that the Shari'a should henceforth be *the* main source of legislation; and that there exists a body of civil legislation in draft in Egypt waiting to be enacted to give effect more nearly to the Shari'a principles.

Bearing in mind the foregoing common features, we may standardise the sources of law prescribed in the codes in the Arab Middle Eastern jurisdictions as the following:

1 The Shari'a.
2 Express legislative provisions in the codes.
3 Contracts between the parties.
4 Custom.
5 The general principles of law, justice, equity etc, the latter being of course the usual sweeping up clause in any code (we recall article 1 of the French Civil Code which provides that a judge is to be prosecuted if he declines to decide a case on the basis that there is no law!).

These sources are not intended to be hierarchical. All are to be expected – there are no surprises certainly to the civilian lawyer whether Arab or no – with the obvious exception of Islam and hence the Shari'a. To the extent to which there is an Arab 'common law' the Shari'a is it. Now, I should stress that I do not make any claims to be a Shari'a lawyer – in my opinion to be so requires may years of concentrated study in an idiom in many ways foreign to that of the common and civil law systems, and of course essentially in classical Arabic. My own superficial dabbling in the subject persuades me that it is an incredibly difficult subject – one key note is the lack of certainty where modern commercial transactions are concerned: allied of course to the fact that many aspects of such transactions, in particular many aspects of loan agreements, are anathema to the Shari'a and illegal.

It is, as I have said previously, essential to assess what might be the role of the Shari'a in any particular jurisdiction; in particular assurances should not be accepted that because there are civil courts as distinct from Shari'a courts, the Shari'a will not apply. So to do would be to confuse jurisdiction with the law to be applied in the jurisdiction. The converse is however true: a Shari'a court would not apply civil law or commercial law contrary to the dictates of the Shari'a.

Many precepts of the Shari'a do not accord with what man has made of international or transnational commerce – and we now come close of course to the whole rationale of Islamic banking, inter alia. Now I quote from the late professor Coulson who put the matter with his usual lucidity:

> "Muslim jurisprudence is the real will of God, a divinely ordained system preceding and not preceded by the Muslim state, controlling and not controlled by the Muslim society."

This philosophy reflects the difficulties to be anticipated if the Shari'a applies to a commercial problem: there are many.

To quote from Al Sanhouri in 'Masaadir al Haqq', in isolating the three main features of the Shari'a which create difficulty in modern commercial law and, may we say, loan agreements in particular – riba, gharar, and a multiplicity of transactions in one contract.:

> "You will observe that each of these three matters had a profound effect on detailed provisions to the extent that, in many such, the Islamic jurisprudence distanced itself from the requirements of the transactions. If it were possible to clarify our understanding of these three matters in accordance with the development of civilisation then much of the reasoning which stops the Islamic jurisprudence from going along with the requirements of such development would disappear."

The obvious and classic difficulty is riba, because of its identification in the context of loan agreements with interest on monies lent. In fact, of course, the principle goes much further.

Let us reflect somewhat upon the ironic situation that since the Iraqi/Kuwaiti troubles, both Kuwait and Saudi Arabia have become really for the first time borrowers in the international market.

To revert to some of the extremes which I have already mentioned above – the commercial code of Kuwait permits interest in a commercial loan: the Shari'a, the basic law of Saudi Arabia does not. Bahrain in its new commercial code in 1987 makes express provision for interest to be assumed where none is expressly specified. In other jurisdictions there are varying shades. In some there is ambiguity.

Where Shari'a precepts spring, as does that of riba, from sources in the Quran and Sunna, basic nusuus, then there is no denying them. We have no time here to go into the great debate over riba – in this respect I might refer you to Chibli Mallats' recent and excellent thesis on the subject.[2] However, what is I believe beyond debate is that riba itself must be beyond the law. It may be a question of definition, but unless and until there is a common definition then the whole subject is one of great uncertainty and indeed risk. I had forgotten which Khalifa it was, but Professor Frank Vogel of Harvard — with us today – reminds me that it was Umar who expressed that wish that before the Prophet died he had provided a definition of riba.

I have given above the main elements of a modern syndicated loan agreement. It will be apparent from a glance at these elements, that it is to the relationship between lenders and borrower that the law of the borrowing jurisdiction may be relevant, despite the choice of law in the contract. The relations between lenders, between lenders and agent, between lenders and guarantor etc., are likely to be governed by the proper law of the contract and it may be thought unlikely that the law of the borrowing jurisdiction will be invoked. The contrary may obtain in the case of the borrower, and those considerations to which we are adverting here may be particularly relevant in the case of a sovereign borrower. At the end of the line, it may be of little comfort that practically speaking at the present time there may be little chance of a sovereign borrower invoking the Shari'a to plead the illegality of a loan agreement as going against its public policy or indeed even its constitution. It is fair to say that in my experience, I have only known of one case in which a member of the syndicated banks has withdrawn from the loan because of this possible risk: I do believe, however, that in the future the position will be viewed with more caution. The prizes at the end of the road are not so glittering; the states involved are not so credit worthy.

I have quoted from the late Professor Coulson: may I now quote from the first Coulson Memorial Lecture given by Sir Norman Anderson:

> "Finally, we noted the contemporary emergence of Islamic fundamentalism which seems to me to be a two-sided phenomenon: on the one hand a very understandable revolt against the dominance and (until recently) the colonialism of western powers; on the other hand a reaction against what might be termed the western philosophy of life, which, although basically founded upon Christian faith and ethics, has become so engulfed in liberalism and agnosticism, that it has largely lost both its cutting edge and its persuasive power."

Well, in my personal experience, Al Islam has certainly not lost its cutting edge or its persuasive power. We do not need to refer to 'fundamentalism' which envisages something extreme and possibly even violent in modern parlance: but the belief is there, that with the helter skelter adoption of secular codes on the civil model to the exclusion of the Shari'a, something is wrong and I believe this to be a universal malaise.

I have referred to the 1980 amendment to the Egyptian constitution. I have referred to the commercial codes of Kuwait and Bahrain at one end of the scale: but at the other end we may point to the civil code of the Yemen, which is Shari'a based, as is the Civil Transactions Code of the United Arab Emirates. We might also refer to the charter of the Islamic International Court of Justice promulgated by the Islamic conference in 1987:

> "Article 1 – The Islamic Court of Justice is the principle judicial organ of the Islamic Conference Organisation, and is founded on the principles of Islam and the sources of the basic rules of the Islamic Shari'a.
>
> Article 27 – A) The Islamic Shari'a is the basic source relied upon by the court in its judgments. B) The court shall refer to international law and bipartite and multipartite international agreements or international custom in force or the general principles of law or judgments issuing from international tribunals."

Here we may re-call also that two Hague conferences have endorsed the Shari'a as one of the sources of the general principles of law referred to in Article 38 of the statute of the International Court of Justice.[3]

There are of course many other examples, but the potential for application of the Shari'a is ever present. What is urgently, even desperately, needed is a uniform statement of Shari'a principles, adopted as a convention by the Arab states so that those principles may be seen and understood in common form by all.

I have quoted from what Sir Norman Anderson said at the first Coulson Memorial Lecture; I was privileged to give the second Coulson Memorial Lecture in 1988 during which I said the following:

> "Do the Arab States really wish, would they even be advised, to tamper with the existing concepts of riba at the present time? When they look at the world banking system which is based essentially upon interest and which may seem to them at times to be tottering on its base; when they see the most powerful nations in debt rather than in credit . . . may this not provide, apart from basic beliefs which exist anyway, a powerful argument that what the prophet uttered so long ago was entirely right, and that the principle of profit sharing and partnership is better not only from the religious point of view but in practice? Is Islamic banking not true merchant banking? Why then, they may say, erode the principles of riba as they exist, when it may be contended that

> they provide the only solution to impending chaos? I am not saying that I subscribe to such extreme view – I am simply not sufficient of an economist – but it is a solemn thought."

I have long been and still am of the opinion that a reassertion of the Shari'a is coming. How this will manifest itself on the ground in the context of loan agreements remains to be seen, but it is sobering to reflect that quite apart from the legal pressures inherent in the Shari'a for change in the system of conventional banking, we have actually found the IMF advocating the replacement of some of the burden of debt by equity investment – shades indeed of mudaaraba and mushaaraka at the Shari'a![4]

In my introduction to 'Islamic Law and Finance' a previous conference held here in 1988 I ventured to include three propositions:

1 That in jurisdictions where the Shari'a applies, contracts not in accordance with its precepts are quite simply illegal: in our present context, banking transactions based upon the conventional western system of interest;
2 That in Muslim eyes not only is a system of economics not based on Shari'a principles antireligious, illegal and sinful: in the world today such a system is not working; that for material reasons alone the Islamic system is better.
3 That the alternative to some cooperation in the international financial field is a clash, a confrontation.

In that introduction also I quoted from myself in the second Coulson lecture in 1988 as follows:

> "What, if anything, can be done by the Western lawyer, other than to sit back and wait for an inevitable crash application of the Shari'a? First of all, realise the existence of the problem, and problem it is! Secondly, Western lawyers must show a great sympathy and understanding for this powerful religious and cultural background, and we have to devise where necessary (not as yet in all jurisdictions) our bridges – if indeed these can be built. There are many ifs. The Shari'a is a sacred subject, and apart from understanding on the Western side, any dialogue must require the cooperation of the Muslim side in what in many quarters is regarded as a forbidden subject. Certainly, let us never underestimate the importance of this subject at this time – a classical and rigid application of the Shari'a to modern

economic agreements could be catastrophic, and it is sobering to reflect that this could occur in most of the Arab jurisdictions with no need for prior legislation. Let it not be thought either that such application is relevant only within a Muslim jurisdiction – what of the situation in a Western court directed by its conflict rules to apply to a contract the Shari'a law, proved by expert evidence to be the law applicable as the proper law of contract? Also, what of the enforcement of foreign judgments in the Muslim jurisdictions? These are grave matters."

I went on to say:

"Perhaps what is required in today's climate is not just a restructuring of the Shari'a to fit Western economic concepts, but some restructuring of those concepts in order to meet the Shari'a: a study of just how far Western and Shari'a concepts are incompatible in the light of a new ijtihad. In so far as dialogue is possible, let us pursue it. We must take the opportunity for discussion while wise and moderate men are available to participate in it. Really, this can only be done by lawyers, and, in the final analysis, Muslim lawyers at that – such is the difficulty where the law is identified with religion. The political implications are, of course, obvious; but for the issue to become an international political issue, or to be overtly treated as such, is, I hope, unthinkable – to say that that would be counter-productive is to understate the obvious. We are too apt to write learned memoranda based upon the material pros and cons of a situation. Despite the obvious difficulties, I am optimistic enough to believe that something may be achieved."[5]

Yet, we find that when we try to include Shari'a subjects in lectures or in our Middle East Legal Practitioners Forum, no one is interested. All I can say is that everyone, and in particular we lawyers, had better become interested before it is too late! This is an area where CIMEL and MELPF could make a vast contribution.

Notes

1 Syndicated Lending: Practice and Documentation. Tony Rhodes, General Editor – 1993 Euromoney publications.

2 Now included in his book 'Islam and Public Law'.
3 See 'Arab Comparative Commercial Law – The International Approach' Vol I. pp. 112, 113 (1984). Graham & Trottman and the International Bar Association.
4 Islamic Law & Finance: being proceedings of a conference convened by the Centre for Near & Middle Eastern Studies and the Law Department of the School of Oriental & African Studies, University of London, April 1988: Abbas Mirakhor 'The Progress of Islamic Banking' at pp. 91 et sequ. Published Graham & Trottman 1988.

XVII

Construction Contracts in the Arab Jurisdictions

You will see from your syllabus that the original title suggested for this lecture was 'Construction under Middle East Law Systems'. I have changed that title for two main reasons: firstly, 'Construction' might imply that I am engineer; I am not, I am a lawyer: secondly, I am not at all sure what the geographical designation 'Middle East' means to most people. Such designation would certainly include Israel as to whose laws I have no knowledge; it would probably also include Turkey to which the same consideration applies. The title now chosen is more apposite to my subject.

An audience cannot fairly be expected to direct relevant questions to me unless it knows something of my own professional background. Although I come before you with an academic title, of which I am justly proud, the whole of my professional background is that of the practising lawyer: I teach Arab comparative commercial law as a visiting professor at SOAS. That apart, I have been actively concerned in the practice of the law, Arab laws in particular, for a period of 55 years – with a slight hiatus during the years 1941 to 1946 during which I was flying aeroplanes. I paid my first visit to Bahrain in 1948 and opened my first office there in 1951; thereafter offices were opened in Kuwait and the southern Emirates as well. I have thus had the privilege of watching at first hand the development of the modern legal systems of the Gulf States.

As to your background – I have ascertained that the majority are common law trained, some are civil law trained, there are very few with any Arab experience; there are virtually none with any experience of comparative law.

The Arab jurisdictions

We do not, happily, have to try to define here what is mean by 'Arab', as that is more difficult than it sounds. Suffice it to note that we are concerned with eighteen separate jurisdictions from Morocco in the west through to Oman in the east; that is the significance of the word Arab in our present context. Eighteen separate jurisdictions, taking the United Arab Emirates as one jurisdiction, although it itself comprises seven Emirates each with its own peculiarities in law.

Now, while all these jurisdictions have laws in common they do not have a common secular law. I stress here the word 'secular' because we have to recognise at once the ubiquitous presence of the *Shar'ia*, the religious law of Islam, about which I shall have to say quite a lot in a moment. I think we must right at the outset get this into perspective. If we ask ourselves the questions is there a *lex arabica*, is there a *lex mercatoria arabica*, we must return a negative answer at the present time. In many cases in practice in the Arab world there is a valid transnational approach between the various jurisdictions; in these jurisdictions, that is to say the Arab jurisdictions, the comparative approach has as we shall see a peculiar relevance because of the common features which exist between them: these common features exist (notably of course the *Shar'ia* itself) to an extent which is not discernible in other jurisdictions: but that is very far from saying that there already exists a *lex arabica*. To assume that there is a body of law which can be so entitled would be a dangerous error at the present time. The comparative process which is so relevant may in the future lead to a truly common body of law but such a designation would only truly be safe to assume, in my view, if there occurs common legislation by the Arab States to justify it. Unfortunately at the moment there are few signs of this and thus each jurisdiction must be taken as individual. Now, as in other, non-Arab, jurisdictions where authority is not available within the particular forum, it may be relevant to adduce authority, doctrine and jurisprudence from other Arab jurisdictions in priority over other sources, but that is at the moment as far as it goes. However, among the common processes which we can adduce from an overall study there is of course the one element which is unique to the Islamic States and that is the *Shar'ia* law. The role of the *Shar'ia* law and its extent in the jurisprudence of the Arab States is therefore of fundamental importance and let there be no mistake: in today's climate, political, economic and social, this is a subject of overwhelming and increasing importance. I do not think that any student of contemporary history could doubt that for a moment: the increasing reassertion of the *El Islam* and hence the *Shar'ia*, is apparent.

Not so long ago I delivered a paper on syndicated loan agreements in the Arab jurisdictions. I commenced by saying that in considering those contracts, there was basically nothing different from the consideration of any other contract – the same goes for construction contracts. The fundamental differences in law, or possible fundamental differences, between the Arab and the Western jurisdictions affect or could affect all contracts. It might have been better to entitle this talk 'Contract in the Arab Jurisdictions'; we have to cover general aspects initially and develop specific features as far as possible in discussion.

Now the main feature by far to be considered initially is that these are all,with the exception of Lebanon, Islamic States and that Islam is the religion of the State and the Islamic law, the *Shar'ia*, is constitutionally either *the* main source of legislation or a main source.

There are other special common features which we shall consider.

So, first of all I must try to set the scene against a general backdrop of principle. Some of this may seem rather strange territory to most of you.

We shall be dealing with the *Shar'ia* to the extent to which it applies, and the *civil law* system. There is alas little relevance left to the common law in the Arab jurisdictions. There are vestiges left for reasons which are now historical in Bahrain and certain of the Emirates. The common law may ultimately contribute in the comparative process as one of the general principles of law, particularly in arbitration, but such occasions are increasingly rare.

Now what are the features which we find to be common to the Arab jurisdictions overall? I think these can be distinguished as follows:

1 *El Islam*.
2 The *Shar'ia*, the Law of Islam.
3 The Arabic language.
4 The constitutions.
5 Civil and commercial codes on a common model.
6 An interchange of Judges.
7 The influence of Egyptian writings and judgments.

Taken in the aggregate these factors represent a powerful cohesive force which dictates a degree of propinquity between the various Arab jurisdictions which it may be said does not exist elsewhere. It is, of course, true that some of these features are equally common as between Western jurisdictions – in the West we find common constitutional models; we find of course common origins for the great European codes; we find where there are *lucunae* in the law of a particular forum that it may be relevant to invoke authority from another. However, for reasons which will become apparent to us, where such common features exist in the West they in no way provide the cohesive force which they constitute in the Arab world; and of course in addition we have the unique features of Islam, the *Shar'ia* and the Arabic language.

We must now consider briefly each of these sources.

El Islam, the *Shar'ia*

We can bracket these two together: the *Shar'ia* is of course the cannon law of *El Islam*.

As I have said, in dealing with the Arab world we are dealing with all Islamic States (with one marginal exception the Lebanon). It is perhaps not so obvious that this is not at all the same as that in dealing with the Western world we are dealing with Christian States! For the Arab his religion is inextricably interwoven with his life. The precepts of *El Islam* are present in his thoughts and speech. The Koran says 'Ye who believe mention (or remember) God often praise him both early and late' and the cry of the *muezzin* rings out five times daily from the mosque calling the faithful to pray. The *Shar'ia* is the law of that religion. In looking at the strong reassertion of Islam which we are witnessing in the Arab world we are looking also at the reassertion of the *Shar'ia* law.

Just as the constitutions of the Arab States describe *El Islam* as the religion of the State so do they in greater or less degree prescribe the *Shar'ia* as a source of legislation. There are degrees of such prescription. In Saudi Arabia and Oman for example there are no written constitutions as we understand them (this is not strictly so: Saudi Arabia had the old written Declaration of the *Hijaz* and now has a new 'constitution' but this is not a constitution in the modern sense; nonetheless it prescribes *El Islam* and the *Shar'ia* as the only source of law). The extent to which the *Shar'ia* does in fact apply as a source of legislation must be one of the main objects of study in this subject and as I have said there is diversity: for example in Qatar and since 1980 in Egypt the *Shar'ia* is *the* main source of legislation. In Kuwait, Bahrain and the UAE the constitution prescribes the *Shar'ia* as *a* main source of legislation. In the constitution of Jordan, although as would be expected *El Islam* is clearly stated to be the religion of the State, there is no mention of the *Shar'ia* as a source of legislation but nonetheless it has its place. The modern civil code of the UAE is largely *Shar'ia* based and has its origin largely in the Jordanian codes.

Thus in dealing in any particular jurisdiction in the Arab world, the practising lawyer must ask himself at the outset the degree to which if at all the *Shar'ia* is applicable to the problem which he is considering. In some jurisdictions (e.g. Egypt, Kuwait and now since its new commercial code Bahrain) in commercial cases, it may have no relevance; in others such as Saudi Arabia it may be paramount. The lawyer who does not undertake this preliminary investigation is acting very much at his peril; for as we shall see, at the *Shar'ia* many modern contracts would simply be illegal and void. This essential element is often neglected even by Arab lawyers.

The Arabic language

One cannot possibly over-emphasise the importance of the language in the study of Arab laws and of course in the formation and construction of contracts. There can be no doubt that the availability of the Egyptian codes as drafted by that great jurist Al-Sanhoury in the Arabic language played a large part in their being adopted, as adapted by Sanhoury, by many other Arab states - Iraq, Syria, Libya, Kuwait, Qatar – and as models for many others. Allied to the exigencies of the language, the genius of Sanhoury spread the format of these codes throughout the Arab world. However, the matter goes further than that: the official language of all these countries is Arabic, the Courts accept pleading and documentation only in Arabic, as would be expected, and the thought processes involved in and reflected in the Arabic language introduce an additional element into interpretation and construction. I have experienced the most dreadful mistakes perpetrated by English lawyers who obtain an English translation of an Arabic contract and then apply to it English rules of construction. In one classic case a very eminent international lawyer, who should have known better, based his argument upon the existence of a semi-colon in such a translation – there are no semi-colons in Arabic!

In my experience and practice of both common and civil law I have found that the fundamental difference between the civil and the common lawyer lies in a basic difference of approach which probably defies a succinct analysis. In the Arab countries, this difference is compounded again by the veneer of Arab thought reflected in the language.

One of the most difficult tasks which I have in trying to teach is to instill in non-Arabists some understanding of the atmosphere inherent in Arab thought as reflected in the language; concomitant with this, is to instill some idea of the thought processes involved in the *Shar'ia*. In the classical writings on the *Shar'ia* we find what the Western lawyer would regard as an obsession with grammatical analysis of language. I cannot dwell on this, but as a matter of construction let me take a short example: the hallowed precept in the continental codes, the civil codes: '*Al'aqd shari'at al muta'aquidain – les conventions legalement formeés tiennent lien de droit a ceux que les ont fait.*' Now this or something like it can be found in the French code, the Italian code, the German code, really wherever we look. It of course reflects the basic maxim *pact sunt servanda* and we can usually translate it that contracts legally concluded constitute the law of the parties. It is not surprising to find that because of the civil basis of the Arab codes it is common to them also. Now literally translated that means that 'the contract is the law of the parties' but of course left at that it is absolutely meaningless. In searching further for a meaning, in interpreting that provision, the Arabic brings into play another element in construction.

Now on the question of sanctity of contract let us make a short *excursus*: it illustrates as we go along one of the distinctions which we shall have to make between the *Shar'ia* and the secular laws.

The *Shar'ia* recognises in full the sanctity of contracts. I quote from a modern decision, the remarkable award of Professor Rene Dupuy in the Texaco arbitration:

> "The observance of contract generally speaking is proclaimed by the Koran (see in particular sura 5(1)) and the practice of the prophet which is the second source of law in Islam (*Bukhari* 3(187)). The writings of Muslim jurists uphold the same principle, in particular Ibn Qudama, a jurist of considerable authority in the *Hanbali* school which is predominant in Saudi Arabia . . . this principle applies not only to agreements completed by private persons but also agreements entered into by the sovereign. Thus, under the *Shar'ia* nobody, neither the sovereign nor any official, is exempt as a matter of privilege."

and further:

> "To both the common lawyer and the civilian the sanctity of contract in municipal law and of treaties in international law are among his most fundamental principles. Without them he cannot

> conceive of an orderly and peaceable society. It is therefore reassuring to find that the principle of *pacta sunt servanda* is common to all the major legal systems including with certain qualifications Soviet law.' (Jenks '*The Common Law of Mankind*' 143 (1958). The author supports his conclusion by reference to Muslim, Hindu, Hebrew, Chinese, Japanese, African and Russian sources). [*Texaco and Another v. Libya* 53 ILR 422]"

The principle is also a major precept of international law. 'Every treaty in force is binding upon the parties to it and must be performed by them in good faith'. (The Vienna Convention on the Law of Treaties 1969, Article 26).

In the course of the arbitration between American Independent Oil Company (Aminoil) and the State of Kuwait (in which I was of counsel for Aminoil), the agreed '*compromis*' provided for the application of general principles of law. Opinions were filed by leading jurists (English law: Professor CJ Hampson Q.C. and Mr Mark Barnes; French law: Professor Loussouarn; German law: Professor Iur Bernd Stauder; Kuwaiti law: Professor Sulaiman Morqos and Dr Saba Habashi; Swiss law: Professor Bucher; US law: Professor Willis Reece), whereby the general principles were dealt with on a comparative basis. the principles dealt with included *pacta*, estoppel or preclusion, respect for acquired rights, the prohibition against abuse of rights, the prohibition against unjust enrichment, reparation for injury. The proceedings in that arbitration including all those opinions have been placed in the law libraries of many Universities including Cambridge and Oxford and constitute an invaluable study of comparative law.

The eminent jurist Professor Bertholdt Goldmann was asked to prepare a synopsis of the opinions given. In dealing with pacta, Professor Goldmann stated:

> "The answer here is unanimous: the principle *pacta sunt servanda* which means that parties who freely and legally enter into a contract are bound to fulfil the obligations undertaken through it, is one of the basic principles of the six legislations'. Proceedings Vol. 5 Goldmann at page 17."

And again at page 23:

> "12. It thus appears that *pacta sunt servanda* is a fundamental principle under the six municipal laws, hence at common law,

civil law and Muslim law and that the conditions under which by virtue of this principle contracts are binding for the parties are identical or close to one another under these laws. Accordingly, it is, in respect of municipal laws, a 'general principle' in the sense of Article 3(2) of the arbitration agreement."

So we find that the principle of sanctity of contract constitutes a general principle of law and is embraced in particular by the *Shar'ia*. Well, as a general principle that is fine: but when we look into it more deeply, we find the basic differences which distinguish the *Shar'ia* philosophies from those of modern Western systems. May I here translate a passage from '*Masaadir Al-Haqq*' of al-Sanhoury: he puts it, in Arabic of course, better than I can and he is an outstanding authority. He does not follow the usual course and put the main difficulty on the basis that the *Shar'ia* knows no general theory of contract *per se* but only types of nominate contract, although that is of course the case. However, he is of the opinion that we can in our time go far to extracting by analogy from the specific examples of nominate contract given by the *Shar'ia* a general theory. No he does not put the difficulty there *i.e.* in the matter of nominate contract; he highlights the matter somewhat differently:

"Thus, those nominate contracts mentioned by the doctors of law are only those contracts which most frequently occur in the transactions of the time. If civilisation has evolved other contracts which satisfy the conditions laid down in the jurisprudence, such contracts are lawful. It is on this legal (*Shar'i*) policy that the new Iraqi civil legislation is based' (let us record in passing here that it was Sanhoury who drafted the civil code in Iraq among others)."

Article 74 of the Iraqi code enumerates the types of contract in accordance with the objects.

Then this is followed by a general provision (Article 75) as follows:

"The contract may embrace anything else in respect of which the obligation is not forbidden by law or contrary to public order or morals."

Al-Sanhoury continues

"However, the scope of public order in Islamic jurisprudence is wider than that in Western jurisprudence. The prohibition of

> contracts contrary to *riba* or *gharar* greatly extends such scope in the Islamic jurisprudence: so also does the theory of condition as applied to the contract increase the extent of such scope to a large degree. Thus, the principle in the Islamic jurisprudence is freedom of contract within the bounds of public order; *but the multiplicity of the principles which are considered to go to public order narrow such freedom.*"

As a general rule we find the principle of the sanctity of contract enshrined in both *Shar'ia* and secular legal systems but qualified everywhere by the necessity to achieve contractual justice. Thus, for example, statute has of necessity restricted absolute freedom on contracting but the methods prescribed by *Shar'ia* and secular law differ in many respects.

Let us return and complete our list of similarities:

The constitutions

It suffices to note at this stage that where there are written constitutions, these are more or less based on the common form. As the reason for this is basically the same as the reason why there are common codes I shall now pass immediately to:

Civil and commercial codes on a common model

I have already briefly alluded to this in reference to the genius of Al-Sanhoury and the subsequent availability of the basic codes in Arabic.

In 1949 Egypt promulgated its civil code. This was drafted by Sanhoury and has survived virtually unamended for nearly 50 years. In 1942 when he was working on the code Sanhoury announced that he had used comparisons of more than 20 modern codes, the jurisprudence of the Egyptian Courts and the Islamic *Shar'ia*. However, it was quite apparent that Sanhoury's preoccupation and main difficulty in drafting the Egyptian code was to try to build a bridge between the *Shar'ia* and the dictates of modern commerce. In this context we have to point up the conflict between the immutable tenets (i.e. the Koran and *Sunna*) of the *Shar'ia*, and, in particular, the modern economic scene. In 1980 I wrote:

> "The problem is that the Arabs have to a greater or lesser degree in wishing to adopt the existing international world of

> commerce, come face to face with the classic situation: an irresistible force against an irremovable object. As is not uncommon in these circumstances (not by any means only in the Arab world) the question has been begged on all sides. It will be to say the least interesting to see for how long and to what extent this apparent anomaly can continue". [Ballantyne, *Legal Developments in Arabia*, (1980) p. 121]

Well the anomaly does continue and increasingly the position is accentuated by current political circumstances. The dream of Sanhoury was that the *Shar'ia* could be increasingly adapted to the needs of modern commerce and that modern codes could be increasingly made to conform more with the *Shar'ia* so that by some kind of compromise the two would meet. There is not much sign of that happening and indeed I regard it as in the ultimate analysis probably impossible.

Interchange of Judges

It suffices to note under this heading that there has been a considerable importation of foreign Arab judges into the Gulf jurisdictions in particular (notably from Egypt) by reason of the lack of suitably qualified persons in the jurisdictions concerned.

The influence of Egyptian writings and judgments

Jurisprudential writings in many of the Arab jurisdictions are simply not to be found: in particular again in the Gulf area. It is not surprising that the one work which is certain to be found at the right and of every judge sitting in an Arab court is the monumental *Al Waseet* of Al-Sanhoury, his ten volume commentary on the Egyptian civil codes. The other book which almost always is present somewhere is the *Majellat Al Ahkam Al 'adliya*, commonly known as the *Majella*, the Ottoman codification of the *Shar'ia* which was put together in the Nineteenth Century. Most judges have this available just in case a *Shar'ia* point comes up.

So we have all these unifying factors; let us remind ourselves of what they are

1 *El Islam*
2 The *Shar'ia*.

3 Arabic.
4 The constitutions.
5 Civil and commercial codes.
6 An interchange of Judges.
7 The influence of Egyptian writings and judgments.

This situation encourages us, particularly where there are *lacunae*, where there are gaps in any particular system, to adopt the comparative approach and look for points of uniformity, for points of concordance in order to fill them. Of course we find that this approach is to a limited (if increasing) extent valid also in Europe – let us remind ourselves of the French judge for example who cannot decline to give judgment on the basis that there is no law; he must deduce a principle from somewhere. Due to the factors which I have briefly outlined this is a much more potent consideration in the Arab jurisdictions than it is in Europe.

The *Shar'ia*

I cannot of course assume that my audience has any knowledge of the *Shari'ia* and I would like to quote from the late Professor Noel Coulson's book in which he puts the difficulty with his usual incisiveness:

> "Muslim jurisprudence . . . is the revealed will of God, the divinely ordained system preceding and not preceded by the Muslim state, controlling and not controlled by Muslim society."

Now, this is really concentrated. Let me elaborate a little. In considering the adaptation or modernisation of the *Shar'ia* to fill the needs of contemporary circumstance, we are immediately dealing with an essential contradiction: the whole essence of the *Shar'ia* as a religious law is that it is not intended to develop according to the dictates or needs of society; quite to the contrary, society and its circumstances are to be controlled, circumscribed, by the basic tenets of the *Shar'ia*. Society is supposed to evolve according to the dictates of the *Shar'ia*. Now clearly, if that had happened then there would be no conflict and no irresistible force against an irremovable object. But it did not happen, and there is now much talk of new *Ijtihad*, new emerging doctrines based on the *Shar'ia* which will, so to speak, update it and bring it into line with modern conditions. This, of course, involves a basic conflict, essentially attempts to surmount *immutable* provisions of the *Shar'ia*. It is in this that lies, I feel, the whole really insurmountable problem in seeking to adapt the *Shar'ia* to some concepts of western law, and in particular commercial law, which offend basic and immutable provisions of the *Shar'ia*.

I hope that the novelty of some of the foregoing concepts to this audience, may have justified the length at which I have felt it necessary to introduce what is after all a very complex subject. Now, against the foregoing backdrop, what are the difficulties inherent *if* the *Shar'ia* should apply to a modern contract, in particular in our present context a modern construction contract? Such difficulties could be manifold and uncertainty must be stressed as the main one but Al Sanhoury with his usual genius reduced the main difficulties to three: (1) *riba*, (2) *gharar*, and (3) a multiplicity of conditions in one contract, virtually the notion that a contract should deal with only one transaction at a time.

These concepts are of course complicated and have been debated by learned jurists for centuries. Very briefly:

1 ***Riba*** means any unearned accretion: the classical and most tiresome example in the modern context being interest on money.
2 ***Gharar*** is uncertainty, the object of the contract must be certain and defined and in existence.
3 Is self evident. In particular one example: any condition which is extraneous or additional or a *fortiori* inconsistent with the object of the contract is void and indeed may avoid the whole contract.

Now it will be apparent that any of these principles could well entirely avoid a modern construction contract if strictly applied; the basic difficulties were very early recognised, for example, in the field of international arbitration.

In *Petroleum Development Ltd* v *Sheikh of Abu Dhabi* (18 International Law Reports, page 144) the question before the arbitrators was, what were the rights of the oil company with respect to all underwater areas over which the Ruler of Abu Dhabi had or might have sovereignty jurisdiction control or mineral rights. The arbitrators differed and the award was given by Lord Asquith of Bishopstone. The possible difficulties inherent in an application of the *Shar'ia* were summarily (and in my opinion quite wrongly) dealt with in the following passage:

> "This is a contract made in Abu Dhabi and wholly to be performed in that country. If any municipal system of law were

> applicable, it would *prima facie* be that of Abu Dhabi. But no such law can reasonably be said to exist. The Sheikh administers a purely discretionary justice with the assistance of the Koran; and it would be fanciful to suggest that in this very primitive region there is any central body of legal principles applicable to the construction of modern commercial instruments. Nor can I see any basis on which the municipal law of England could apply. On the contrary, clause 17 of the agreement, cited above, repels the notion that the municipal law of any country as such could be appropriate. The terms of that clause invite indeed prescribe the application of principles rooted in the good sense and common practice of the generality of civilised nations – a sort of 'modern law of nature'. I do not think that on this point there is any conflict between the parties."

In thus giving his award, the learned Umpire not only failed entirely to advert to the *Shar'ia* he also completely ignored the fact at that time the British Crown exercised extra-territorial jurisdiction in Abu Dhabi under the Foreign Jurisdiction Acts and concomitant Orders in Council which prescribed a body of Anglo-Indian law to which he could well have referred.

That arbitration was immediately preceded by *Petroleum Developments (Qatar) Ltd* v *Ruler of Qatar* which appears in the same volume of the ILR at page 161. Once again, the two party arbitrators disagreed and it was up to Lord Radcliff to deliver the award. A report in the ILR merely gives the findings without the reasons and the full award was unreported. However, I am aware that the two experts who gave evidence on the *Shar'ia*, Professors Anderson and Milliot both expressed the view that the concession in practice, viewed in the light of the *Shar'ia*, would be found in many of its aspects to be void. Thus, the learned Umpire effectively ignored the *Shar'ia*.

A third arbitration to which reference may valuably be made is that of the *State of Saudi Arabia* v. *The Arabian American Oil Company* the award in which was given on 23rd August 1958 (the famous '*Aramco*' arbitration). The arbitration tribunal found little difficulty in deciding that it was the law of Saudi Arabia which applied to the concession, nor that such law was the *Shar'ia*. It did however face difficulties when it tried to apply that law to the regime of oil concessions.

> "The regime of mining concessions and consequently also of oil concessions has remained embryonic in Muslim law and it is not

the same in the different schools. The principles of one school cannot be introduced into another unless this is done by an act of authority. *Hanbali* law (i.e. the law of Saudi Arabia) contains no precise rule about mining concessions and *a fortiori* about oil concessions.

The rule *pacta sunt servanda* is fully recognised by Muslim law.

It is obvious that no contract can exist in vacuo, i.e. without being based on a lega system.

In as much as the law in force in Saudi Arabia did not contain any definite rule relating to the exploitation of oil deposits, because no such exploitation existed in that State before 1933, this *lacuna* was filled by the 1933 concession agreement whose validity and legality under Saudi Arabian law are not disputed by either side. The present dispute only concerns the effects of the provisions contained in the agreement.

The concession agreement is thus the fundamental law of the parties and the arbitration tribunal is bound to recognise its particular importance owing to the fact that it fills a gap in the legal system of Saudi Arabia with regard to the oil industry.

In so far as doubts may remain on the content or on the meaning of the agreements of the parties, it is necessary to resort to the general principles of law and to apply them in order to interpret and even to supplement the respective rights and obligations of the parties.

Matters pertaining to private law are in principle governed by the law of Saudi Arabia but with one important reservation. That law must, in case of need, be interpreted or supplemented by the general principles of law, by the custom and practice in the oil business and by notions of pure jurisprudence, in particular whenever certain private rights – which must inevitably be recognised to the concessionaire if the concession is not to be deprived of its substance – would not be secured in an unquestionable manner by the law in force in Saudi Arabia."

I trust that I have quoted enough from this award to point out the difficulties; the endeavours of the Tribunal to extract itself from such difficulties may be likened to the wiles of a fox endeavouring to escape the inevitable result of the hunt, or a trout whose antics are nonetheless quite useless to dislodge the hook in its jaw. To those interested in following up the subject, this award should certainly be read in full.

So, the first question which the practising lawyer must ask himself in his initial consideration of the contract in any Arab jurisdiction is 'Could the *Shar'ia* apply'? In many cases in a contract, *a fortiori* in a commercial contract, the answer will probably be No – Egypt, Jordan, Kuwait, Bahrain are clear examples – in other cases the *Shar'ia* must be taken *seriatim*: examples are Saudi Arabia where it is still paramount, Yemen, the UAE and Oman.

The reason for a negative answer in many *commercial* cases is that faced with the dilemma to which I have referred many of the Arab states have enacted commercial codes which adopt secular legal principles firmly – notably in the acceptance of the matter of interest on monies. However, many *civil* codes nonetheless contain much of the *Shar'ia* – it is thus essential to identify whether a contract is of a 'civil' or 'commercial' nature and this must be determined according to its proper law. *A fortiori*, we must note carefully that a construction contract may be either: civil or commercial.

The contract of *Muqaawala*

In the Arab civil codes generally, the construction contract comes under this heading. Definitions of *Muqaawala* tend to be more or less uniform and we may take one of the most modern codes as an example. The civil code of the United Arab Emirates reads as follows:

> "*Article 872*: *Muqaawala* is a contract whereby one of two parties undertakes to make something or perform a work against a consideration undertaken by the other party."

This is of course a wide formula which embraces also contracts other than construction contracts.

It is important to note that a contract of *Muqaawala* may be 'civil' or 'commercial'. To quote from Al Sanhoury (*Al Waseet* Volume VII page 21 and 45, Arabic):

> "The construction agreement from the contractor's side is sometimes civil and sometimes commercial. It is civil if it is not considered a commercial activity. Liberal professions are considered civil activities. So, if the physician contracted with the patient to treat him, or the solicitor contracted with his client to defend him or the architect contracted with a person to prepare a design requested by the latter or the sculptor contracted with a client to make a painting or a statue, the contract in all

> these cases is a civil one, even from the side of the contractor who is a professional. We have seen also that the contract is also considered civil from the employer's side. However the professional may perform commercial activities that consume much of his efforts like the architect who prepares a design and bill of quantities, supervises the work and carries out the construction works by supplying material, machinery and required labour. In this case the contract cannot be divided and shall be deemed commercial with respect to the architect."

I am sure that I do not have to tell this audience that in practice modern construction contracts tend to be of immense bulk and complication, with general and special conditions and specifications running often to many volumes and going from definition of the works through to settlement of disputes usually by arbitration.

Increasingly, and not unexpectedly, the contract is expressly subject to the law of the country where it is to be performed. On those rare occasions where a foreign law or, even more rarely in a major international contract, general principles of law are chosen, it cannot of course be assumed that such a choice necessarily excludes all the incidents of the lex solutionis. This is of course of itself a complicated subject. It is however worthy of note that the *Shar'ia* has been defined in two Hague Conferences as constituting one of the general principles of law referred to in Article 38 of the Statute of the International Court of Justice.

So – returning to *Muqaawala* – a contract of *Muqawala* may be either civil or commercial.

So whereas in advising initially on a construction contract in a specific Arab jurisdiction the first question to be asked is whether the *Shar'ia* has any application overall, the next step is to refer to the civil code or the civil and commercial codes as the case may be.

It is not inconceivable that even express provisions of the code may be challenged before a constitutional court, as being contrary to a constitutional dictate to observe the *Shar'ia*. This is rare but in a recent case the Kuwaiti Constitutional Court considered whether those provisions of the commercial code sanctioning the charging of interest were unconstitutional as offending against the *Shar'ia*. The court decided that as the *Shar'ia* was expressed in the constitution to be *a* principal source not *the* principal source, of legislation, the provisions were valid. [Judgment of the Constitutional Court, 28 November 1992]

As it is normally the commercial codes which contain leading exceptions to *Shar'ia* principles, whereas the civil codes often enshrine such principles, the importance of defining the construction contract as 'civil' or 'commercial' becomes apparent.

Specific laws

We have thus far of necessity painted with a broad brush; but of course in considering a construction contract in any particular Arab jurisdiction there will normally be a multiplicity of specific legislation also to be considered: we do not have anything like the time to go into all these although we might well develop some of them in discussion afterwards. Examples of principles found to be general in most if not all of these jurisdictions are the following:

In-built protection of the rights of nationals
Foreign capital investment control.
Commercial agency and distributorship laws.
Generally restrictions upon the carrying on of business by foreigners and the need for a 'sponsor' or 'agent'.

Arbitration clauses - increasingly submission to foreign arbitration is disliked.

The effect of arbitration clauses in any event according to the respective codes: *a fortiori*, whether the courts will regard their jurisdiction as excluded by a valid clause.

Whether the jurisdiction concerned is party to the New York Convention or other treaties etc. etc. It is endless, and of course we have no time to consider all these incidents here tonight. We may however end by adverting to two specific and difficult matters:
Decennial liability; and
Imprévision

The principle of decennial liability will I am sure be known to all or almost all of you, certainly to those civil lawyers amongst you. As a general rule, it is a ten year liability imposed upon architects and engineers and the contractor for the safety of buildings designed or erected by them. The liability normally goes to collapse of the structure but has been extended often to include basic defects which endanger the structure.

The provision is regarded as going to *ordre public* (*alnizam al'am*) and therefore cannot be excluded by contract; it may however sometimes be excused by *force majeure* or provisions of the codes going to *imprévision* or unforeseen circumstances.

Basically, the decennial provisions stem from old French law – the Code Napoleon – hence through Egypt to the modern Arab codes – e.g. Egypt, Kuwait, Iraq, Syria, Algeria; the Kuwait Civil Code of 1980 etc. etc. Thus, this is an important feature of Arab construction contracts and must be insured against. Many of the Arab systems indeed provide for compulsory insurance against the decennial liability.

This brings me to *imprévision*: intervening circumstances of a general nature which could not have been foreseen at the time of contracting.

I have already referred to the recognised necessity in virtually all jurisdictions known to me, not just the Arab, of mitigating the strict application of the rule of *pacta sunt sevanda* in the search for contractual justice. The principle of *imprévision* is a good example of this. We may refer this time to the Kuwaiti code for the basic rules.

> "*Article 198:*
> Should there occur, after contract and before full performance thereof, general exceptional circumstances not to be anticipated at the time of its conclusion, and there result from such occurrence that performance of the obligation arising therefrom, if not becoming impossible, has become oppressive for the obligor, so as to threaten him with grievous loss, the judge may, after weighing up the interests of the parties, restore the oppressive obligation to what is reasonable, by narrowing the scope thereof or increasing the consideration therefor. Any agreement to the contrary is void."

This rule of course also goes to public policy; the discretion given to the judge to alleviate the contractual burden cannot be avoided by contract. It is an exception to the rule of autonomy of the parties and is as I have said one of the outstanding examples of the mitigation of the strict *pacta* rule in order to achieve contractual justice. The doctrine of *imprévision* owes much in origin to French administrative law but the French courts have set their face against its extension into the general field of contract. Not so the Arab codes, which have adopted it as a general rule. It gives to the Judge a general discretion which is however very sparingly exercised.

However, although in secular law *imprévision* may be an exception to the general rule, the *Shar'ia* takes a rather different view. The late Professor Coulson pointed this out with his usual brilliance:

> "Baldly stated, the difference between English and Islamic law in this respect is that the latter sees unilateral rescission of such a contractual relationship as quite natural and acceptable in circumstances where the former would insist upon its continuation. Where changing circumstances affect a party's outlook and he is simply unhappy because the situation is turning out to be different from his original expectations, then Islamic law releases him from his original promise while English law holds him to it. I believe that this distinction reveals a profoundly different psychological approach to the notion of contractual commitment, the surface of which may be scratched but no more than that by the following remarks.
>
> In English law the sanctity of contract means that the promise endures despite the normal vicissitudes of fortune. It is right that the promise should be kept 'for better or for worse', 'through thick and thin', because this is in line with the popular belief that tenacity of purpose to some degree controls events and that the human will determines the future. The promise must dominate the circumstances.
>
> For Islam precisely the converse is true. Circumstances dominate the promise. Future circumstances are neither predictable nor controllable but lie entirely in the hands of the Almighty. In the face of the predetermined march of events human activity assumes a relative insignificance and the contractual promise becomes a relatively ephemeral thing. If the tide of affairs turns then the promise naturally floats out with it. The ubiquitous phrase of the vernacular, *Inshallah* (if Allah so wills) is no empty expression. It could in fact be read as a vital proviso to any contract for future performance.
>
> Other symptoms of this recognition of human fallibility are found in the legal texts. Assessment of possible variant solutions for a legal problem invariably ends with the words '*Wa Allah a'lam*' or 'Allah alone knows'. Calculation of damages never takes into account anticipated profit because this is a future and unknown quantity. Briefly, therefore, the reluctance of the jurists to hold a contracting party to his promise in the face of changed circumstances may appear as a natural expression of an attitude of

> resignation or fatalism deriving from their total submission to the will of Allah which the faith of Islam itself demands.
>
> It is because of the force of this ingrained philosophy that the traditional *Shar'ia* right of unilateral rescission in contracts of a continuing personal commitment cannot be ignored or regarded as totally superseded by any apparent contradictory terms of modern statutory enactments. Extreme caution is required in placing reliance upon the ostensibly binding nature of a contractual commitment of this sort. At the very least, even if unilateral withdrawal during the specific time period is to be treated as a breach of the contract, the quantum of damages recoverable for such breach will, because of the fundamental *Shar'ia* principles involved, fall far short of the mark which might reasonably be anticipated under English law." [Coulson – *Commercial Law in the Gulf States: The Islamic Legal Tradition* (1984) at p. 81]

Perhaps no passage could more forcibly point out the inherent dangers.

One hardly needs to stress the disaster inherent in a situation where a long term construction contract probably, these days, for a huge project might have its overall stability threatened by the application of such principles, admirable as they may be.

In framing this talk I did bear in mind that I would have to temper it to suit the background and experience of my audience. It was thus my first task to ascertain at the outset to what extent, if at all, my audience was familiar with the basic legal tenets obtaining in the Arab jurisdictions. Depending upon the answer to that enquiry, it was my intention to include or omit the greater part of this talk which has been devoted to a general introduction to the subject; also upon such determination must depend the proportion of this session which could be devoted to lecturing or to discussion. The enquiry revealed that, with the exception of a few of my own LLM students who are present, this audience had virtually no prior knowledge of the subject. I have thus been obliged to devote what would otherwise have been a disproportionate section of this lecture to the general background at the expense of considering specific incidents in Arab construction contracts. Perhaps the latter could at some stage form the subject matter for a second lecture – maybe next year!

Thank you for your attention.

XVIII

The Shari'a: Bridges or Conflict?

> 'Dispute not with the People of the Book save in respect of what is better – except those of them who do wrong: Say to them "We believe in that which is revealed to use and revealed unto you, and our God and your God are one God and we all surrender unto him".'

and

> 'Say: Oh people of the Book, come in equal parlance between ourselves and yourselves.' (The Holy Qur'an)

By these revelations Muslims, Christians and Jews are directed to make common cause between them.

Yet there is growing evidence that, politically, Al Islam is being polarised as the enemy of the West. There is no need for this, and it will be an overwhelming tragedy if material interests which thrive upon dissension, allied to incomprehension, are allowed to create a head-on clash, instead of mutual understanding, tolerance and even affection.

Lawyers operating increasingly in the international field, in particular the international commercial field, can make an invaluable contribution to such understanding; but for bridges to be built, there must be knowledge on all sides of the basic elements and problems involved.

Our Arab Forum is concerned with 18 States, jurisdictions, stretching from Morocco in the West to Oman in the East: (there are seven additional 'sub' jurisdictions if we consider the seven constituent elements of the United Arab Emirates). All these States, with the marginal exception of Lebanon, are Muslim States, whose constitutions prescribe Al Islam as the religion of the State, and the Shari'a, the religious law of Al Islam, as *a* or *the* main source of legislation. The latter prescription varies in degree between the various states: at one end of the scale, in Saudi Arabia, the Shari'a reigns supreme, alloyed only by such secular regulations as are not contrary to its provisions; at the other, in such jurisdictions as Egypt, Bahrain, Kuwait, the Shari'a may, at the present time, be expected to have little relevance in a commercial transaction.

To say that these are Islamic states is not at all the same as saying that the states of the Western world are Christian. For the Muslim Arab, his religion is inextricably interwoven with the whole of his existence. The Holy Qur'an says, 'Ye who believe remember God often, praise him both early and late' and the cry of the mu'athin rings out five times daily from the mosque, calling the faithful to prayer. Islam is a living faith and the Shari'a is the holy law of that faith. When we talk of the reassertion of Al Islam in the Arab World, we are inevitably looking also at a reassertion of the Shari'a.

There are in excess of one billion Muslims in our world today. In advising on any jurisdiction in the Arab world the practising lawyer must ask himself at the outset the degree to which, if at all, the Shari'a is relevant to the problem at issue. As we have seen, the answer to this question will vary, but the lawyer who does not ask it acts at his peril and is short-changing his client; for under the Shari'a, many modern commercial contracts, many Western economic concepts, are strictly viewed as illegal and therefore void.

It is impossible in a note of this length to give detailed examples. The main difficulties were summarised by that great Egyptian jurist, *Al Sanhouri*, in the following passage from *Masaadir Al Haqq* (The Sources of Jurisprudence in the Islamic Fiqh): 'There are three things which the Islamic jurisprudence considers as unlawful: they are *gharar* (uncertainty), *riba* (unearned accretion, interest) and a multiplicity of transactions in one contract. If it were possible to simplify the understanding of these three things in facilitation of the development of civilisation, many of the reasons which prevent the Islamic jurisprudence from going along with the requirements of such development would fall away'.

These three precepts constitute formidable difficulties. The veto on *riba* alone, viewed even in its narrow sense as interest on monies lent, constitutes ostensibly a direct opposition to the economic system of the capitalist world. Many of the Arab states have dealt with this problem by a direct defiance of the Shari'a principle, by sanctioning interest in their commercial codes, but the moral unease and debate continue. In a recent case in the Constitutional Court of Kuwait, the legality of these provisions in the Commercial Code was challenged as being unconstitutional where the Constitution prescribes the Shari'a as 'a principal source of legislation'. The Court declined this plea, but opined that the position might be different where the Shari'a was prescribed as '*the* main source of legislation' (as it is, eg, in Egypt and Qatar). Had the Court been dealing, *ex hypothesi*, with the constitutional position in Saudi Arabia, where the Shari'a is the *sole* source of legislation, it would, on its own analysis, have faced an insoluble dilemma!

Our world today is ruled by economics, finance and money. The basic clash of ideologies apparent from the foregoing example points up the dangers inherent in the situation, and the need for urgent consideration of the ideological problems which may very swiftly spark political confrontations which must be avoided.

As a compelling thought: when we look at the contemporary macro-economic scene today, its conventional banking system, can we really dismiss the Islamic precepts as inappropriate: for example, more equity sharing as distinct from lending at interest, still basically *anathema* to Western bankers? To quote from an excellent recent supplement to the *Economist* 'Islam and the West': 'Despite this (ie the disadvantages) some people in the West have begun to find the idea attractive. It gives the provider of money a strong incentive to be sure he is doing something sensible with it. What a pity the West's banks did not have that incentive in so many of their lending decisions in the 1970s and 1980s. It also emphasises the sharing of responsibility, by all users of money. That helps to make the free market system more open: you might say more democratic.'

There is in my opinion an urgent need for dialogue in this subject par excellence; it embraces inevitably the much broader spectrum of overall comparison between the Shari'a and secular laws. The Arab Forum can make a vital contribution to this subject and a conference should be convened to that end.

I end this Note with a quotation from Professor Stephen Hawking of Cambridge, with which I concluded my speech at the IBA's 3rd Arab Regional Conference held in 1993 in Casablanca: 'Man's greatest achievements have come about by talking and his greatest failures by not talking'.

For Product Safety Concerns and Information please contact our EU representative GPSR@taylorandfrancis.com
Taylor & Francis Verlag GmbH, Kaufingerstraße 24, 80331 München, Germany

www.ingramcontent.com/pod-product-compliance
Ingram Content Group UK Ltd.
Pitfield, Milton Keynes, MK11 3LW, UK
UKHW010956180926
475701UK00004B/388
* 9 7 8 0 4 1 5 6 6 6 9 5 4 *